HISTORY OF RICE IN INDIA
Mythology, Culture and Agriculture

History of Rice in India
Mythology, Culture and Agriculture

Tuk-Tuk Kumar

GYAN

Published by

GYAN

Gyan Publishing House
5, Ansari Road
Daryaganj, New Delhi-110002
Phone: 011-47034999, 9811692060
E-mail: books@gyanbooks.com

Distribution Network
gyanbooks.com
India, USA, Canada, UK, Australia, France

ISBN: 978-81-212-0240-4 (HB)

Reprint in India, 2024
First Published, 1998

Printed at: Gyan Press, Delhi.

History of Rice in India: Mythology, Culture and Agriculture
Author: Tuk-Tuk Kumar

Foreword

The present book is the first major work on the history of a single crop in India. That it is on such an important crop as rice gives it an added importance. What also lends this work distinction is the fact that it has tried to encompass all categories of relevant data—archaeology, literature, botany, ethnography and linguistics. On each of these categories there has been a rcasonably thorough and systematic discussion. What has emerged in the end is a precise and analytical picture of the history of rice in the protohistoric and early historic periods of India. In the historiography of studies on history of agriculture in India the present venture by Dr. Ms. Tuk-Tuk Kumar (*nee* Ghosh) must be considered a highly successful major attempt.

In recent years the study of the history of Indian agriculture has been primarily devoted to the identification of plant and crop remains found in archaeological excavations. Professor Vishnu-Mittre of the Birbal Sahni Institute of Palaeobotany in Lucknow has played a stellar role in this regard, and after his retirement the mantle has fallen on Dr. K.S. Saraswat (Lucknow), Dr. G.M. Buth (Srinagar) and Dr. M.D. Kajale (Pune). It will, however, be quite incorrect to imagine that the archaeological records of plant and crop remains in India are in any sense complete or even adequate.

The number of scholars involved in this kind of study is quite marginal in such a large country as India. I remember that I could not get a leaf impression on clay dating probably around 1000 B.C. identified in a major university department of Botany. At the same time the importance of synthesizing the presently available data is always there and I am thankful to Ms Kumar that she gave her best in the course of her Ph.D work with me. What stands out in this work is her fairly exhaustive analysis of the different types of sources. It is surely possible to dispute some points raised by her but this work is likely to remain unparalleled as a richly documented history of rice in early India for some years to come.

It had been my privilege to be associated with this work from its inception to conclusion and it gives me great pleasure that it is now published.

Dilip K. Chakraborti

Author's Note

I would like to dedicate this book to my mother, whose continued support was invaluable.

I would also like to thank Dr. Dilip K. Chakraborti, University of Delhi, ICHR and the staff of the various Libraries and Research Institutions who have helped in some form or the other, in giving the book its present shape.

It is evident that more work is required in this field of study and it will be well worth the wait to see the fruits of research efforts coalesce over a period of time.

Tuk-Tuk Kumar

Contents

Contents

List of Maps

(CHAPT. 3)

1

Introduction

THE nineteenth century, especially the latter half, witnessed an aroused spirit of research which contributed much to the study of Indian civilisation and antiquity. This has formed the basis of much of the later studies. In order to trace the early research on the history of Indian agriculture, it is to this period that one must turn.

Though not very detailed, some relevant works were produced. Among them the most conspicuous is that of Alphonse de Candolle (1886). He aims primarily at discovering the condition and habitat of each species before it was cultivated, and—what is of immediate interest to us—the length of time during which each species has been in cultivation and how its culture spread in different directions. India has been mentioned as the centre of origin of many plants It is in connection with this that a brief historical background has been attached. However incomplete and hazy, we can detect some significant features of early Indian agriculture in de Candolle's work.

Providing limited but some useful information as far as the history of agriculture is concerned are, among others, W. Roxburgh (1832) and J.D. Hooker (1897). They focus on the Sanskrit equivalents of the names of plants (thereby suggesting their antiquity), the regions where they are found wild (suggesting that the plant may be indigenous) and those areas in which they have a long tradition of cultivation. The work of G. Watt (1908) may be said to be in the same tradition. However, it is more directly relevant to our purpose as a historical background has been appended to each of the commercial products he has dealt with.

In the strictly historical and general works of the period on ancient India, agriculture is often discussed in rather superficial terms. We may cite Dutt (1891) as an example. His work is divided into Vedic, Epic and Rationalistic periods, in which agriculture figures only occasionally and that, too, briefly.

Specific historical works on the economic conditions in ancient India began to be produced with the beginning of the twentieth century (e.g. Subbarao, 1911 ; Iyengar, 1912 ; Das 1925). Though all of them were not exhaustive studies, they were an advance on the earlier historical studies. However, agriculture was treated in one section only. On account of this factor, there remained many gaps in knowledge. G.P. Majumdar (1927) deserves special mention for attempting a detailed study of plant life. He shows that in Indian treatises and traditions there is an abundance of scientific observations, classifications, generalisations, theories and applications relating to plants. In his view the basic value of such a study as this is historical. About agriculture, he makes some general observations and traces the beginnings of agricultural science to its development during the Mauryan period. Besides, he discusses the Krisi Parasara and Amarakosa on agriculture. However, the idea behind the work is to stress the contrast between a glorious past and a dark present.

Other works of a similar nature which followed were those of R. Gangopadhyay (1932) and S.P. Raychaudhuri (1941). U.N. Ghoshal (1930) underscored the importance of agriculture to the economy and therefore to the state. Pran Nath (1929) and A.N. Bose (1942-45), while discussing the general economic conditions in ancient India, also discussed agricultural conditions. All the above scholars, however, based their findings mainly on literary texts, both indigenous and foreign.

A little later an important botanical work shed significant

light on the early Indian plant economy, though in a somewhat indirect manner. This was the work of N.I. Vavilov (1951). India figured, in his analysis, as a very important centre of origin of some plants.

In the Post-Independence era, as far as history writing was concerned, a change was noticeable. While the volumes like those the *Bhāratīya Vidyā Bhavan* series (1951-55) devoted proportionately less space to economic conditions, and agriculture in particular, a trend to treat social and economic conditions of smaller time periods with more objectivity and less glorification was seen developing. Agriculture was included in their ambit of discussion.

A monograph dealing with agriculture in ancient India published by the Indian Council of Agriculture Research (1964) must be mentioned in some detail. Here, agriculture has been discussed in all its aspects. Land and its divisions, irrigation and drainage, tillage and tilling implements, manures and manuring, cultivation of crops, sequence of cropping, protection of crops from diseases and pests, agricultural meteorology, livestock in agriculture, etc. have been dealt with at length. Many indigenous treatises relating to the subject have been consulted for information. Among them may be mentioned Charaka, Suśruta, Śurāpala, Kāshyapa, Parāśara and Varāhamihira.

It will be clear from the foregoing that our knowledge of early Indian agriculture, barring a few notable exceptions, is neither detailed nor complete. Works of a general nature preponderate over others which are more specific in nature. Even in the monographs, the conclusions are based mainly on literary sources, both foreign and indigenous. What we get in most cases is therefore a compendium of references scattered in various texts. There are a few exceptions in some general works, but the use of archaeological evidence has more often than not been of marginal significance.

Moving sharply away from this trend are works on early Indian agriculture based mainly on archaeo-botanical evidence. The most significant contribution in this field has been made by Vishnu-Mittre (for a general survey of the literature, Vishnu Mittre 1974) but other researchers have also been active in this area (cf. Chowdhury, Saraswat and Buth 1977). The contribution of these works is undeniable. They are important for the following reasons. Firstly, they constitute a departure as far as works on Indian archaeology are concerned. Though excavation reports contained sections on excavated plant remains, the analyses were not integrated into broader works. Secondly, in most of these works the archaeological evidence, subjected to a thorough scientific investigation, is supplemented with a botanical interpretation. Lastly, not only is an evolving picture of crop plant evolution presented but the position regarding the entire subcontinent is greatly clarified.

However, not all the works provide as complete an account as the above points may be seen to convey. Some of the works purporting to discuss agriculture, do not deal with the theme in all its aspects. There are a few which concentrate only on the study of a few specified sites. There is also the more or less complete sidestepping of literary texts. The position seems quite the reverse of the earlier situation. Some recent works, however, try to correlate literary and archaeological evidence (cf. Bose, Sen and Subbarayappa, 1971, Randhawa, 1980).

We notice, on the completion of this brief historiographical survey, three broad phases. Of course, they are not crystal clear and well defined. They are as follows. In the first phase works—both on botany and history touching on Indian agriculture—were few and even they were not very detailed. In the second phase the focus shifted from general history to economic history and consequently agriculture received more attention in its historical perspective. In the third phase archaeology, or more precisely archaeobotany, stepped into study plant remains and other themes related to early agriculture. What remains for the future is the general appreciation of a multi-disciplinary approach to, and interpretation of, the subject. Perhaps more specified studies could be undertaken on these lines and coordinated, at a later stage, into a study which would provide many new insights into early Indian agriculture.

The purpose of the study is specific, and limited to the early history of one item in the agricultural complex—rice.

Rice was chosen as the subject as it happens to be one of the oldest crops in India and remains a dominant crop in the plant economy till the present times.

To secure a well rounded picture, a multi-disciplinary approach has been adopted. To begin with, rice will be exhaustively studied in different historical contexts. The main sources used are literary texts, inscriptions and excavated sites. We may consider each of these sources.

Literary Sources

As far as the literary sources are concerned, the most representative texts of different periods from the Ṛgveda to the 7th—8th century A.D. have been discussed. What was kept in view while going through these texts related to the antiquity of rice, its varieties, modes of its cultivation and utilisation (apart from that as a cereal) and the areas in which it was cultivated. Where evidence regarding the general agricultural background was available, it was mentioned too.

The limitations of the available source material may be outlined. Literary sources are overwhelmingly religious in character and therefore do not purport to provide more than a glimpse of the existing economic conditions. Secular texts are either literary, political or scientific treatises with not many exhaustive references. Most of the conclusions are in the form of inferences drawn from allusions. The nature of the references is mainly repetitious. Occasionally, however, they do provide a wide range of information which, when assimilated into a composite picture, is illuminating.

The chronology—or rather the lack of it—is another major problem to be contended with. In order to present an evolving picture, it is imperative to have a fairly accurate time bracket within which to place the data. The texts which have been consulted can, at best, only be provided with a roughly relative chronology with all its inherent limitations.

Another handicap is the general difficulty in determining the geographical background of the texts. Such a determination is essential especially when one is dealing with a cereal which is linked with, and dependent on, geographical factors. Only in some cases are such specific references available, whereas in others, the generally assumed territorial background of a text is taken for granted. Therefore, a study of regional variations in crop pattern, land use etc., cannot be attempted in any detail.

Yet a cautious appreciation of the available literary evidence does go a long way in building up a complete picture of the early history of rice in India. In any case, we shall try to make clear the nature of our literary references to rice in various texts up to the 7th—8th century A.D.

Inscriptional Evidence

The inscriptional evidence from around the third century B.C. to the fourteenth century A.D. was scrutinised. The points relating to antiquity, geographical background and uses (other than the primary one) of rice were probed.

The obvious advantages of inscriptions are linked to four factors. Firstly, they can be more precisely dated than literary sources. Secondly, they provide a more precise idea of the geographical context. Thirdly, since they deal more succinctly with socio-economic matters, some details are particularly revealing. Fourthly, there is little likelihood of interpolations. The material available may therefore be regarded as fairly authentic. The later inscriptions were scrutinised because the earlier ones in most cases lack in suitable data.

This is not meant to imply that there are no shortcomings in this source. On most occasions, the references tend to follow a particular pattern and hence appear repetitious. Sometimes the references to rice are fairly indirect. In fact, of the corpus of inscriptions, very few have many significant details on rice.

However, on balance, it seems that these disadvantages do not obscure, the advantages outlined above.

Archaeological Evidence

Archaeological evidence, by its very nature, is precise in character. The material recovered can be subjected to direct scrutiny and inferences drawn therefrom. The spatio-temporal issues pose few problems. The issues related to rice which were looked into were its antiquity, varieties, uses (apart from that as a cereal), and regions of its cultivation.

Certain shortcoming of archaeology as a source must be mentioned. Not all the excavated rice remains have been scientifically or historically analysed. There are also some problems relating to scientific investigation of remains which leave much for controversy and dispute. Beside. the information yielded by the remains is often disappointingly meagre. This evidence also can prove to be of as limited use as the innumerable repetitions in the literary sources.

The evidence from these three sources constitute the core of the historical evidence. The utilisation of a multi-disciplinary approach had been mentioned at the outset. The material from the other disciplines relate to botany, linguistics and ethnography. We may discuss the approach to each separately.

The botanical issues relevant to the early history of rice were taken into consideration. The main focus was on the problems of origin and evolution, domestication, varietal differentiation and spatial spread. The study was thus provided with a sound theoretical underpinning in the light of which historical data could be processed.

As for linguistics, one aspect of it, i.e. the terms for rice in Indian language families, was discussed. This may be said to provide a link with the earlier literary sources. Such an exercise enable one not only to locate the developments within a language family but also to trace inter-relationships among different families. Besides, on the basis of such a study, the cultural significance of rice in a given context emerges very strongly. A better historical understanding follows from such an exercise.

Ethnography in this study serves two purposes. Firstly, it provides us with the details regarding rice cultivation which were lacking in the historical sources. This is crucial to the study of land use, cropping patterns and regional variations which are significant in studies such as the present one. Though this data cannot be treated as purely historical data, its use lies mainly in facilitating interpretations and providing the basis for hypothesis-building.

Secondly, ethnographic data have been used to highlight the use of rice among a few primitive tribes in their socio-religious rites and customs. This was mainly because the bulk of evidence from historical sources had pointed to the abundant use of rice in these contexts. Such a study enabled one to understand why such a mode of utilisation was prevalent what the views held on it were and a few other illuminating details. A couple of features of the historical data can be more easily explained on the basis of the survey.

As it is amply clear, the purpose of the present study is to draw on certain historical details relating to rice and supplement them with details and interpretations from other relevant disciplines. Hopefully, a better understanding of the early history of rice in India will emerge. The contribution will not lie in the use of this approach alone, but also in that many significant points will have been highlighted and compiled into one coherent whole.

2

The Textual and Inscriptional Evidence

THIS chapter proposes to evaluate and make explicit the nature of the literary and inscriptional source–material on the early history of rice in India. The survey of the ancient texts and inscriptions may not be exhaustive but, hopefully, enough has been cited to provide a clear insight into the nature and implications of the data.

I. The Texts

1. *The Ṛgveda* (Griffith, 1963 ; Vishvabandhu, 1964-5)

It would not perhaps be quite correct to presume that the Ṛgvedic people were only pastoralists. References in the "Family Books" reveal considerable familiarity with agricultural practices. The following is among the most graphic addressed to Kṣetrapati, a term which has been explained by Monier Williams (1899 : 332) as denoting the lord of the soil, as also a kind of tutelary deity.

(a) "*Śuna* and *Sīra* welcome ye this land, and with the milk which ye have made in heaven, bedew ye both this earth of ours" (IV. 57.5).

(b) "Auspicious *Sīta*, come thou near : we venerate and

worship thee. That thou mayst bless and prosper us and bring us fruits abundantly" (IV. 57.6).

(c) "May Indra press the burrows (*Sīta*) down, may Pusan guide its course aright. May she ...be drained for us through each succeeding year" (IV. 57.7).

(d) "Happily let the shares (*phāla*) turn up the ploughland. Happily go the ploughers (*kinaśa*) with the oxen...grant us prosperity, *Śuna* and *Sīra*" (IV. 57. 8).

Sīra has been described as a plough by Monier Williams (1899 : 1219) and Macdonell and Keith (1958 : 451). The latter describe *Śuna* and *Sīra* as the names of two agricultural deities, the personifications probably of the share and the plough (Macdonell and Keith 1958 : 386). *Sīta,* according to Monier Williams (1899 : 1218) means not only a furrow but a deity invoked as presiding over agriculture of the fruits of the earth. There are no other meanings attributed to *phāla* and *kinaśa* besides the ones mentioned already.

Kṛsh is the term generally used to denote cultivation. Monier Williams (1899 : 306) describes it as meaning drawing or making furrows or ploughing. There are many references to cultivated fields which are referred to as *urvara* (IV. 38. 1 ; IV. 41.6 ; VI. 20.1 ; VI. 25.4 ; VIII. 21. 3 ; VIII. 91.5) and Kṣetra (V. 62. 7 ; IX. 85. 4 ; IX. 91. 6). There is also mention of sickles (*dātra*, VIII. 78.10). reaping (X. 131.2) and garners (II.14.11). Crops were probably dependent on rain (II. 56.10). The importance of agriculture is attested not only by prayers for agricultural prosperity but also by the use of the cereal cultivated in rituals (I. 135. 8).

A certain uncertainty arises when it comes to identifying the cereals cultivated. The term generally used to denote them is *Yava.* According to Monier Williams (1899 : 847) and Macdonell and Keith (1958 : 187) in the earliest times, it was probably any grain or corn yielding flour or meal. It is translated as barley by Benfey (1866 : 737) and Apte (1959 : 455). Occasionally the term, *dhāna* (V. 53. 13 ; IV. 24. 7 ; I. 16.2) refers to the creal commonly used.

Monier Williams (1899 : 514), however, states that it may be taken to denote rice, too. Macdonell and Keith (1958 : 345) on the other, hand, assert that the term in the Ṛgvedic context cannot be taken to denote rice.

Enough attention has not been focused on this point. Whether *Yava* and *dhāna* signified generic terms for cereals or a particular crop, remains to be determined. The contexts themselves are hardly useful for a precise identification.

However, the following point needs emphasis. There are enough references to rice in the later Vedic texts to suggest that rice was one of the most important cereals during the period and that rice was an integral part of the rituals including the household ones. It is quite unlikely that the occurrence of rice in the later Vedic texts did not have a long antecedence in India and that this antecedence does not go back to the Ṛgvedic period.

We have to depend upon the *Saṃhitās* of the Yajurveda. Sāmaveda, Atharvaveda, the Brahmaṇas, the Araṇyakas and the Upanisads, all religious works, for the later Vedic period, which roughly speaking, comes down to 500 B.C. (Sharma, 1968 : 15).

2. *The Taittirīya Saṁhitā of the Black Yajurveda* (Vedic Sansodhana Maṇḍala 1972 ; Keith 1967)

Agricultural practices are described in the course of rituals.

(a) "...He ploughs with a (team) of six oxen ; the seasons are six ; verily with the seasons he ploughs him. In that (he ploughs) with (a team) of twelve oxen (he ploughs) with the year. This (earth) was afraid of excessive burning by Agni ; she saw this of two sorts, ploughed and unploughed, (it serves to prevent) her being excessively burned...." (V. 2.5).

The mention of the "keen shared plough" (*phala*, IV,IV. 2.5. (r) is significant. It may be taken to mean a metal share, though one cannot be specific about the details. Wells, probably used for irrigation, are mentioned (IV. 2.5 (n). Fourteen types of plants are mentioned; seven domesticated and seven wild (V. 2.5). Though no details are available, the diversity of crops is worth noting as also the acquaintance with their wild relatives. A few of the crops are mentioned in IV 7.4. They are rice, barley, beans, sesams, kidney beans, vetches, wheat, lentils, millet, *panicum miliaceum*, *panicum frumentaceum* and wild rice. (*Vrīhi*, *Yava*, *Māsha*, *Tila*, *Mudga*, *Khalavasha*, *Godhuma*, *Masura*, *Śyāmaka*, *Priyangu*, *Meṇava*, *Nīvara*). With special reference to rice what is important is the mention of both wild and cultivated rice. The mention of different varieties of rice is significant.

(b)"....To Agni, lord of the house, he offers a cake of black rice (Krişṇanām Vrīhina) on eight potsherds.... to Savitṛ of true instigation, a cake of swift growing rice (*Aśunām Vrīhina*) on tweive potsherds...to Bṛhaspati, lord of speech, an oblation of wild rice (*Naivāram*) ; to Indra, the noblest, a cake of large rice (*Mahāvrihīṇam*) on eleven potsherds...." (I. 8.10).

(c) "....From the house of a village judge further on he should take rice ; he should separate out the white and the black ; of the white (*Śukla Vrīhi*), he should offer an oblation to the Adityas...of the dark ones he should offer an oblation to Varuna...." (II. 3.1).

Different sizes of rice grains were known. This, too, may be taken as indicative of different varieties of rice, though it cannot be so confirmed.

(d) "...He should divide the rice grains into three parts ; the mean size he should make into a cake on eight potsherds for Agni, the giver, the largest he should give as a mess to Indra, the bestower, the smallest to Visnu . ." (II. 5.5).

No further details are available regarding the varieties of rice. There may have been more than one rice crop in a year though there is specific mention of the rice crop being harvested in autumn.

(e) "...He gave to the spring the sap, to the hot season barley, to the rains, plants, to autumn rice, beans and sesamum to winter and the cool season" (VII. 2.10).

It ts clear that rice was an important item in rituals.

(f) "...What then is the five-fold character of the sacrifice ? Fried grains, mush, rice grains, the cake, clotted milk, thereby the five is made up ...." (VI. 5.11).

Rice broken by nails, husked and unhusked rice grains (I. 8.9) and after-shoots of rice (II. 3.4) were also offered to the various deities.

The terms most commonly used to denote rice in the *Taittirīya Samhitā* is *Vrīhi* to which different varieties have been appended. Monier-Williams (1899 : 1043) and Macdonell and Keith (1958, I : 345) briefly define it as rice. What can be suggested from a study of the text is that rice, with its different varieties, occupies an important place among a great diversity of crops, as also in the realm of religious rituals.

3. *The Vājasaneyī Saṁhitā* (Griffith 1957)

The Vajasaneyi Samhita belongs to the white Yajurveda. The use of rice in rituals is emphasised in the text. (I. 1-22 ; XVII ; XX ; XXI). The preparation of the cakes is described at length, from taking the rice grain from the cart, winnowing and pounding it and cooking an offering. However, it must bc noted that we know of the use of rice in rituals from the commentary appended to the text. Otherwise, the passages appear too obscure. Besides the ritualistic aspect there is little significant information. This in itself is important as it is comparable with evidence from the *Taittīriya Saṁhitā.*

4. *The Sāmaveda* (Griffith 1963)

Of the terms used to denote rice in the earlier texts, there is no mention in the Sāmaveda. This may be attributed to the fact that it is mainly based on the Ṛgveda and possesses little, if any, originality. Most of the references speak of the offering of barley and corn to deities (I. II. 7). There are a few prayers to the gods to send rain and plentiful food (II. IV. 3).

5. *The Atharvaveda* (Griffith 1916-1917 ; Vishvabandhu 1960-2)

References to agriculture are copious. Description of agricultural operations and the concern for a successful crop can be seen in the following hymns.

(a) "...Let homage to their ploughs (lāṅgala) be paid, our homage to the pole and yokes" (II. 8.4).

There is mention of keen shared plough, too (III. 17.3) as in the *Taittīriya Saṁhitā.*

(b) "...Cause this corn (*dhānyam*) of ours to be exhaustless" (III. 24.4).

(c) "...Let the ripe grains (*bījam*) come near and near the sickle" (III. 17.2).

(d) "...Bring higher increase of the corn prepared and yet to be prepared" (III. 24.5).

There are prayers to protect corn from lightning (VII. II. 1), famine (IV. XVII. 6) and pests (VI. XL. 1).

Products like rice (*Vrīhi*), barley (*Yava*), millet (*Śyāmaka*), beans (*Māsha*), Sesamum (*Tila*), sugar cane (*Ikshu*), besides some fruits and vegetables are mentioned, some of which have not been found to occur in earlier texts. Among the agricultural products, rice and barley are specially important.

Different varieties of rice are not mentioned apart from *Vrīhi*. Besides being an important cereal, rice was taken to possess—along with some other items—medicinal and recuperative powers.

(e) ".... Barley and rice (*Vrīhi*) are healing balms, the sons of Heaven who never die" (VIII. 7.20).

(f) "Auspicious unto thee be rice (*Vrīhi*) and barley, causing no painful sickness or consumption, these deliver from calamity" (VIII. 2.18).

It is closely identified with Prāṇa or breath (XI. 4.13) and prosperity (X. 6.24). These passages may be taken to reiterate the importance of rice in the economy.

Equally significant is the offering of rice to various deities in religious rituals. Such offerings may be in the form of *Odana* (XI. 4.13) etc. *Charu* (XVIII. 4.16 etc.) and *Purodāśa* (XII. 4.35). This provides the earliest reference to forms of offering common in later rituals. Macdonell and Keith (1958 : 124) and Monier-Williams (1899 : 390, 635) define the above as denoting mess, usually of grains cooked to be offered to the gods. The importance of these offering appears in the following hymns.

(g) "...The sacrificial word, all worlds are to be won with *Odana*" (XI. 3.19).

(h) "*Odana* which Prajapati, the first born of order, dressed with fervour for the Brahman, which guards the worlds from breaking at the centre,—I with this *Odana* will conquer Mrityu" (IV. XXXV. 1).

(i) "...That *Odana* with hundred streams, sky reaching, hath in its might pervaded heaven and earth." (XII. 3.5).

Taṇḍula was also used in rituals. (X. 9. 26) Monier-Williams

(1899 : 432) has described it as grain, especially of rice, obtained after threshing and winnowing.

It has been observed that most of the references to rice related to them as offerings. This may be taken to attest the significant role of rice in the social life of the people. No direct evidence is available on other aspects related to rice production.

6. *The Aitareya Brahmana* (Haug 1977)

With reference to the agricultural background, an interesting detail which emerges from the text is the mention of cereals growing in the southern countries (I. 2.7). Sāyana explains the passage as follows in the commentary. To the north of the Vindhya mountains, chiefly barley and wheat are cultivated, which ripen in February and March whilst in the countries south of the Vindhyas, rice prevails, which ripens in November and December. However, being a late authority, the above explanation cannot be accepted wholly. But it may be assumed that this text embraces a wider ambit than the earlier texts. The other references to agriculture relate to ploughing (III. III. 38), irrigation (VII. 7. 24) and harvest offerings (VII. 2.9). Little new light is thrown on the subject.

Most of the references to rice occur in rituals where it is offered as *Charu* (I. 1.1), *Purodāśa* (II.I. 9 ; II. III. 23 etc.) and *Pāyasa* (II. III. 23). The symbolical significance is enunciated in some cases.

(a) "The *purodāśa* is the animal which is killed. The chaff and straw of the rice of which it consists are the hairs of the animal, its husks the skin, its smallest particles the blood, all the fine particles to which the rice is ground represent the flesh, and whatever others substantial part is in the rice, are the bones"(II. 1.9).

Rice was also used in coronation ceremonies.

(b) "Next he shall order to bring four kinds of grain from vegetables viz. rice with small grains, rice with large grains, priyangu and barley...rice with large grains represents universal sovereignty... the priyangus...represents enjoyment of pleasures...barley represents the skill as military commander. By bringing their sprouts he places such a skill in him (the king)" (VIII. 4.16).

The different sizes of rice grains mentioned in the above

context may be taken to indicate different varieties of rice but there is no direct reference.

Though not much new light is thrown on the topic, a few useful points, viz. agriculture in the south and the use of rice in different ceremonies, may be said to have emerged.

7. *The Śatapatha Brāhmana* (Eggeling 1966 ; Chowkhamba Sanskrit series 1964).

This is the best known, the most extensive, and doubtless, also on account of its contents, the most important of all the *Brahmana.*

There are many interesting references to agriculture. Bringing of land east of the Sadānīra under the plough is mentioned (1.4, 1.15). Its identification is not definite though it has been taken to denote the river Gandak. The agricultural prosperity of the Asuras is also mentioned (I. 6.1.3.). They may be taken to represent the non-Vedic population in certain areas. Crops not referred to in earlier texts are flax and hemp (VI. 6.1.24). Fruits also figure in hymns (V. 5.4.10). Seventeen kinds of food are spoken of (V. 2.2.3) but they remain unspecified. Homage paid to agricultural implements is mentioned (VII. 2.2.4). Assurance of food seems a constant concern (III. 2.1.30). Though agriculture was flourishing, the mass of the peasantry was an oppressed lot (VI. 1.2.25).

References to rice relate mainly to rituals. There are elaborate descriptions of the preparation of the rice cake (I. 1.2.5 ; I. 1.4.20 ; I. 1.4.23). The *Anvāhārya* mess is another preparation of rice which is offered beside the rice cake (I. 2.3.5). Different varieties of rice are mentioned and why they are offered to particular deities.

(a) "For Savitri Satyaprasava (of true impulse), he prepares a cake from fast grown (*plāśuka)* rice on either twelve or eighteen potsherds ; for Savitri is the impeller of the gods. "May I be quickened, impelled by Savitri ! thus (he thinks). And as to (its being) of fast grown rice, " may they quickly impel me, "he thinks" (V. 3.3.2).

(b) "For Agni Grihapti he then prepares a cake on eight potsherds from quick grown (*āśu*) ; for the house lord's position means prosperity : as much as he (the king) rules over, over that Agni, the houselord, leads him to hold the position of a master of the house. And to its being of quick grown rice : "May they quickly lead me ! So he thinks" (V. 3.3.3).

(c) "For Brahaspati Vak (speech) he then prepares a pap of wild rice (*nīvāra*) ; thereby Bṛhaspati quickens him for speech. And as to its being prepared of wild rice, Bṛhaspati is the Brahmaṇ and they, the wild rice plants are ripened by the Brahmaṇ : Hence it is prepared of wild rice." (V. 3.3.5).

(d) "For Indra Jyestha (the most excellent) he then prepares a pap of red rice grains (*hāyāna*) : thereby Indra, the most excellent, leads him to excellence or lordship. And as to its being prepared of red rice : outstanding doubtless are those plants, the red rice, and outstanding is Indira : therefore it is prepared of red rice" (V. 3.3.6).

There are references to black rice, too.

(e) "He cooks the pap for Nirrīti of black rice, after splitting the grains with his nails" (V. 3.2.13)

Different sizes of rice grains are mentioned.

(f) "They divide the rice grains into two parts : the smaller and broken ones belong to Bṛhaspati, and the larger and unbroken ones to Mitra..." (V. 3.2.7).

It appears that a greater variety of rice crops were known than in the earlier period. The varieties not mentioned in the foregoing texts are *plāśuka* and *hāyāna.* The former has been described by Macdonell and Keith (1958 : 56) as an epithet of rice in the sense of shooting up rapidly. This is comparable to *āśu*, described by Monier-Williams (1899 : 157) as rice ripening quickly in the rainy season. The latter, states Monier Williams (1899 : 1297), is a sort of red rice. In other words, the terminological study confirms the description provided in the text.

Malted rice also appears as part of the offerings in certain rituals. It is grain that has germinated and subsequently become dry.

(g) "There are grains of rice and grains of millet, grains of wheat and kuvala jujubes, Indra grain and badara jujubes, malted rice and barley...both cultivated and wild grain food he thereby secures" (XII. 7.2.9).

The auspicious quality of rice is clear from the following passages.

(h) "...From his (Indra's) bones his sweet drink flowed and became the nyagrodha tree ; from his marrow his drink, the soma juice flowed, and became rice : in this way his energies, or vital powers, went from him" (XIL. 7.1.9).

(i) "At first, namely, the gods offered up a man as their victim...when he was offered up, the sacrificial essence went out of him...

It entered into this earth. They searched for it by digging. They found it (in the shape of) those two (substances), the rice and barley : therefore even now they obtain those two by digging ; and as much efficacy as all those sacrificial animal victims would have for him, so much efficacy had this oblation (of rice) for him who knows this. And thus there is in this oblation also that completeness which they call the five-fold animal sacrifice" (I. 2.3. 6-7).

Though the references to rice in the text are fairly numerous, they are mostly of a rather stereotyped nature. There is not much that can be gleaned from them save the varieties of rice offered, the mode of preparing these offerings and the mythical explanation of these offerings. Besides, little specific evidence on rice is available. Agriculture, in general, appears to have been well developed which may be taken to account for the numerous agricultural products which figure in various rituals.

8. *Other Brahmaṇas*

Brahmaṇas like the *Panchaviṁśa Brāhmana* (Caland, 1931) and the *Jaiminīya Brāhmaṇa* of the Śāmaveda (Bodewitz, 1973) and the *Gopatha Brāhmaṇa* of the Atharvaveda (Mitra 1972) also contain references to offerings of rice, the advantages thereof and rites relating to them. However, no new light is thrown on either the agricultural background or the cereal, rice, in particular.

9. *The Upaniṣads* (Max Muller 1965 ; Vidyarnava 1933 ; Swahananda 1956)

The Upaniṣads are mainly philosophical treatises and, as

such, do not provide direct evidence on our topic. However, a few relevant allusions may be said to occur.

The kinds of cultivated crops are mentioned such as barley, sesamum and kidney beans, millet, panic seed, wheat, lentils, pulses and vetches (Brihadāraṇyaka Up. VI. 3.13) which have been found in the foregoing texts, too. The importance of harvest sacrifices is stressed (Muṇḍaka Up. I. 2.3).

As far as the cereal, rice, goes it figures in various philosophical analogies. This underlines the importance of rice in the daily lives of the people. The following passages may be said to substantiate it.

(a) "That person, under the form of mind (*manas*) being light indeed, is within the heart, small like a grain of rice (*Vrihi*) or barley. He is the ruler of all, the lord of all, he rules all this, whatever exists" (Brihadāṛanyaka Up. 6.1).

(b) "From him the many Devas, too, are begotton, and sadhyas, men, cattle, birds, the up and down breathings, rice and corn (for sacrifices), penance, faith, truth, abstinence and Law" (Muṇḍaka Up. II. 1.7).

The use of rice in various religious rituals also occurs.

(c) "The father, when going to depart, calls his son after having strewn the grass...and having laid the sacrificial fire, and having placed it near a pot of water with a jug (full of rice), himself covered with a new cloth and dressed in white" (Kausitaki Up. II. 11.15).

A couple's fertility is also meant to be enhanced after partaking of various rice preparations.

(d) "...at the end of the three days...the husband should make her pound rice (*Vrīhi*). And if a man wants that a white son should be born to him, and that he should know one Veda, and live to his full age, then after having prepared boiled rice with milk and butter, they should both get fit to have offering ..." (Brihadaṛanyaka Up. 4. 13-14).

The only term used to describe rice in the Upanisads is *Vrīhi.* No Varieties are mentioned. The only new light thrown on the topic is in the form of analogies in philosophical contexts. The use of rice in ceremonies is not illuminating. A deeper explanation, not available, is needed for the fertility enhancing powers of the cereal, if it is not to be dismissed as a mere myth.

10. *The Śrauta Sūtras* (Dandekar 1962, 1973).

The nature of the texts being such, i.e. related to the treatment of sacrifices, different authorities quote the same rituals with but slight variations. Not much new light is thrown on the agricultural background. Rice figures in plenty of ceremonies and a tabulation will be better able to project the general nature of references (Table 1).

Though there are many such references, some which are more relevant to our study are also found. Black and white paddy are mentioned often.

(a)"...(If one does not regain his kingdom), he should fetch paddy from the house of a person who may be agitating on behalf of the village from outside. He should separate the white and black. It is said in the Brahmaṇa—one should pour out for the Adityas, the grains that are white...one should pour out for Varuṇa the grains that are black..." (Baudh. 13.21).

Other types of rice are syamaka and nivara.

(b) "One who fears impotence, should offer to Vajin some cooked *śyāmaka rice*" (Baudh. 13. 26).

The mention of syamaka rice is interesting for syamaka elsewhere is taken to refer to millet.

(c) "...One who desires that others should regard him as equal to men of high status, should perform this sacrifice. He should offer...a cake of *nīvāra* grains on eleven potsherds to Marutvant Indra..." (Man. 5.1.10. 1-9).

Black and white paddy have been mentioned in earlier texts, but not much is known about them. Nivara, we know, refers to wild rice.

(d) "A cake of *apatānta* rice on eight potsherds to Gṛhapati Agni, cooked *śyāmaka* rice to Vacaspati Bṛhaspati, a cake of *hāyāna* on eleven potsherds to Jyestha Indra..." (Man 5.2. 720-22).

Hayana refers to red rice but the meaning of apatanta rice is not clear. Different sizes of rice grains (Man. 5.1.10.61-62) probably convey the sense of different varieties.

It is clear that rice played a very important part in rituals. Different varieties were available as is obvious from the foregoing. The importance of a rice offering is clear from the following passage :

TABLE 1

Rice in the Rituals of the Srauta—Sutras

Purpose of Sacrifice	Rice Offering	Authority	Details of Reference
For one though learned has not attained success	To Soma-Rudra rice cooked in the milk of a white cow	Kātyāyana	(15.3.22)
To regain the kingdom from the conqueror	To Adityas rice cooked in clarified butter	Mānava	(5.1.8)
For one who is desirous of a village	To Visvedevas-rice grains should be fixed together	Baudhāyana	(13.30)
For one suffering from a pulmonary disease	To Adityas-rice cooked on a new moon day	Baudhāyana	(13.28)

For one overtaken by misfortune	The Adhvaryu should go through the rites up to the pouring out of paddy for crushing	Baudhāyana	(13.33-34)
To be endowed with Rasa	To Agni-rice cooked in goat's milk	Baudhāyana	(13.7)
For rain	Rice to be cooked in earthen pitcher and on Ahavaniya fire	Varāha	(1.3)
If one's army rises against him	To Indrani-cooked rice	Mānava	(51.9.36)
Animal sacrifice	From taking up the winnowing basket to preparation of Apyas	Baudhāyana	(4.8-10)
For one desiring heaven	To Anumati and Asa, cooked rice	Kāthaka	(p. 639)

(e) "...When there is no specific injunction the havis (paddy and barley should be regarded as the oblation)" (Baudh. 24.9).

Rice was used to prepare the following items: rice flour (Āpast. 8. 1-4), rice dough (Kat. 15. 7. 30-34), *surasoma* (Baudh. 17. 31. 38), pop corn, tari and masara (Charaka Sautramani). The last two items were used for preparing wine.

The rice-in-ritual motif predominates. *Apatānta* rice and different preparations of rice are the only additions to our information regarding the cereal in the period.

11. *The Gṛhya Sūtras* (Oldenberg 1964)

References to the agricultural background are mainly in the form of sacrifices connected with the different stages of the agricultural operations. The repetitive and ritual mention of rice offering in various ceremonies is overwhelming. They are part of the ceremonies performed from the wife's confinement (Gobhila-II. 7.9) to the birth of the child (Āpastamba-VI. 15.6), daily oblations (Hiranyakeśin-I. 2. 7. 21), marriages (Hiranyakesin-I. 6. 21. 6.) and funerals (Āpastamba-VIII. 21. 12). They are also used in some special ceremonies (Gobhila-I. 5. 19). There is not much information about the cereal in these references. Different preparations of rice were offered. In one sacrifice, the fallings-off of rice grains is used (Khadira-IV. 3. 6.) though its meaning is not clear. It was considered meritorious to distribute rice after certain ceremonies to Brahmanas (Śānkhyāyana-III. 2. 16).

Not much that is directly relevant can be gleaned from the above references save that rice was an important agricultural product which played a significant role in the social life of the people.

12. *The Dharma Sūtras* (Buhler 1965)

These have been dated by one source to the period spanning c. 500-200 B.C. (Sharma, 1968 : 15). Details regarding agriculture, in general, are not very significant. Rice figures in rituals similar to those mentioned in the previous texts. Interest ingly, it figures in various penances enjoined on those who transgress the sacred law.

(a) "If (a wife) has been mentally unfaithful to her husband, she shall live on barley or rice boiled in milk during three days and sleep on the bare ground." (Vāśishtha XXI. 6).

There are restrictions regarding trade in rice which are significant.

(b) "Among the various kinds of grain, he (the Brahmana) shall especially not sell sesamum or rice..." (Āpastamba-I. 7. 20).

(c) "He who sells sesamum, forsooth, sells his ancestors ; he who sells rice, forsooth, sells his life, he who gives away his daughter, making a bargain, forsooth, sells portions of his spiritual merit" (Baudh. II. 1. 2. 27).

However, it appears that barter was permitted.

(d) "It is permitted to barter sesamum, rice, cooked food, learning and slaves (each for its own kind and the one for the other)" (Vāśistha II. 39).

It is recommended for a householder that he obtain husked rice from "virtuous men" (Baudh. III. 2. 13). The reasons behind such restrictions are not clear. It is probably another reflection on the supposedly sacred character of rice. There are similar telling references relating to restrictions of the use of rice (Vāsishtha-XIV. 37).

Besides, liquor obtained from rice is mentioned (Vasishtha XX. 19).

The value of the Dharmasutras lies in the fact that besides its use in rituals, rice, in these texts, figures in restrictions and penances which we have not come across in earlier texts.

Though none of the works of the Buddhist literature can possibly date back to the period of Buddha himself, isolated texts preserved in these works may probably be regarded as words of Buddha. Their component parts may be said to belong to different times. They were probably committed to writing in the first century B.C. The Tripiṭaka consists of three so-called *pitakas* or "baskets" namely (1) Vinayapiṭaka, "basket of the discipline of the order"; (2) Suttapiṭaka, "basket of Suttas"; (3) Abhid-hammapiṭaka, "basket of the higher subtleties of the doctrine". The first two "baskets" have been consulted for our purpose.

13. *The Vinaya Piṭaka* (Horner 1940, 1942, 1949, 1951, 1952).

This section contains all that refers to the monastic community, the rules of the discipline of the order, precepts for the daily life of the monks and nuns, and so on. There is some information which throws new light on the agricultural background in general viz. an enumeration of all the agricultural processes from ploughing of the field to the storage of the crop (VII. 3) and the mention of crops like *kangu* (millet), *Varaka* (bean) and *Kudrusaka* (rye) XXV in the commentary.

References to rice are fairly numerous. However, most of them described rice as a cereal. The two varieties mentioned are *Vrīhi* and *Sāli*. The former is the Pali version of the Sanskrit term *Vrihi*. According to Macdonell and Keith (1958 : 376) Sali is a later word for rice. Monier Williams (1899 : 1067) states that it has ten varieties. Suryakanta (1975 : 580) describes it as rice which is sown in the rainy season and harvested in winter.

Prepared rice appears by various names like *Odana* (XXXV), *Bhatta* (XXVII) and *Sukkhākura* (XXXVIII). The last term conveys the meaning of dried boiled rice which may be moistened for purposes of consumption. Whereas in the earlier texts the emphasis has been on the ritualistic use of rice, the Buddhist texts unambiguously stress that rice was the staple article of diet of the Ganges valley. Laymen generously gave away rice, prepared in different ways to the Buddhist monks by way of alms (II). The size of the monk's bowl was measured according to the amount of rice it held (XXI). Most of the references relate to how monks should collect and utilise the rice they receive. Stealing (II) and coveting others' share (II) is frowned upon as is wastage (III). Shortage of rice is spoken of when there would be a drop in alms giving (II). Mention of wagon loads of rice, on the other hand, would give an indication of plenty and trade (VI).

Though references to rice as a cereal predominate we get some insight into rice cultivation, in particular, regions of its production and a few other uses of rice. There is in the *Mahāvagga* a description of what is supposed to be an extensive terraced rice field.

(a) "Then the Lord having stayed in Rājagaha for as long

as he found suitable, set out on tour for Dakkhinagiri. The Lord saw the field of Magadha laid out in strips, laid out in lines, laid out in embankments, laid out in squares, and seeing this he addressed the venerable Ananda saying, "Are you able Ananda, to provide robes like this for the monks ?" (VIII. 12. 1).

This is one of first references to a rice field in a particular region. Other regions associated with rice production are Champā (II), Sāvatthī (II), and Rājagaha (VIII).

Liquor obtained from cooked rice is mentioned (I. 1). In certain ailments, rice was not the suitable diet (VI).

The Sutta Piṭaka is the most reliable source for Dhamma. It consists of five Nikayas or "Collections" namely (i) Dīghanikāya, (ii) Majjhimanikāya, (iii) Samyuttanikāya, (iv) Anguttaranikāya and (v) Khuddakanikāya. The last named comprises the following texts : 1. Khuddakapatha, 2. Dhammapada, 3. Udana, 4. Itivuttaka, 5. Suttanipāta, 6. Vimānavatthu, 7. Petavatthu, 8. Theragāthā, 9. Therīgāthā, 10. Jātaka, 11. Niddesa, 12. Patisambhidamagga, 13. Apadāna, 14. Buddhavamsa and 15. Cariyapiṭaka.

14. *The Majjhima Nikāya* (Horner 1954, 1957, 1959)

References to the agricultural background are not very illuminating. Mention of rice is mainly with regard to it as a mode of subsistence and variations thereof. Hill paddy, wbich we have not come across earlier is mentioned (10). There are no details about it. Wild rice (12) and rice from which the black grains have been removed (77) also occur. The last variety is similar to a reference mentioned while discussing the Srauta Sutras which speaks of the separations of white and black paddy. However, the exact connotation is not clear. There is reference to a mythical large grained rice (12) compared to the existing, presumably smaller grains.

Different preparations of rice are boiled rice (91), rice cooked in milk (35), gruel and powder of rice husks (12). There are many repetitions, besides, especially relating to the distribution of rice by the laity to the monks (35).

It appears that the mention of hill paddy is more significant among the other details regarding agriculture and rice available from the study of this text.

15. *The Saṃyutta Nikāya* (Davids and Woodward 1950-56)

The "Collection of Grouped Discourses" contains relatively few references to rice. It again appears as the staple food. As for varieties, only choicest rice is mentioned (XXII. 96) which in itself is not a specific reference particularly useful to us. Rice distribution, as alms, recurs, with special mention of Sāvatthī (I.81.3). Interestingly, there is a reference to a Brahmana offering a preparation of rice with ghee in a religious ceremony (VII. 1.8) as in the earlier Vedic texts.

The mention of choicest rice in the text is significant but there are no details available. Not much can be gathered regarding our topic, besides.

The Khuddaka Nikāya

16. *The Jatakas* (Fausboll 1877-97 ; Cowell 1957)

These are described as "stories of former births (of the Buddha)". Some of the poems and a few of the prose narratives may reach back to the time of the Buddha or a still earlier time. For the great mass of the verses, however, no greater antiquity than the third century B.C. can conscientiously be urged, certainly not proved, and much of the prose assuredly belongs to the Christian era, (Winternitz, II, 1972, p. 122). Taken together, they provide some valuable references.

Agriculture, on the whole, seems well developed judging by the description of current practices. The use of iron plough-shares was common. A diversity of crops was known. Extension of agriculture in virgin territory was being carried out.

Among the varieties of rice mentioned prominent is hill paddy.

(a) ". . . The king replied, 'No leaves for me, that is not my fare ; give a bowl of pure hill rice, cooked with a subtle flavouring of meat to make the pottage nice" (XXII. 538).

The original Pali term used for this variety is *Sali* which we have come across earlier.

Wild rice, described in Pali as *Nīvāram* and *Sayamjātisālim* is spoken of, often with reference to where it may be found. These are significant for the regions where wild rice is available are rarely mentioned in the other literary texts.

(b) ". . . he flew to the Himalaya hills . . . eating his fill of the clumps of rice that grew wild there" (XIV. 484).

(c) ". . . one day, having along with his flock eaten the wild rice that grew in a certain pool in the plains of India, he flew through the air, and he flew slowly as in sport to Cittakuta" (XIII. 476).

Red paddy (*Rattasālivam*) in water deep as elephants can stand in, is mentioned once (XVI. 514). *Vrīhi* is referred to (1II. 276). Other types are not specifically mentioned though there is reference to superior quality rice (I. 5).

(d) " . . . Thus answer made the monarch great . . . Fine rice has been their food . . . If they must feed on wild-tree fruit, what will the children do . . . Take herbs, roots, honey, meat and rice, thc whitest and the best : Enjoy it at your will, O King . . . ." (XXII. 546).

Rice grains were known as *taṇḍula* (II. 23). While preparations of rice were known as *bhattam* (IX. 432) and *pāyasa* (I. 146).

The importance of rice is clear from the following passage.

(e) "One, who like, rice, Sire, was the refuge of the people, stole the property. When that is recovered, why ask about the thief" ? (IX. 432).

Gandhāra (I. 28) ; Benaras (I. 23) ; Sāvatthī (I. 6) and Magadha (I. 11) seem to be closely associated with rice production. The mention of Gandhāra in the Northwest is significant for it is not a traditionally rice growing region.

Agricultural operations related to rice cultivation are specified. There is mention of huge estates where rice was grown (*Sālikhettam*).

(f) " . . . There stood a Brahmin village . . . he held an estate of one thousand acres, where he grew rice . . ." (XIV. 484).

A field with ripening rice crop is well described in the following passage.

(g) ". . . Now he one day had gone to his paddy field and seeing a head of rice bursting the husk, went about to tie it up with a wisp of rice, and taking a handful of it he tied the head to a post. Then it occurred to him, "From this field I have yet to give the king his due, and I have taken a handful of rice from an untithed field . . ." (III. 276).

Preparation of the field is described at length in the Kāma Jataka (XII. 467). An important reference, therein, is to the preparation of little embanked squares for water. Lack of irrigation facilities brought a drop in yields.

(h) ". . . But there was not much rice in it, and the Great Being said, "Why, Madam, there is very little rice here !" "We got no water". "You mean when your field was in growth you got no water upon it". "Even so, master" (XXII. 546).

There is reference to both excess rain damaging the rice crop (II. 199) and drought when no rice was available (I. 36). On the other hand, times of plenty are indicated by the mention of storage of rice in overflowing granaries (I. 131) and wagon loads of rice crossing highway (I. 115). The latter provides evidence of trade in rice. Fresh (V. 366), matured (I. 23) and scented rice (I. 73) were in common use.

Rice was utilised in a number of ways. Distribution of rice as alms to monks by the better-off laity finds plentiful mention and is lauded (I. 109). Rice seems to have been a form of remuneration for workers, both domestic and agricultural (VIII. 421). The king probably received some tax in kind, specifically rice (III. 276). Such a reference has not occurred before. Other uses of rice were as an ingredient of liquor (XVI. 512) and in religious offerings by Brāhmaṇas (II. 162). The medicinal use of rice is also focused on.

(i) "...So Kappa gave him broth made of millet and wild rice together with leaves sprinkled with water, without salt and spices, and at that very instant, the dysentery was assuaged" (IV. 346).

(j) "...Took some husked rice and cooked it as a prophylactic and...gave it to the hundred and odd warrior princes to drink as a prophylactic, and so all of them were satisfied..." (XXI. 537).

A unique use of rice is that in preparing arrows.

(k) "...Now at that time the arrow maker had heated an arrow in a pan of coals and had wetted it with sour rice gruel, and, on closing one eye, was looking with the other while he made the arrow straight..." (XXII. 539).

Various birds and animals who figure in the birth stories also partook of rice (XVI. 511; I. 23).

From the above, it appears that rice was very important in the social and economic lives of the people. An observation states that without rice or grain, one's word has no weight in the midst of one's kinsfolk (XXII. 546). The varieties of rice known, the details regarding its cultivation and numerous uses reflect the importance of the cereal and also give a well pieced together picture of the existing conditions.

17. *Suttanipâta* (Chalmers, 1932)

References are mainly in the nature of the use of analogies from agriculture to expound philosophical questions (I. 4). On the basis of the description of agricultural operations and numerous crops, it may be said that agriculture was prospering. However, as far as these details are concerned, they are mostly in accord with the other texts. Rice is usually offered by way of alms (II. 7). There is not much information, besides.

18. *The Thera Gāthā and the Therī Gāthā* (Davids 1964)

These are religious poems of the Elders of the Order. About agriculture, in general, little that is not known earlier is mentioned. There is mention of threshing of rice (CCXI), pounding (XLVIII) and boiling (XXXVI). Rice was offered to the Buddha and his followers (XXIII). Wild rice appears to have been available in a forest glade, three leagues from Rajagaha (CCXX). The term *Kura* is also probably wide rice in same form or another, found at *Sāvatthī* (CLX).

19. *The Dhammapada* (Burlingame, 1969)

It is the best known and the longest known work of Buddhist literature. That agriculture was flourishing is attested by the use of its analogies in philosophical questions, the diversity of crops known and description of agricultural operations and implements in detail, as in the foregoing texts.

A number of varieties of rice are mentioned like red rice (XVIII. 10 d.), hill paddy and wild rice (IV. 3a). Purest rice is also spoken of (II. 2). These are comparable to the varieties mentioned in the Jātakas.

A detailed description of a rice field occurs as also how rice is prepared for storage.

(a) "... At that time two brothers ... caused one great field to be planted with rice. One day Cula Kala went to the rice field, hulled a kernel of rice, and ate it, and found it unusually sweet. Shortly afterwards he desired to make a gift of unripe rice to the congregation of monks ... when he went back to the field and looked at it again, he saw the entire field was filled with heads of growing rice bound together, as it were, in sheaves ... When the rice was in the ear, he gave first fruits of rice in the ear ... When the rice was reaped, he gave the first fruits of the reaping; when it was in the sheaf, the first fruits of the sheaf; when it was in the shocks, the first fruits of the shocks ; when it was in the rick, the first fruits of the ricks ; when it was threshed, the first fruits of the threshing floor ; when it was ground, the first fruits of flour; when it was measured, the first fruits of its measuring when it was put away in the store house, the first fruits of the store. Thus he bestowed the first fruits of a single crop nine times. Whatever, he took away was made up and he had a bumper harvest" (I. 8c).

This is a significant passage as such a detailed picture of rice cultivation is not easy to come by. Other important references relate to the ploughing festival in which the king participated, (VI. 40), ditches by the roadside for irrigating fields (VI. 5) and quarrels over the river Rohini's waters for irrigation purposes (XV. 1). Women appear to have been employed as keepers of rice fields (IX. 3). References to famine are plentiful (I. 10). Storage of rice, under such circumstances appears to have been possible for the better-off sections of society (XVIII. 100d).

The geographical regions associated with rice are Uttarakuru (XXVI, 33b), Benaras (V. 126), Sāvatthī (XX. 5), the territories of the Sakiyas and Koliyas (XV. 1) and Kosala (XV. 6). They correspond to the Gangetic Valley save for Uttarakuru which lies to the west of it.

As for uses, rice was primarily used as a cereal. It was liberally donated to tne congregation by all sections of society (XXVI. 21). An interesting reference points to the fact that five hundred cart loads of rice, along with other agricultural implements, appear to have been part of a trousseau (IV. 8). Remuneration by way of rice is mentioned (II. 2).

Though references to agriculture and rice are fairly numerous, the one aspect on which some new details are available is with respect to rice cultivation. The uses and varieties of rice are similar to those we have come across earlier.

20. *Pāṇini's Astādhyayī* (Vasu 1962)

The date of Pāṇini has been the subject of frequent controversy. Keith places him "not later than 300 B.C." whereas Macdonell believes that Pāṇini "lived after, probably soon after, 500 B.C." Ramakrishna Bhandarkar argues that Panini flourished around "the beginning of the seventh century B.C." (these references are cited in Tripathi 1960 : 54n).

There are plentiful references to agriculture but there is little that is new either by way of crops mentioned or methods employed. Different varieties of rice are mentioned. They are *Vrīhi*, (I. II. 58), *Śāli* (IV. IV. 100), *Lohita Śāli* (II. I. 57), *Hāyāna* (III. I. 148), *Mahāvrīhi* (VI. II. 38) and *Nīvāra* (III. III. 48). *Lohita Śāli* appears to be another variety of red rice. Of these, *Śāli* is specially praised.

(a) "...Suitable or excellent for food" (IV. IV. 100).

(b) "...a rice above all praise" (V. 2.68).

A particular field is described as being fit for growing rice (V. II. 2). There are no other details. There is mention of rice being sown in summer (IV. III. 44) and ripening in autumn (IV. III. 43) An interesting reference relates to rice in Kashmir (III. II. 114). This is significant as majority of the earlier references speak of rice in the Gangetic valley.

A great number of references speak of the use of rice as a cereal, *Odana* (I. IV. 106). Flattened rice was known as *Pṛthuka* (II. I. 35). However, rice figures in religious offerings, too. The offerings are known as *Purodāśa*, (V. I. 4) and *Charu* (V. I. 2) as in the earlier Vedic texts. There is a reference to rice grains, *Taṇḍula* being suitable for the preparation of a religious offering (V. I. 4).

The significance of the text, for our purpose, lies in the fact that a new variety of rice, *Lohita śāli* is mentioned and that rice seems to be associated with the northern region of Kashmir. Other references are not very illuminating.

21. *Kautilya's Arthaśāstra* (Kangle 1963. 1965, 1966)

The importancc of this text is that it is widely used to study the Mauryan economy of the 3rd B.C. It contains a section on agriculture. The details available are very different from those available in any of the foregoing text. The importance of agriculturists to the State was explicitly recognised. Incentives were provided by the state to increase production, in the form of favours and exemptions. Irrigation works were built with natural water sourcess or water brought from elsewhere. Agriculture, oppressed by the troubles of fines and taxes, and herds of cattle, by thieves wild animals, poison and crocodiles as well as by diseases, was protected by the State (II. I. 19).

The Director of Agriculture was to collect seeds at the right season. Different treatment was prescribed for different seeds. In the case of grains, they were to be soaked in dew by night and dried in the heat by day for seven days and nights. Land suitable for each crop was selected and ploughed several times. The amount of rainfall was divined through a study of the planets. The distribution of rainfall in different areas seems to have been well ascertained. Harvesting, threshing and storage of grain are mentioned but there no details (II. 24.41).

Śāli rice, *Vrīhi* rice, *kodrava*, sesamum, *priyangu*, *udaraka* and *varaka* were the first sowings. Udaraka and varaka have been mentioned by Om Prakash (1961 : 87) to be two new varieties of rice introduced in this period. However, this cannot be stated with any certainity. *Śāli* rice has been described, in the Arthasastra to be among the best of crops.

A use of rice to which attention has been drawn is in rituals.

(a) "And those learned in the Vedas and ascetics may take flowers and fruits that have fallen on the ground for worship of the gods, rice and barley for the agrayana sacrifice..." (II. 24. 41. 30).

The Arthasastra may be counted among those texts which are important mainly for prdviding a detailed picture of the prevailing agricultural conditions. Details regarding rice are mainly in conformity with those which were mentioned in earlier texts. This is because the treatment of individual crops is not as exhaustive as that of the general agricultural background and the role of the state in that sphere.

22. *Patanjali's Mahābhasya* (Puri 1957)

This is a commentary on Pāṇini's grammar. He is taken to belong to the Sunga times i.e. second century B.C. Agricultural processes do not show an advance upon earlier times. But a few interesting details are worth noting. A good crop was an indication of the prosperous times ahead which could be found out from a single grain of rice (I. 2.58). *Vrīhi* and *Śāli* are the two varieties mentioned. Magadha is said to be famous for *Sali* rice (I. 1.2). The banks of the river Devika are also specially suitable for growing paddy crops, (Agrawal, 1953 : 201). It is the mention of these geographical regions which is of some significance, though the last cannot be specifically located.

23. *The Milinda Panha* (Horner 1963-4)

This text probably looks back to the reign of the Greek King Menandros who ruled in northwest India in the first century B.C. The work is likely to have been written in the first century A.D. (Winternitz, II, 1972, 175). Rice is mentioned as one of the important crops. Two kinds of red rice, one healthy and the other, not, is spoken of (VI). The latter is known as *Parumbhaka* which having cropped up in between wilts away. This variety has not been mentioned in earlier texts. In Aparanta (a territory in western India) rice is said to to ripen in five or six months (VIII). The "extensiveness of rices" is mentioned in the same context suggesting its widespread cultivation and utilisation. It is specifically mentioned as food fit for a king and contrasted with another kind of grain meant for slaves and work people. This emphasises the prominence of rice among the available agricultural products.

Ayurvedic Texts

24. *The Suśruta Saṁhitā* (Bhishagratna 1963)

This is a representative work of Āyurveda. It appears that from time to time many hands were in operation on what passes as the Suśruta Saṃhita today. It is stated that the original Saṃhita was written at least two centuries before the birth of the Buddha while its final recension was made about the second century B.C. (Bhishagratna, 1963, I : VI). If this date be accepted, the text may be taken as roughly contemporaneous with the above mentioned ones.

The chapter on food and drink is extremely important for our purpose. A great variety of agricultural products are mentioned. However, the details regarding the varieties of rice are particularly striking. We do not come across such information in earlier texts. These are interspersed with some general observations.

The varieties of *Śāli* mentioned are *Lohitaka, Śāli, Kalama, Kardamaka, Paṇduka, Sugandhaka, Shakunahrita, Pushpandaka, Pundarika, Mahāśali, Shita-bhiruka, Rodhra-pushpaka, Dirgha-shuka, Kanchanaka, Mahishn-mastaka, Hayanka, Dushaka* and *Mahadushaka*. There are no details available regarding these species either in the text or in the bilingual dictionaries which we have consulted.

As for their properties, the following is said. "The several species of *Śāli* rice are sweet in taste, cooling in potency, light of digestion and impart strength to those who use them. They subdue the pittam and slightly generate vayu and kapham. They are demulcent and tend to constipate the bowels and reduce the quantity of fecal matter. Of these, the red species (*Lohitaka*) is the most efficacious, and subdues, and deranged humours. It is diuretic, spermatopoietic, refrigerant, eye-invigorating, cosmetic, tonic and pleasant. It improves the voice. Its efficacy has been witnessed in case of fever and ulcer and in all other diseases. It is a good disinfectant and anti-toxic. The other species differ a little in their properties from the preceding one and are successively inferior in quality in their order of enumeration."

To the *Shashtika* group belong the following species. *Shashtika, Kanguka, Mukundaka, Peetaka, Pramodaka, Kakalaka Asana-pushpaka, Maha-shashtika Churnaka Kuravaka* and *Kedaraka.* Shashtika, probably connotes quick-ripening varienties.

Of them it has been said that "they are sweet in taste and digestion and pacify the vayu and kapham. Their properties are somewhat identical with those of *Śali* rice inasmuch as they are constructive, tonic, spermatopoietic and increase the kapham. The *Shashtika* is pre-eminently the most efficacious of all the other species and leave an astringent after-taste in the mouth. It is light, mild, demulcent and imparts strength and firmness to the body. It is astringent and sweet in digestion and exhibits properties similar to those of the red *Sali.* The remaining varieties are inferior in quality, each succeeding one being inferior to the one immediately following it".

The several species of *Vrīhis* are as follows : *Krishna-Vrīhi, Śāli-Kukha, Jātumukha, Nandīmukha, Lavakshaka, Taritaka, Kukkutandaka, Paravataka* and *Patala.*

"They have a sweet and astringent taste, are sweet of digestion and hot in their potencies. They tend to slightly increase the secretions of the internal organs and bring on constipation of the bowels. Their general properties are mainly identical with that of the aforesaid *Shashtikas.* The species, *Krishna- Vrīhi* is the best of them all. It is light and leaves an astringent after taste, the remaining varieties gradually deteriorating in quality from the one under discussion".

Of the genus Kudhanya, the following varieties are mentioned : *koradushaka, shyāmaka nīvāra, shantanu, varaka uddalaka, priyangu, madhulika, nandimukhi, kuravinda, gavedhuka, varuka, todaparni, mukundaka* and *venuyava.* Of these, it is *nivara* which is more relevant for our purpose.

As a whole, "they generate heat and have a sweet and astringent taste. They are parchifying and pungent of digestions, subdue the kapham and tend to produce retention of the urine and enrage the bodily vayu and the pittam. Of these the species known as *kodrava, nīvāra, shyāmaka, shantanu* have a sweet and astringent taste and prove curative (in certain cases)".

Some other general observations of a similar nature are

found in the text. "Rice of once transplanted paddy plants or of those transplanted several times in succession is light, easily digested and comparatively more efficacious. It acts as a constructive tonic and is not followed by any reactionary acidity after digestion, destroys ihe deranged humours and is diuretic. Rice, of paddy plants, sprouting from the stubbles of a previous harvest is parchifying. It supperesses the evacuation of stool, has a bitter and astringent taste, subdues the pittam, is easily digestible and generates kapham. The use of new (harvested within a year) rice tends to increase the secretions of the internal organs, while that of a year's maturity is light. Rice threshed out of paddy which has commenced sprouting is heavy, and is long retained in the stomach. It can be but imperfectly digested and tended to effect the organ of vision. Rice of two years' standing should be regarded as well matured in time and excellent in quality. A thing which is hard to digest like *Vrīhi*, is made by frying".

Needless to say, the amount of knowledge, outlined above presupposes, is phenomenal. If the chronology and regional background were certain, these details would have an enhanced value.

25. *The Charaka Saṃhitā* (Ray and Gupta 1965)

The extant Charaka Saṃhita is a redaction, by Charaka of the original work of Agnivesa. Its date is disputed. P.C. Ray places the date of compilation in the pre-Buddhistic period. Filliozat assigns it to the second century or first century B.C. Winternitz places it at 100 A.D. (cf. Ray and Gupta 1965 : 3).

Different varieties of rice are mentioned about a dozen of which are common to the various groups mentioned in the Susruta Saṃhita. They are as follows : *Raktaśāli, Māhāśāli, Kalama, Sakunihṛta, Turṇaka, Dirghasuka, Gaura, Paṇḍuka, Langula, Saribhakya, Promodaka, Patanga, Tapaniya, Yavaka, Hayana, Pamsuvapya, Naisadhaka, Svastika, Gaura svastika; Varaka, Uddalaka, Cina, Sarada, Ujjvala, Dardura, Gandhana, Kuruvinda, Vrīhi* and *Patala*.

Of the medicinal use of rice the following may be said. *Nīvārā*, or the wild rice plant was used in haemotheria (c l.

4. 36). *Taṇḍula* was generally used as a vitaliser and roborant (c I. 4. 73).

Though not as detailed as the Susruta Saṃhita, the Charaka Saṃhita provides some valuable information by way of varieties of rice and its medicinal uses. It may be assumed that rice was among the more important agricultural products.

The Epics

26. *The Mahābhārata* (Roy 1955, 1956 ; De 1940 ; De 1936 ; De 1958)

It is only in a very restricted sense that we may speak of the Mahabharata as an 'epic'. It is not the work of one single author or of one time, but consists of earlier and later portions which belong to diflerent centuries. Between the fourth century B.C. and fourth century A.D. the transformation of the epic Mahabharata into our present compilation took place probably gradually. (Winternitz 1972, I : 475).

The more important references deal with the agricultural background. The importance of agriculturists is realised and the king's contribution towards their welfare stressed.

(a) "...Are the agriculturists in the kingdom contented ? Are large tanks and lakes constructed all over thy kingdom at proper distances, without agriculture in thy realm being entirely dependent on the showers of heaven ? Are the agriculturists in thy kingdom wanting in either seed or food ?" Grantest thou with kindness loans (of seed grains) unto the tillers, taking only a fourth in excess of every measure by the hundred ?" *Sabhā Parva*, Scct. IV).

(b) "...Let not the agriculturists in thy kingdom leave it through opperession ; they, who bear the burthens of the king support the other residents also of the kingdom ..."(Śānti Parva, Sect. LXXXIX).

As far as the gcographical distribution of grain crops goes, the following passages are significant.

(c) "...Surrounding the kingdom of the Kurus, are many countries, beautiful and abounding in corn (*anna*) such as Panchala, Chedi, Matsya, Surasena, Pattachchara, Dasarna, Navarashtra, Malka, Salva, Yugandhara, Saurashtra, Avanti and the spacious Kuntirashtra..." (*Virāṭa Parva*, Sect, 1).

(b) "...And for this reason the land of the five rivers and the whole of the region called Kurujangala and the forest of Rohitaka which was uniformly wild, and Ahichchatra and Kalakuta and the banks of the Ganga and Varana and Vatadhana and the hill tracts on the border of the Yamuna...full of abundant corn (*dhana*) and wealth, was entirely overspread with the army of the Kauravas (*Udyoga Parva*, Sect. XIX).

(e) "...Before much time had passed he reached the country of the Videhas...there he beheld many populous villages, and many kinds of food drink...He beheld many fields abounding with paddy and barley and other grains..." (*Santi Parva*, Sect. CCCXXVI).

These refer to the Gangetic Valley and regions to the west and south of it and western India. A curiously interesting reference states that in the *Kaliyuga* men will seek those countries where wheat and barley form the staple food (Vana Parva, Sect CLXXXIX).

As far as rice, in particular, is concerned there are not many details. Varieties of rice mentioned are few.

(f) "...That man who regards good *Śāli* rice and hard thick rice as equal, is emancipate...*Santi Parva*, Sect, CCLXXXIX).

(g) "...That virtuous ascetic who liveth on rice growing wild (*nīāvra*), or roots or potherbs,...is indeed the foremost of his brotherhood..." (*Udyaga Parva* Sect. XXXVIII).

Besides its use as a cereal, rice was mainly used as part of religious rituals.

(h) "...And commenced auspiciously, and all impediments removed, and furnished with abundance of wealth and corn, as also with plenty of rice and every kind of food, it was properly watched by Kesava. And Yudhisthira in due time completed the great sacrifice..."(*Sabhā Parva*, Sect. XLV).

Sundried rice and fried paddy were considered auspicious

(i) "...Vessels full of sundried rice and other auspicious articles..."(*Droṇa Parva*, Sect. LXXXII).

(j) "...And fair maidens honoured him by showering upon him, fried paddy and perfumes and floral garlands..."(*Drona Parva*, Sect. CXII).

Distribution of rice was highly lauded (*Sambhava Parva*, Sect. CXXXIV).

It appears that the references relating to agriculture are significant. On the other hand, those relating to rice are more of a stereotyped nature with hardly any new details.

27. *The Rāmāyana* (Shastri 1952, 1957, 1959, Bhatt 1960; Vaidya 1960)

It is probable that the original *Rāmāyana* was composed in the third century B.C. by Valmiki on the basis of ancient ballads and that it acquired its present from and contents towards the end of the second century A.D. The later parts of the Ramayana, especially Books I and VII are separated from the genuine Rāmāyana of Books II and VI by a long interval of time. (Winternitz 1972, I : 516-17).

The references to agriculture are not as significant as those in the *Mahābhārata*. On rice, too, there are a few stereotyped references. It was mostly used in different ceremonies.

(a) (Marriage ceremonies) "...Dishes filled with parched corn and rice were placed there, and darbha grass spread about. the sacred formulas being pronounced over them"(*Bāla Kaṇḍa* Ch. 73).

(b) (Daily oblations) "...Shri Rama entering the chamber of his mother beheld her offering oblations into the sacred flame ; he beheld there the sacrificial articles prepared for the worship of the gods ; curds, rice, butter, sweetmeats, rice cooked in milk..." (*Ayodhyā Kāṇḍa*, Ch. 20).

(c) (Funeral ceremonies) "...O Prince, it is said that water and rice offered by a beloved son, grants imperishable bliss to one departed..." (*Ayodhyā Kāṇḍa*, Ch. 101).

That rice was considered truly auspicious emerges from the following :

(d) "...He beheld the royal high way adorned like the pathway of the gods in heaven, with every auspicious mark, such as curds, rice, sandalwood, parched grains and milk..." (*Ayodhyā Kāṇḍa*, Ch. 17).

Rice was gifted by the munificent.

(e) "...O Lakshmaṇa, bestow on them eighty camels apiece loaded with jewels, a thousand bullocks loaded with rice and two hundred bulls for tilling the ground..."(Ayodhyā Kānda, Ch. 32).

Allowing for poetic exaggeration, abundance of rice is depicted in statements like:

(f) "...Send out in advance, a hundred thousand loads of rice in good condition..." (*Uttara Kāṇḍa*, Ch. 91).

(g) "...Hot rice in heaps as high as mountains ..."(*Bala Kanda*, Ch. 53).

A beautiful description of a rice fields is available in the following passage.

(h) "...Fields of rice with ears resembling Khajura flowers, bend gracefully under the weight of the grain..."*Araṇya Kāṇḍa*, Ch. 16).

From the above mentioned references it may be concluded that the rice-in-ritual motif continues to be prominent.

28. *The Smṛtis* (Jolly 1965 ; Jolly 1965 : Buhler 1964)

The Dharmasutras developed into the Smṛtis written in verse. The oldest and the most well known of the Smṛtis is that of Manu. Its style and contents suggest its final composition in the first or second century A.D. The Visṇu Smṛti seems to have been composed in the same period. The three completely legal Smṛtis are those of Narada, Bṛhspathi and Kātyāyāna. The first two belong to the fifth century A.D. and the last probably to the sixth century A.D. (Sharma, 1968 : 16).

Being legal treatises, these texts contain many references to laws regarding land agriculture. A householder's house and his field were considered the two fundamentals of his existence and the king was advised not to upset either of them (Nār. XI.42). Agriculturists were described as the middle class of hired servants (*Nār*. V. 23). The disputes concerning agriculturists were to be settled by themselves.

"(In disputes) among merchants, artisans, or the like persons subsisting by agriculture...it is impossible for outsiders to pass a sentence ; and the passing of the sentence must, therefore, be entrusted to persons acquainted with such matters" (*Nar*. I. 5).

There were rules laid down regarding partnership in tillage (*Brh*.. XIV. 21), boundary disputes (*Nār*. XI. 1), non payment of wages to agricultural labourers (*Nar*. VI. 3), destruction of grains by cattle (*Nār*. XI. 28), stealing of grain (*Bṛh*. XXII), lending of grain (*Brh.* XXVII, 22-23), forcible use of plough, mortar, pestle (*Nār.* VII. 14-15) etc. which provide a fairly good insight into the agricultural background.

A few interesting details regarding rice are available though there are many stereotyped references, too. Of the varieties, *Vrīhi*, *Śāli* (*Manu.* IX. 39) and wild rice (*Vis.* LI. 35) are mentioned.

Of the uses of rice, the most significant is in judicial proceedings. The reference to the rice ordeal is of great interest.

"Now I will proclaim the rule regarding the grains of rice which have to be chewed (by the defendant). This rice ordeal should be administered in cases of larceny, but on no other occasions whatsoever. That is the law.

Let the judge, who must have cleansed himself previously, use white grains of rice, but not (the grains) of any other fruit, and let him place in an earthen vessel in the sight of (an image of the deity of) the sun.

After having mixed them with water in which (an image of the sun god) has been bathed, he shall leave them in that place for a night. At day break, after having prepared them three times, a worshipper of the gods shall himself give them (to the defendant) who must be facing the east and must have bathed and fasted, after having proclaimed the charge himself, in order that right may be discerned from wrong.

When the defendant has chewed the grains, he shall cause him to spit them on a leaf. If a leaf of the holy fig tree be not available, he shall take a leaf of the birch tree (for that purpose).

Should blood issue forth, or the tooth flesh be hurt, or the limbs shake, he must be pronounced guilty (*Nār.* I. 25.337-342).

Rice also appears to have been used in the fire ordeal.

"...If it does not appear whether (either of) the two hands is burnt, he shall take and seven times crush grains of rice in his hand with all his might.

The grains having been crushed by him, if the members of the court should declare him to be unburnt, he shall be honourably released as being innocent. If he is burnt, he shall receive due punishment" (*Nar*, I. 21. 302-3).

The crushing of grains of rice served the purpose of making

visible such wounds as might have been overlooked previously.

Besides this important use, rice figured in rituals (Vis. IX. 7) and penances (*Manu* XI 93). There were fines or penances for stealing boiled rice (*Manu*, VIII. 329) or wantonly cutting wild and cultivated rice (*Vis.* L. 50). Liquor distilled from rice was forbidden to Brāhmaṇas (*Manu*. IX. 95). An interesting reference speaks of the assignment of a measure of a rice by a king to the widow of one whose property had lapsed in escheat (*Bṛh*. XXV. 67)

A great variety of crops is mentioned in these texts and of rice and barley, the following is said,

"...Clothes made of other material than silk, cattle other than cows, and metals other than gold, are (termed) articles of middling value, and so are rice and barley" (*Nār*. XIV. 15).

The Smṛtis are important for providing some new light both on the agricultural background and on rice.

29. *Amarasiṁha's Amarakoṣa* (Sardesai and Padhye 1969; Sardesai and Sharma 1941)

The Gupta period (c. fourth century to the fifth century A.D.) was said to have been distinguished by a number of intellectual celebrities. Among them may be counted the lexicographer, Amarasimha who compiled the Amarakoṣa. (Tripathi, 1960 : 272).

There are a few details with respect to agriculture and rice but they are not very striking. The varieties of rice were *Vrīhi* (IX. 15), *Śāli* (III. 22), *Nīvāra* (IX. 25), *Kalama* and *Saṣṭika* (II). There were fields which were fit for corn and rice (IX). Rice cultivation depended on rain or river water (II. 13). The rice crop was probably harvested in autumn as it is referred to as ripening during the rainy season (IX. 15). Rice in pods (IX. 24) and the husk of rice (IX. 22) are mentioned. A pestle for cleaning rice, both cultivated and wild figures in the text (IX.25). The different preparations of the cereal were flattened rice, *Prthuka* (IX. 47), boiled rice, *Bhisma* (IX. 48) and rice gruel, *Odana* (IX. 50).

30. *The Purāṇas* (Shastri, 1967 ; Wilson 1972 ; Pargiter 1904 ;

Akhtar 1972 ; Shastri 1968 ; Tagore, 1976, 1978; Shastri 1969, 1970, Shastri 1973).

It is difficult to determine the exact position of the Purāṇas in the history of Indian literature, both according to contents and chronologically. They are for the later Indian religion, Hinduism, approximately what the Veda is for the oldest religion or Brahmanism. They undoubtedly reach back to great antiquity but those works which have come down to us are of a later date. All that can be safely concluded is that the earlier Puraṇas must have come into being by the seventh century A.D. (Winternitz 1972, I : 525).

Some information regarding agriculture and agriculturists is available. Useful grains have been described as being of seventeen kinds (*Vishnu Pur.*, L. VI). They are rice, barley, wheat, millet, sesamum, panic and various sorts of lentils, beans, peas, *māsha, priyangu kulattha* pulse, *śyāmaka, nīvāra, jartila gavedhuka, martaka* and *venu-yaya* which we have come across in the earlier texts. Some agricultural processes are also described but they do not throw new light on the subject. Though agriculture, on the whole was flourishing, the condition of the agricultural worker seems to have been pitiable (Bhag. Pur. V. IX. II).

The reference to rice in religious rituals is virtually overwhelming. As for the varieties, red rice (*Agni Pur.* XCIII), *Śāli*, rice (*Agni Pur*, CLXXV), *Vrīhi* (*Matsya Pur.* II. CCLXVI). *Aman* rice (*Markandeya Pur.* XV. 8), white rice (*Matsya Pur.*, LXII), black rice (*Agni Pur.* CCXXX), *Nīvāra* (Vishnu Pur. III. XVI), *Saṁthi* rice (*Matsya Pur.* II, CCXXXIX), plain rice (*Matsya Pur.* II. CCLXVIII), small grained rice *Mārkandeya Pur.* XXXII.2), *Syāmaka* rice (*Linga Pur.* LXXXIII 23-26), and *Saṣṭik* rice (*Śiva Pur.* XVIII. 43-46) occur. It is clear that some of these varieties have not been mentioned earlier. *Aman* rice and *Saṃthi* are commonly grown in modern times. The former is winter rice while the latter is described to a race with short, strong stem, ear partially enclosed in theheath and grain husk, dark coloured or black. There are no elaborations regarding plain rice and short grained rice.

As regards rice cultivation, the following passages are significant.

(a) "...The ploughman should then drive his plough made after the sanctioned patterns and worship the...gods for a good harvest of paddy...The above ceremonies should be conducted on the occasions of transplanting or mowing down the rows of paddy plants...whereby a good harvest would be gleaned and gathered home..."(*Agni Pur*. CCLIX).

(b) "...The Brāhmaṇa who picks up for his own use a small quantity of pot-herbs, rice etc. from a field without the knowledge and consent of its rightful owner, should be pardoned for the smallness of his crime..." (*Agni Pur*. CCXXVII).

The different parts of a rice plant are explicitly described in the course of a philosophical discourse. Such descriptions are rare.

(c) "...As all the parts of the future plant, existing in the seed of rice, or the root, the culm, the leaf, the shoot, the stem, the bud, the fruit, the milk, the grain, the chaff, the ear, spontaneously evolve when they are in approximation with subsidiary means of growth (or earth and water). gods, men, and through beings involved in many actions become manifested only in their full growth, through the influence of the energy of Vishnu..." (Vishnu Pur., VII).

Evidence is provided regarding different uses of rice. Predominant was its use in rituals in the course of offerings to deities (*Garuda Pur*. LXXXVI), special rites (*Agni Pur*. CLXXIX), vratas (*Matsya Pur*. LXII), sin expiations (*Garuḍa Pur*. CIV), oblations to ancestors (*Matsya Pur*. XVI) and distribution of alms to Brahmanas and the needy (*Markandeya Pur*. XLI), among others. Boiled rice was the most common form of offering (*Agni Pur*. XL). Among other offerings may be unripe grains of rice (*Garuda Pur*. C), unhusked rice (*Matsya Pur*. XVI), uncooked rice (*Matsya Pur*. LXXII), unbroken grains or rice (*Bhag. Pur*. X. XXII.2-3), sundried rice (*Agni Pur*. CXVII) and fried paddy (*Agni Pur*. LXXXI). Special rice offerings were known as *Charu* (*Agni Pur*. LIX), *Arghya* (*Matsya Pur*. CCLXVII), *Havishya* (*Agni Pur*. CLXII), *Bhutabli* (*Agni Pur*. XXXIX), *Payasa* and *Krisara* (*Agni Pur*. XL). Rice was used to decorate the sacrificial ground (*Matsya Pur*. LXXIV). Rice was used to make images in various ceremonies (*Garuda*

Pur. CXXXIV). Its auspicious quality is constantly reiterated (*Bhag Pur*. I. XI. 14-15).

Another aspect of rice on which attention is focussed is its medicinal properties.

(d) "...The red species of *Śāli* paddy destroys the three doshas, allays thirst and arrests perspiration. *Mahāśali* is highly restorative...*Śyāmaka* is parchifying, absorbent, anticholeric and phlegmagougic...*Taṇḍuliya*...is antitoxic...*Manda* made of fried rice is appetising and digestant" (*Garuda Pur*. CXCII).

Suitable rice diet for particular ailments has also been laid down.

(e) "...Chronic dysentery...grains of old and matured *Śāli* rice should from the staple food of the patient. A man suffering from any of the intestinal tumours should carefully avoid wet, though boiled rice...Consumptive patient...boiled rice made from grains matured in the granary at least for a year ...Asthmatic...boiled *Śāli* rice, with all husks and extraneous matter carefully exempted..." (*Agni Pur*. CCLXXIX).

A unique use of rice is mentioned in the following passage.

(f) "...The process of cleansing and perforating the pearl seeds, is as follows : first, all the pearls should be collected and kept in a bowl of boiled rice, previously saturated with the expressed juice of the Jamvera fruits (lime). Then the whole contents of the bowl should be kept simmering for a while after which the pearls should be taken out and rubbed with the liquid extract of boiled rice. Thus softened, they should be piercest through as desired..." (*Garuḍa Pur*. LXIX).

Liquor distilled from wild rice (*Bhag. Pur*. I. XV. 22-23) is mentioned. There is also a reference to the hypothecation of paddy and the rules pertaining to it (*Agni Pur*. CCLIV). There appear to be certain restrictions regarding the sale of rice particularly for religious purposes as is clear from the following passage.

(g) "...At that juncture, men will open markets to sell boiled rice, the Brāhmaṇas will sell the Vedas and the women will earn their living by selling their hair" (*Matsy Pur*. XLVII).

On the basis of the foregoing, it may be surmised that rice was a fairly important agricultural product during the period of the *Purāṇas*. New light is thrown on the varieties and uses and a few notable details are available regarding the mode of cultivation. The only gap is with respect to the geographical regions producing rice. A fitting conclusions would be the following passage.

(h) "...Everything is founded on cooked rice...the vital breaths are stabilised in cooked rice..." (*Liṅga Pur.* LXXXI, 39-45).

31. **The Periplus of the Erythraean Sea** (Schoff 1912)

It is the first Mediterranean record of organised trading with the nations of the East. This is a plain and painstaking log of a Greek in Egypt, a Roman subject, who steered his vessel into the waters of the great ocean and brought back the first detailed records of the imports of the markets and of the conditions of its peoples. The nearest single year that suggests itself as the date of the Periplus is 60 A.D. (Schoff 1912 : 15).

This text provides definite, dated evidence with regard to rice production in Western India. The hinterland of Saurashtra has been described as a fertile country, yielding wheat, rice, sesame oil, clarified butter and cotton (41). The production of rice must have been considerable for there is reference to the export of rice. It was exported from Barygaza (modern Broach) to Egypt (14). Some traders made voyages specially to this and other market towns while others exchanged their cargoes while sailing along the coast. In this context, the trade at Dioscorida (modern island of Socotra,) is mentioned where traders from Barygaza brought rice, wheat, Indian cloth and a few female slaves and took for their exchange cargoes, a great quantity of tortoise shell (31).

Thus, though not many details of either the agricultural background or rice in particular, can be gathered, this text sheds much light on one aspect i.e. export of rice for which there is no parallel.

32. **Hiuen Tsang's Si-Yu-Ki** (Beal 1885)

Hiuen Tsang was a Buddhist pilgrim from China who visited India during the regin of Harsavardhana (c.606—647 A.D.). The records of his travels are of some importance. He states that since the climate and quality of the soil were different, the produce of the land was of a varied character. Different crops were cultivated in the appropriate seasons. Among the agricultural products rice and corn were the most plentiful (II. 17) (Beal 1885, I : 88).

A kind of rice called keng-t'ao is mentioned. What its special qualities were is not known. The kingdom of K'iu-chi was said to have soil suitable for rice including that of the above mentioned variety and corn (I. 2). The exact location of this region is not clear through it belongs to the north west of the subcontinent. Po-li-ye-to-lo, probably to the west of Mathura, was said to have abundant grain. A strange kind of rice, ripening in sixty days was said to be growing in this region (IV.6). This probably refers to the *Saṣṭika* variety of rice.

An interesting observation had it that though Indians had saucepans and stewpans, they did not know of the use of steamers used for cooking rice (II. 17),

The importance of this text lies in the information it provides regarding the significance of ricc, its varieties, areas of production and methods of preparation.

The time span covered by the literary texts is undoubtedly vast and therefore the picture we get of rice in the different periods cannot be very detailed. Neither are the text uniformly informative as regards the socio-economic background. The evidence contains much that is of a stereotyped nature. Nonetheless, though the chronology remains an unresolved issue and the geographical background dim, we get much significant information regarding the varieties of rice and their diverse uses. Supplemented with the information provide by a study of the archaeological sources and other disciplines these will contribute to a fuller knowledge of rice in the ancient Indlan context.

II. Inscriptional References

A perusal of the basic inscriptional sources (Hultzsch, 1897, 1925 ; Konow, 1929 ; Mirashi 1963 ; Waldschimdt and Mehendale, 1963) reveals that there is no reference to rice in early inscriptions. However, several later inscriptions (Hultzsch, 1890; Burgess 1892, 1894; Mirashi 1955 and Fleet 1963) mention such terms as *charu* and *bali* which, as has already been noted, suggest offerings mixed with rice. Offerings of rice grains as part of religious ceremonies also occur in some inscriptions (Mirashi, 1955).

Perhaps more significant are the references to the grant of paddy and paddy fields.

(i) *The Saṇkheda Plate of Sankargana* dated to the last quarter of the sixth century A.D. was found at Saṇkheda in the Baroda District of Gujarat. The plate was issued from the victorious camp fixed at Nirguṇḍipadraka by Sanṭilla, the Baladhikṛta of Nirihullaka. The object is to record the grant of a field to Anantasvamin to provide for the performance of religious rites.

It states ". . . . There had been granted, with (a libation of) water, on the occasions of a solar eclipse, for the performance of the religious rites . . . a field requiring one piṭaka of paddy (*taṇḍula*) as seed . . . to be enjoyed by a succession of sons" (Mirashi 1955).

(ii) *Fragmentary Chola Inscription,* Tirumalai District, North Arcot, Tamil Nadu : it is engraved in Tamil character of about the twenty second year of a Chola king (whose name is lost). This inscription records the arrangement by which the Jaina temple Tirumalaippalli at Vaigavur was to get 4726 kalam of paddy annually (Indian Archaeology—A Review, 1975-6).

(iii) *Inscriptions from Timmasamudran,* Cuddapah District, Andhra Pradesh : an undated inscription in Tamil character of about the twelfth century engraved on a stone in front of a ruined Siva temple records the assignment of paddy from specified lands out of the monsoon, winter and summer crops for the festival in the month of Masi to god Devagal—joti—nayakar, by Kari Kalasolappidakkalppemmadidevar and (Ti) indisvaras.

(Indian Archaeology—A Review, 1968-9)

(iv) *Inscriptions of Perumpulivakkam District,* North Arcot, Tamil Nadu : eleven inscriptions are noticed in the Agastisvara temple. The third inscription, dated in the thirtieth regnal year of Rajendra, is on a pillar of the ardhamandapa. It refers to the gift of six nali of rice per day to Theru Agastisvara-mudaiyar of Perumpulippakam by Malaiyan Kuntavai, the chief queen of Rajendra I (Indian Archaeology—A Review, 1967-8).

(v) *Inscription inside the Shore Temple* dated to the ninth year of Vira Rajendra Chola : this records the gift of a piece of a land from the great assembly of Siridaviur to Tirukka-dalvallai" ... as exclusive property, with exemption from taxes, five rice fields (tadi), consisting of two thousand kuris (of land) ... where (the temple of) this god stands (Hultzsch, 1890).

From the above, it is clear that the practice of donating paddy is early. Earlier references to land grants also probably refer to rice fields in some cases, but it is the specific mention that is useful for our purpose. The early examples of donation of paddy come from western India. However, later and more profuse references come from south India from the Chola period. An important sidelight on which light is thrown is joint ownership of rice lands by assemblies.

There are a few more interesting details related to the grant of paddy. These references are fairly late and come mostly from the Chola period. They would fall into the following categories.

(i) Payment of rice as revenue.
(ii) Payment of allowances in rice.
(iii) Payment of interest in rice.
(iv) Use of rice for procurement of articles of consumption.

We may discuss them under these different heads.

(i) (a) *The Inscription on the west and south walls of the Virupaksheśvara temple at Veppambattu near Velur* dated to about the fifteenth century. It is a deed of sale of the revenue in gold and revenue in rice of the village of Veppambattu and the village of Sirukadambur. The mentioned village belonged to Andi—nadu, a division of Agaraparru. Both villages are stated to have been granted to the temple of Virupaksha—deva at Veppambattu Bukka Maharayar (of Vijayanagar).

"... We gave as a sarvamanya to last as long as the moon and sun, all the revenues in gold and all the revenues in rice ..." (Hultzsch 1890).

(b) *Inscription on the south wall, second tier in the Rājarājeśvara temple at Tanjavur*. The inscription specifies the revenue in paddy and the revenue in gold and in money which a number of villages had to pay to the stone temple of Rajarajesvara, which Rājarājadeva had caused to be built at Tanjavur. The villages were situated both in the Chola country and in other countries and had been assigned to the temple by Rajarajesvara until the twentyninth year of his reign. The extent of the land is recorded in great detail by a land measure, the name of which is not stated, and by fractions of it. The paddy due to the temple had to be measured by the 'marakkal' called (after) Adavallan i.e. by a corn measure which was preserved at the shrine of the god Adavallan ; and this marakkal was equal to a rajakesari. This term was evidently derived from Rajakesarin, the surname of the reigning king Rajaraja and of other Chola kings, and must be taken as the real name of the royal standard measure, a copy of which was preserved at the temple.

"... (The village of) Palaiyur in Inganadu (a subdivision) of Tenkaduvay . . . the revenue paid as tax is ... one nari of paddy ... (The village of) Arappar in the same nadu ... the revenue paid as tax is three nari of paddy. (The village of) Kirandevankudi in the same nadu ... five nari of paddy. (The village of) Nagank ... in the same nadu ... four nari of paddy. (The village of) Tanniri Kunram ... in the same nadu ... four nari of paddy ... in (The village of) Usikkannangudi in the same nadu ,.. two nari of paddy ..." (Hultzsch, 1891).

(c) *Inscription on the north wall, upper tier of the Rājarājeśvara temple at Tanjavur*. Like the foregoing it was engraved after the twentyninth year of the reign of Rajaraja. This inscription also specifies the revenue in paddy and the revenue in gold to be paid by a certain number of villages which Rajaraja had given to the temple (Hultzsch 1891).

(ii) (a) *Inscription on the outside of the north enclosure of Rojarajesvara temple at Tanjavur*. It records the order of Rājarājadeva by which he assigned a daily allowance of paddy to each of forty eight persons whom he appointed before the twentyninth year of his reign in order to receive the Tiruppadiyam in the temple and to two persons who had to accompany the others.

"...These fifty persons were to receive from the city treasury of the lord a daily allowance of three kuruni of paddy each, (measured) by the marakal called (after) Adavallau, which is equal to a rājakesari. Instead of those among these persons, who would die or emigrate, the nearest relations of such person were to receive that paddy and to recite the Tiruppadiyam... accordingly, (the names of these fifty persons) were engraved on stone, as the lord Sri Rajarajadeva had been pleased to order..." (Hultzsch, 1895).

(b) *Inscription on the outside of the north enclosure of the Rājarājeśvara temple at Tanjavur.* This is also dated to the twenty ninth year of the reign of Rajaraja. It records an order of the king by which he assigncd the produce of certain land to a number of men who had to perform various services in connection with the temple, and to four hundred women, evidently dancing girls. Each person received one or more shares, each of which of the produce of one veli of land, calculated at hundred kalam of paddy. This statement is valuable as it enables us to ascertain, by a comparison of the produce in paddy with the extent of the land, that the unnamed land measure which is referred to in other Tanjavur Inscriptions is meant for the veli. According to the Dictionnaire Tamoul —Fransaise, the modern equivalent of veli twenty six square metres (Hultzsch 1895).

(c) *The inscription on the south wall, first and second tier of the Rājarajeśwar temple at Tanjavur.* It is dated to the nineteenth year of Rajendra Chola. It recorded the grant of a yearly allowance of paddy to a Saiva priest of the Rājarājeswara Temple. He issued this order from his palace at Gangaikonda—Sorapuram.

"...2000 kalam of paddy fully measured by the marakkal (preserved) in the temple of this god (and)called (after) Adavaltan, should be supplied every year, as long as the moon and the sun endure, to the treasury in the city, to be enjoyed by the priest of the temple of the lord Sri-Rājarāja—Iśvara, by our lord, the (Sai) vackarya Sarvaśiva—pandita, and by those who shall deserve it among his pupils of this lord and the pupils of his pupils who are natives of Āryadeśa, Madhyadesa or Gauḍadesa...let the Śaiva archaryas of this (spiritual) line protect this charity..." (Hultzsch 1891).

(iii) & (iv) (a) *The inscription in the inner Gopura, on the right of the entrnace of the Rājārajeśvara Temple at Tanjavur.* It is dated to the twenty ninth year of the reign of Rājāraja-deva. It records two deposits of money, which were made by a manager of the Rājarājeśvara Temple and lent out to the inhabitants of a certain village. The interest of the first deposit was to be used for procuring various articles of consumption on thirteen procession days.

".... (one) padakku by the Adavalan (measure) of old rice for boiling (ponaga-para-ariṣi) (is required) for the offering to the god who is carried in procession (at) the festival, and one (kuruni) of old rice for boiling (is required) by his consort, after (both) images have entered (the sacred hall) at the procession on (each of) thirteen festival days,...Five nari, (one) uri and one arakku of paddy (are required) for (one) nari, and (one) arakku of pulse.... Five nari and (one) uri of paddy (are required) for one arakku, one sevidu and three quarters of a sevidu of pepper...Two nari, (one), urakku, (one) arakku and one sevidu of paddy (are required) for (one) arakku and one sevidu of mustard...(one) nari of paddy (is required) for three quarter, three twentieth and three eight of a savidu of cumin...Two nari, (one) uri, (one) arakku of four sevidu of paddy (are required) of three palam and (one) kasu and a half of sugar...(one) kuruni and seven nari of paddy (are required) ...(one) arakku, three sevidu and three quarter of a sevidu of ghee...(one) nari of paddy (is required) for eight palam of tamarinds...(one) kuruni and one nari of paddy... (one) urakku of paddy (is required) for three sevidu of gram for tamarind curry. Five nari of paddy (are required) for a curry of eighteen plantains...six nari of pacdy (are required for curry and one arakku of paddy (are required) for (one) urakku and (one) arakku of salt for curry and curds. Two nari of paddy (are required) for twelve young leaves on which boiled rice (is offered). Four nari and one uri of paddy (are required) for thirty areca nuts and sixty betel leaves. (One) nari of paddy (is required) for (one) kasu of bark. (One) kuruni and six nari of paddy (are required) for firewood. Altogether, (one) kalam, (one) tuni, and (one) padakku by the Adavalan (measure) of mixed paddy for the thirteen monthly festivals, which are celebrated every year. In order to realise (these), seventy eight kasu were deposited under the condition that, as long as the moon and the sun endure, an interest of three kuruni of paddy per year for each kasu should be delivered into the large treasury of the lord at Tanjavur...

....The members of the assembly of (Perunangaiman) galan, a brahmadeya in Venni-Kurram (a subdivision) of Nittavinoda-valanandu, have to measure every, as long as the moon and the sun endure, nineteen kalam, (one) tuni and (one) padakku of paddy into the large treasury of the lord with the marakkal called (after) Adavallen, which is equal to a rājakeśari, for the seventy eight kasu, which they have received (out of) this money atfer (the harvest of) the pasan in the twenty eight year (of the king's reign)—the rate of interest being three kuruni of paddy per year for each kasu (Hultzsch 1892).

(ii) *The inscription on the south wall, second tier of the Rājarājeśvara Temple of Tanjavur.* The inscription describes a number of gifts which were made until the twentyninth year of Rajarjadeva by Arvar Parantakan Kuṇḍavaiyar who was the elder sister of Rājarājadeva and the queen of Vall-Varaiyar Vandyadevar.

In records the gift of gold to two goddesses whose images in the temple had been set up by her. She also deposited certain sums of money which were subsequently borrowed on interest by the inhabitants of certain villages from the shrine of Chand-esvara, the saint in whose name the monetary affairs of the temple were generally transacted. The interest had to be paid yearly into the treasury of the Rājarājesvara Temple either in paddy or in money. In the former case, the interest was three kurnni of paddy for each kasu and in the latter, twelve and a half per cent. If it is to be assumed that the rate of interest was the same in both cases, kasu would correspond to the value of twenty four kuruni of two kalam of paddy. The value of various daily requirements is given in measures of paddy, the whole list probably represents the daily wants of a single priest (Hultzsch 1891).

(c) *Inscription on the south wall, first tier of the Rājārajeś-vara Temple at Tanjavur.* It is dated to the sixth year of the reign of Rajendra Chola and fixes the interest to be paid to the temple by certain villagers for a sum of money which has been contributed by several donors and by the treasury..."the rate of interest being three kuruni of paddy per year for each kusu"(Hultzsch 1891).

(d) *Inscription on the south wall, first tier of the Rājārajeś-vara Temple at Tanjavur.* It is dated to the tenth years of the reign of Rajendra-Chola, and fixes the interest, "...the rate . . being three kuruni of paddy per year for each kasu", which the inhabitants of a certain village had to pay for the benefit of the image of Kratrjunadevar, and one of the images of Mahameru-Vitankar and his consort (Hultzsch 1891).

The inscriptional references are apparently limited, and although most of them belong to the later period, they generally, underline the ritualistic and economic significance of rice, a fact which is well demonstrated by the textual references. The justification of using some inscriptions which are much later than our chosen chronological framework up to the 7th-8th century A. D. lies in this fact.

3

The Excavated Contexts

RICE occurs in a large number of excavated sites and it may be convenient to discuss the evidence according to the following order—the Harappan civilisation, the neolithic-chalcolithic Iron Age cultures outside the Harappan orbit and the subseqent early historic sites.

I. The Harappan Civilisation

The occurrence of rice has been argued at the following Harappan sites : Rangpur and Lothal in Gujarat, Kalibangan in Rajasthan and Hulas in Saharanpur, western U.P.

1. Rangpur

Of the three, only the rice remains from Rangpur have been analysed at length. However, evidence of cereals at this site is meagre compared to charcoals. The cereals are rice from Phase IIa (Harappan, 2200-1700 B.C.) and bajra from Phase III (Post-Harappan). Rice occurs in Trench RGP 7 in the form of rice husk embedded in mud plaster. Some of the specimens of mud plasters were flat and measured about 1.50 cm. × 2.0 cm. Here some impressions of plant-like materials were noticeable when examined carefully with a lens. The lumps were therefore soaked it water in a watch glass. Under the hand lens, the characteristic chess board pattern of the rice husk become clear at once. When examined under a microscope, ridges and grooves were also apparent as well as thick zigzag epidermal cells in parallel rows. This characteristic pattern in surface view immediately confirmed the structure of husks of rice (Oryza sp.). From the nature of their use, it appears that husks were used with mud as binding material for the purpose of plastering. Though no grain or spikelet of rice has been observed, the manner of utilisation of this byproduct indicates the prevalence of rice in this region. Due to the highly deteriorated nature of specimens, determinations have to be confined to the generic level of the plants (Ghosh and Lal 1962-3).

2. Lothal

At Lothal, too, on the coastal flats at the head of the Gulf of Cambay, the rice remains have come in the form of impressions on three potsherds. Details are meagre, not finding more than a passing mention in S.R. Rao's report on Lothal and the Indus civilization (1973). Vishnu-Mittre provides a few statistical measurements (1974 : 17). They are as follows: Length is 5.00—7.00mm. and breadth is 2.50—3.00mm. Earlier, he had raised some points regarding the indeterminable status of the rice finds at Lothal and contended that they were not sufficient evidence of rice cultivation in the Harappan civilisation (Clutton—Brock et al 1960 : 30 n). However, this opinion appears to have been altered as the rice recovered belongs to the cultivated and not wild species and also because a similar use of the cereal has been found in many other sites (Vishnu-Mittre 1969 : 233). The date of Lothal is roughly contemporaneous with that of Rangpur. The difference in the nature of the two records is that at Lothal, besides husks, impressions of rice spikelets also occur. Essentially, however, the use of the cereal is the same. The incorporation of spikelets—an obviously useful stuff—remains inexplicable unless we assume that the food grains were produced in quantities exceeding consumption limits.

3. Kalibangan

Kalibangan is situated on the banks of the now dry course

of the river Ghaggar, 120 miles south east of Harappa. Rice records from Kalibangan have been reported in M. D. Kajale's general survey of ancient grain remains (Kajale 1974). Dated to 2300 B.C., the remains are stated to be in the form of rice husks and chaff in terracotta cakes. However Vishnu-Mittre and R. Savithri (1973) contest this identification. They state that the carbonised food grains from this site were found to belong to barley, wheat, *Cicer arietinum* and *Pisum arvense*. The absence of rice in the carbonised plant remains from this site necessitated the reinvestigation of plant remains embedded in terracotta cakes and pai from this site. The absence of chess-board pattern characteristic of rice on the husk remains in terracotta cakes and pai is highly suggestive of the absence of rice remains in them. The identification of the sub-fossil cuticles derived from terracotta cakes and pai to wheat (*Triticum* sp.) establishes beyond doubt that the husk impression in terracotta cakes and pai do not belong to rice. It would appear that rice production at Kalibangan, therefore, is not proved.

4. Hulas

The Harappan material at this site in Saharanpur district, U.P. has been assigned by its excavator, K.N. Dikshit, to the late Harappan period. Rice is known to occur in this period (personal information from K. N. Dikshit) but no details are as yet published.

II. The Neolithic—Chalcolithic Cultures outside the Harappan Orbit

1. Chopani-Mando

This site is situated on Terrace T^2 of the old channel of the river Belan at a distance of 77km. from Allahabad in east and south-easterly direction in Meja subdivision of District Allahabad, U. P.

The remains of charred or carbonised rice were found embedded in lumps of burnt clay. These remains come from Advanced Mesolithic (Proto-Neolithic) and have been dated to the 9th—8th millennium B. C. They represent the wild variety of rice. However, the samples are still under examination (Sharma et al 1980 : 23, 69). This promises to be a very important find, particularly in view of the occurrence of domesticated rice in the Neolithic levels at Koldihawa and Mahagara in the same region.

Rice, jujube and bamboo form the botanical remains. The remains comprise seed without pericarp, impressions of caryopsis, stalk, glume and probably also spikelets. The rice seeds are either flattened or puffed. They are oblong to elliptical in shape and have longitudinal ridges and grooves.

They have been found in two conditions : in loose form as well as embedded in potsherds. The imprints of caryopsis, stalk, glume etc. have been found only on potsherds, specially of the cord impressed and rusticated wares. It is obvious that they have been used as temper in the clay for manufacturing the pots. (Sharma et al 1980 : 182).

The remains have been identified as domesticated *Oryza Sativa* (Sharma et al 1980 : 23).

The radiocarbon dates from Mahagara which fall mostly in the second millennium B. C. are not consistent with the chronology postulated for the Neolithic level of Koldihawa. However, Mahagara is located on the Belan cliff which shows gully erosion at this point, and thus the samples were most possibly contaminated and gave younger dates. Besides, it should be noted that a C-14 date for the pre-Neolithic Mahagara is 8080 ± 115 B. C. (Sharma et al 1980 : 3).

4. Chirand

It is situated near the confluence of the rivers Ghagra and Ganga in the Saran District of Bihar.

Paddy husk impressions on some of the pieces of burnt clay as also some grains of charred rice indicate the use of that cereal by the inhabitants in the Neolithic context. From layer 17 of CRD XI, the rice remains have been scientifically analysed by Vishnu-Mittre (1972 : 20) and identification of varieties attempted. The kernels of rice, ten in number, are all five-ribbed. Of these five are slender and five broader. The examination of kernels of wild and cultivated species of Oryza reveals that slender grains are usually produced by the wild species and the broader ones by the cultivated species. There are no other external morphological characters to distinguish the grains of individual species. The statistical evaluation of the various dimensions and the calculation of L/(BxT) indices of the wild and cultivated species of Oryza in India has given reliable information to distinguish various species. The L/(BxT) indices of the carbonised grains are calculated and compared with those of modern species (Tables 1 and 2).

TABLE 1

Dimensions of Chirand Grains of Rice (in mm)

	L	B	T	L/(BxT) Index
Large grains	5.00	2.25	1.25	1.85
	5.25	2.50	1.25	1.67
Small grains	4.25	1.50	1.00	2.83
	4.50	1.80	1.00	2.05

TABLE 2

L/ (BxT) indices of cultivated and wild species of Oryza based upon hundred grains each. The table also includes indices of carbonised grains from Chirand (in mm).

Species of Oryza	L/(BxT) Index
Chirand large grains	1.76
Oryza Sativa var Indica	1.71
O. Sativa Var. Japonica	1.70
O. Sativa var. Spontanea Koenig	1.77, 1.79
O. Perennis Moench	2.20
O. Officinalis Wall	2.36
O. Rufipogon Griffiths	2.64
Chirand slender grains	2.45

L/ (B x T) index of the large carbonised grains approaches that of *O. sativa var. spontanea* and *O. Sativa* (cultivated) and that of the small grains is not different from that of the wild species *O. perennis* and *O. rufipogan*. The differences could be due to carbonisation. These statistical comparisons reveal that the carbonised grains were derived from both the cultivated and wild species of Oryza.

The date of the Chirand Neolithic is controversial because the C-14 dates are not mutually consistent. The date suggested by L.A. Narain (1970 : 347), c. 2500 B.C., seems to be the most acceptable in the present state of knowledge.

5. Miscellaneous sites in Bihar and Orissa : Baidipur, Oriup and Barudih

Baidipur (Mayurbhanj District, Orissa) has yielded evidence of what may be *Oryza perennis*. The evidence is in the form of husks measuring 5.25 mm. in length, 2.38 mm. in breadth, 1.68 mm. in thickness, with a L/ (B x T) index measuring 1.35 mm. as analysed by Vishnu-Mittre (1974 : 17). Although, the find of wild rice is interesting no positive inferences can be made because the date is uncertain and the details remain unpublished. The rice record at Oriup (Bhagalpur District, Bihar) is in the form of impressions. The length and breadth are 5.00—5.50 mm. and 2.25—2.50 mm. respectively (Vishnu—Mittre 1974 : 17). No further details are available regarding the site or rice finds, but this is presumably a black-and-red ware site of the second millennium B.C. The following measurements have been provided for the remains of rice at Barudih in Singhbhum (c. 1000 B.C.) : length—5.12 mm ; breadth—2.12 mm ; thickness—1.35 mm ; L/ (B x T) index—2.65 mm. (Vishnu-Mittre 1974 : 17).

The Neolithic identity of Baidipur, Oriup and Barudih is very uncertain, although these sites have occasionally been mentioned in this context (Thapar 1974 : 61-62).

6. Ahar

Ahar is situated on the river of the same name about 2 miles at the east of Udaipur town. The time spread of the Ahar Banasian culture, on the basis of available radiocarbon dates is c. 2000—1400 B.C. (Agrawal and Kusumgar 1974 : 114). Rice definitely formed part of the daily dish of prehistorlc Aharians. Quite a large number of sherds bearing impressions of rice (husk and spikelets) were found. Vishnu-Mittre has examined these remains (Sankalia, Deo and Ansari 1969 : 230, 234). The study was confined to the external features of the impressions and the size statements were based upon actual measurements of impressions, with no allowance being made for the amount of reduction in size. Thin sections of postsherds were cut to study the anatomical details of spikelets but the fragile and ashy nature of the organic remains in the matrix did not yield anything.

The frequency of impressions on potsherds is variable (Table 3).

The spikelets in all the sherds are oblong, flattened along the sides and strongly ribbed. They are 4.7 mm. in length, usually 5-6 mm, and 2-3 mm in breadth, usually 2.5 mm. The chess-board pattern of the outer surface of the spikelets is well preserved in several impressions. There is hardly anything like rachilla or lemina which can be made out from impressions. From the size of the spikelets and grains it appears that the impressions belong to the long seeded strain of *Oryza sativa Linn var. Sativa Bor.*

7. Navdatoli

Navdatoli, in District Nimad, Madhya Pradesh, is one of the largest chalcolithic settlements in central India. On the basis of radio carbon dates the spread of the Navdatolian Malwa culture has been computed between c. 1700 to 1450 B.C. (Agrawal and Kusumgar 1974 : 116). An analysis of the plant remains has been made by Vishnu-Mittre (in Clutton-Brock et al 1961 : 18-19, 43-44, 51-52). The grains of rice are present only in Phases II-IV. The exclusive collection of rice has been found in samples 2180, Phase III and 14200 in Phase IV. Mixed with the other cereals and legumes, a very low frequency of rice is seen (Table 4).

TABLE 3

Stratigraphical Distribution of rice Impressions at Ahar

Period	Trench	Layer	Reg. No.	Kind of Impression	Average size mm.	Frequency	Remarks
1C	C	3	11776	Rice	7x3	Abundant	Core Black
			803	Rice	5x3	Fair	Reddish clay
1B	D	3	2576	Rice	5x2.75	Fair	Core Black, Red
			271	Rice & Millet	5x3	Little	Black Core
1C	E	1	324	Rice & Millet	7x3	Little	No Black
			325	Rice & Millet	4x2	Little	Core
1B	F	5	756	Rice	6x3	Fair	Thin Black
			757	Rice	5x2.5	Abundat	Rice
1B	H	3	3139	Rice	4.5x2.5		
			3140	Rice	4x2.5	Abundant	Thin Black Core
			3141	Rice	4x2.5		

1b	L	1	485	Rice & Millet	5x2x1	Abundant	Thin Black Core
			2376	Rice	5x3	Less Fair	Black Core Present
			2378	Rice	,,	Abundant	Thiek Black Core
			2379	Rice & Millet	5x3	Poor	Black Core Not Very Thick
			2380	,,	,,	,,	Black Core Absent
			2381	,,	,,	Both Rare	,,
			2410	Rice	,,	Rare	Ext. Thin Black Core
11b	X	2	2411	Ricc	4x2	Rare	Thick Black Core
			2412	,,	5x2	,,	,,
			2413	,,	,,	,,	,,
			2414	,,	5x3	,,	,,
			2415	,,	,,	,,	,,
			2416	,,	6x3	,,	,,
			2417	,,	,,	,,	,,
			2418	,,	5x2	,,	Thin Black Core

11b	X	3	2463	Rice & Millet	6x2.5	Poor	Thick Black Core
			2464	Rice	6x3	Fair	,,
			2465	,,	,,	,,	,,
			2466	,,	5x2	Poor	,,
			2468	,,	6x3	,,	,,
			2469	,,	6x3	Abundant	,,
Ic	X	5	993	,,	5.5x3	Fair	Sherd Very Thin & Fragile Core Black, Light Brown
1a	2	5,6	7777	Rice	4.5x2	Abundant	Core Black

TABLE 4

Rice Finds at Navdatoli

Mound IV, Phase II
Tranch—I
Stratum—6
Site No.—1943
Cereal—Oryza Sativa
Mound IV, Phase III
Trench—I
Stratum—4
Site No.—2180 |
2242 |
2290 |
Cereal—Oryza Sativa
Mound IV, Phase III
Trench—I
Stratum—5
Site No.—5078
Cereal—Oryza Sativa
Mound IV, Phase IV
Trench— —
Stratum—2
Site No.—11268A |
14200 |
Ccreal—Oryza Sativa.

The grains of rice are oblong, flattened on the sides and strongly ribbed. The long hilum is preserved in many seeds. A single species of rice, *Oryza Sativa L.* has so far been identified. The dimensions are given below (Table 5).

TABLE 5

Dimensions of Rice Grains at Navdatoli

	Average	Minimum	Maximum
Lcngth (mm)	4.7	4.3	5.1
Breadth (mm)	2.2	2.0	2.4
Thickness (mm)	1.5	1.2	1.8
L : B (mm)	2.1	2.1	2.2
T : B (mm)	0.68	0.60	0.75

Taking together the Japanese red long and Korean red long as standard for Indica and Japanese red short and Korean red short as a standard for Japonica and comparing the dimensions of Navdatoli grains with these standards, it appears that the Navdatoli grains neither belong to Indica type but possess characteristics of both the types suggesting a hybrid nature of the Navdatoli rice grains

8. Inamgaon

The duration of three cultural periods at Inamgaon (85 km southeast of Pune, Maharashtra, and situated on the right bank of the Ghod) is as follows :

Period I—Malwa (c. 1600—1400 B.C.)
Period II—Early Jorwe (c. 1400—1000 B.C.)
Period III—Late Jorwe (c. 1000—700 B.C.)

(Dhavalikar 1977 : 46)

The botanical remains excavated from these three successive cultural periods of chalcolithic Inamgaon include carbonised remains of cultivated and wild plants. They have been studied by Kajale (1977 : 54-5). The cultivated assemblage comprises wheat, barley, rice, lentil, horse gram, hyacinth bean, grass pea, pea, moong/urd. All the grains exhibit maximum concentration in Period II thereby indicating the richness of agricultural activity in Early Jorwe culture. All the types of grains are represented in Period III in reduced quantities.

It seems that barley cultivation was preferred to wheat since the frequency of barley is twenty one time that of wheat. Rice appeared for the first time in the fifth layer of trenches and it has been suggested that its presence need not necessarily indicate rice cultivation around the site. The chalcolithic people might have brought it to the site from the upstream regions of the Ghod river where greater rainfall (more than 750 mm) and topographic conditions favourable for its natural growth and cultivation are found.

The basis for the above speculation is the fact that Inamgaon is not situated in fertile alluvial tract as is the case with

Daimabad and Prakash. Although there is evidence of what may have been an irrigation channel, it is held that it was not used for rice production. However, given the fact that there are different varieties of rice suited to different geographical conditions, the view that it may not have been cultivated in the region probably cannot be accepted at its face value. According to Vishnu-Mittre (1974 : 17) both charred grains and impressions on potsherds of the cereal were recovered. This implies a certain abundance to which a locally raised crop may indeed have contributed. Though rice was not the main cereal, whether it was imported must remain an open question. We are still in the dark regarding the species and variety to which the recovered rice remains belong.

9. Mahisdal

The time bracket of this black-and-red ware site on the north bank of the Kopai in Birbhum district, West Bengal may be 1300–800 B.C. (Agrawal and Kusumgar 1974: 114). Vishnu-Mittre (1974 : 17) states that the rice material is in the form of grains and impressions and adds that details are not available.

10. Sonpur

It is situated on the bank of the Jamunai river in Gaya District, Bihar. It has yielded evidencc of the use of paddy husks in the manufacture of pottery from the chalcolithic period (*Indian Archaeology—A Review*, 1970—71 : 5–6). Vishnu-Mittre (1974 : 17) provides a few statistical measurements but they refer to the Iron Age finds dated around 637 B.C.

11. Pandu Rajar Dhibi

This site is in the Ajay Valley, Burdwan District, West Bengal. There is only one C-14 date from this site. It is 1012±120 B.C. and belongs to Period II or the chalcolithic level. This may help date the rice find Period I when it was used to make pottery with clay. It has been identified as *Oryza sativa L.*Graminae. No details are available (Dasgupta, 1964 : 14).

12. Atranjikhera

Rice occurs in the Ochre Coloured Pottery (OCP), Black-and-red ware and Painted Grey Ware levels of this site in Etah District, U.P. The OCP level at this site, if the thermoluminiscent dates are any indication, may go back to the first quarter of the second millennium B.C.

The plant remains at Atranjikhera have been subjected to comprehensive analysis (Chowdhury, Saraswat and Buth 1977 : 18-21). The remains were recovered from mud clods and wall plasters lying scattered. Ten entire caryopses, either completely covered with husk or partially so, were included in these remains.

In addition it was possible to recover a few broken caryopses, leaf fragments and stem pieces. It is important to note that these remains were removed from a layer just above the natural soil.

All the caryopses are more or less similar in shape but they vary in size from 5.5 to 7 mm in length and 3 to 4 mm in breadth. The fertile glumes which cover the kernel, are made up of lemma and palea. Thc lemma is boat-shaped with convex outer surface and the palea is partially enclosed by lemma. The apices of lemma and palea form a short solid and blunt apiculus. There is no awn. The outer surfaces of lemma and palea are covered with short hairs. The density of hairs somewhat varies from caryopsis to caryopsis. The surface of the lemma and palea under a binocular microscope shows up tissues arranged in a distinct chess board pattern.

Almost all the caryopses have a small stalk or rachilla. Some rachilla clearly exhibit small sockets indicating where the fruits were attached to the main spikelet. The sterile glumes are present and placed opposite one another. They are short, often lanceolate and sub-equal, with smooth surface. In length they vary from 1.5 to 2 mm. The outer sterile glumes clasp the rachilla at a somewhat lower position than the inner one.

On the basis of the size of the caryopses two distinct categories can be recognised. In the first category can be placed those caryopses which are somewhat oval in shape. These, when measured, show variation in length between 6 to 6.5 mm and breadth about 3.5 mm. In other words, the width is slightly more than half the length. On the other hand, the second category contains caryopses which might be called longish. Here the length varies from 6 to 7 mm and the breadth 2-3 mm i.e. the breadth is less than half of the length. The fruits without husk are slightly smaller than those described above. The length varies from 4-5 mm and the breadth from 1.5 to 2.5 mm. All the kernels were ribbed and the number of ribs varies from three to four. In one of the caryopses without husk, the position of the embryo is well marked.

The cross sections of the caryopsis have not revealed any helpful anatomical character of the structure of the kernel. Here all the tissues, during the process of carbonisation, have been disorganised and turned into a black mass.

In the leaf fragments associated with the caryopses the epidermis consists of long and short cells. The long cells lie in the groove (between the veins) and have thick, well pitted sinuous walls. The short cells occur singly as well as in pairs. Those in pairs are composed of cork cells and silica cells. The silica cells are often prominent and contain crescent-like deposits. The short cells are abundantly present over the veins but they are rather restricted in the groove. Over the veins they are arranged in longitudinal rows. The cork cells and silica cells often alternate with each other. When this happens the structure is said to be "dumb—bell" shaped. This is characteristic of the genus Oryza. The stomata are confined to the grooves. The occur in straight rows and placed far apart. The subsidiary cells are low domed to somewhat triangular in shape.

The cross sections of the stem fragments show the central hollow cavity and sub epidermal band of sclerenchyma cells. The parenchymatous ground tissue has large cortical lacunae. The vascular bundles in the outer zone are small, embedded in sub-epidermal sclerenchyma cells but they become fairly large as they approach towards the centre.

One of the important structures of the cereals examined is the presence of chess board pattern of lemma and palea. This structure is helpful in separating the genus Oryza from the rest of the genera belonging to the grass family. Other characters of importance are much reduced sterile glumes and sub equal lemma and palea. It is useful to classify Oryza based on the differences in sterile glumes. When the length of the sterile glumes is equal to lemma and palea, the caryopses are called "wing glumed." When the sterile glumes attain half of the fertile glumes, they are called "medium glumed." Under the third category called "short-glumed" have been placed those taxa in which the sterile glumes do not cover even a quarter of the lemma and palea. According to this classification, the Atranjikhera Oryza in the O.C.P. level falls under "short glumed."

Considering the age of the Atranjikhera O.C.P. material, the possibility of the West African species, *O. glaberrima* steud, being present in the Gangetic Valley is rather remote. The remains may be placed under *O. sativa L.* from which all wild and cultivated species and sub-species in southeast Asia are said to have originated. Preliminary studies indicate that wild and cultivated rice can be separated by the size and shape of the rachilla along with its prominent socket attachment. By applying these criteria the Atranjikhera remains may be said to belong to the cultivated taxa. It is, however, not possible to place them under the categories of the well-known sub species of *O sativa* L. because the number of the caryopses is too small and very few of them exhibit all the morphological characters that are necessary for further division.

The other agricultural products from the O.C.P. level at Atranjikhera are barley and two types of pulses. Whether rice was the summer crop with barley and pulses being grown in winter must remain in the realm of conjecture.

The overlying stratum at Atranjikhera from which black-and-red ware pottery was recovered was rather thin. This restricted the attempt to collect sufficient plant remains from potsherds. It has been dated to c. 1500—1200 B.C. (Buth and Chowdhury 1971 : 282). Some food plants from this layer were found in the form of impressions on potsherds and mud plaster. This consisted of husk marks and bits of leaves. In *Oryza sativa* remains recovered from Period I anatomical data are available in considerable detail. Here lack of sufficient material prevented a similar intensive study but it was clear that the remains belonged to the genus Oryza and probably *Oryza sativa.*

For the collection of morpoological data a binocular microscope was used. The most important structure observed by this method was the impression of chess board pattern of lemma and palea on a potsherd. Peels from the husk show that the outer layer is made up of thick sinuous walled cells. The epidermis of the leaf is composed of long and short cells. The long cells confine themselves between the veins. Over the veins the short cells are arranged in longitudinal rows with alternating cork and silica cells. The dumb-bell shaped silica body is present, indicating once again its close affinity to the genus Oryza (Chowdhury, Saraswat and Buth 1977 : 34).

The plant remains discovered from the Painted Grey Ware stratum at Atranjikhera way dated around 1 000 B.C. or slightly latter. The came from Trench numbers ARJ-4 and ARJ-3. The layers of deposit were indicated by excavators by numbering them from bottom to top as I—VII. The materials were sorted out under the categories given below :

(a) grains in tar like mass
(b) grains individually separate
(c) mud clods of different size and shape with embedded plant remains
(d) hard mud pieces with grooves all round
(e) potsherd with textile-like impression.

The first stage in the method to study was to recover plant remains from the associated material. Grains associated with tar like lumps were treated with 3-4% acetic acid for 2-6 hours depending on the condition of material. When the grains could be dislodged easily, they were taken out from acid and washed repeatedly in water. The next stage was to centrifuge the grains in water for five minutes in order to get rid of all the extraneous matter. They were then washed in distilled water and left for further treatment. The individually separate grains required 9.5—1% acetic acid treatment for two hours. No further physical or chemical treatments was necessary for them. After washing them in distilled water repeatedly, they were put away for further processing. Some mud clods had natural colour of soil, while others had a look or leaf. Small pieces of soil containing plant material were taken out from the big pieces and soaked in water for 6-8 hours. After removing soil particles attached to the material of burnt mud. Both contained charred grains and bits of stem with a light brush, they were treated with 10% acetic acid for ten minutes. This treatment removed almost all the dirt. The material was then placed in water and centrifuged for fifteen minutes. Small pieces of charred remains were then picked up with a pipette and then washed repeatedly. All the material were fragile and had to be first dried. The next stage was to prepare peels, maceration and sections for microscopic examination after double embedding.

Rice was the most plentiful, and presumably the most important, of the cereals studied. The occurrence is presented below (Table 6).

TABLE 6

Occurrence of rice in the Painted Grey Ware level Atranjikhera

ARJ—4		
VII	—	Charred grains from a pit
VI	—	Mud clods
V	—	Mud clods
IV	—	Mud clods
I	—	Mud clods

There is a great deal of similarity between the individually separate grains found in heaps and the grains that are embedded in a tar-like mass. Both have been grouped together as a distinct lot for analysis. The spikelets vary in length from 5-6 mm and in breadth 2.4-3.3 mm. Some of them show two glumes—one on either side of the caryopsis. These glumes are lanceolate in shape and originate from a slightly different level of the rachilla. In length, the glumes vary from 1.5 to 2mm and show a smooth outer surface. The lemma and palea are boat shaped, the former partially covering the latter. The charred condition of the material did not permit accurate determination of the number of veins on lemma-palea surface. All the same, the outer surface lemma palea shows clearly a chess board pattern. The apiculus is short and often blunt. A large number of rachilla with associated organs has been noticed in this material.

Among the material examined there are many grains without husk. Some of them are comparatively broader in the middle than the rest. They have therefore been put under two categories i.e. broad and narrow.

The cross sections of the caryopses have not revealed any characteristic structure. However, the peels do. Here the epidermis shows squarish cells with thick, sinuous walls. Some epidermal cells also show hairs with bulbous base and pointed apex. Peels from the glume have only long cells but no short cells or stomata.

The peels from leaf-like fragments exhibit some interesting anatomical structure. Here the epidermis reveals long and short cells. The long cells with thick sinuous walls occupy the groove along with the short cells. The short cells are single or in pairs showing both cork and silica cells. An important difference between the short cells in this region and those that occur on the ridges has been observed. In latter, the short cells are distributed in a long row with dumb-bell-like silica bodies. The stomata are stictly confined to the groove and there is none on the ridges. They are in rows of 2-4 in between the ridge. The subsidiary cells are triangular or low domed.

The above morphological and anatomical study leaves one in no doubt that the plant remains are nothing but *Oryza sp.* In the case of *Oryza sativa* remains from the O.C.P. stratum it was not thought worth while to trace it to recognised subspecies because of the non availability of sufficient remains. In the PGW stratum there are plentiful rice remains and an attempt may be made to find out the greatest similarity it shows to three well recognised sub-species.

Since a large number of rice remains from the PGW stratum was in husked state, it was necessary to take measurement of the three sub-species in husked condition. For var. Indica and var. Javanica fifteen samples each were calibrated and for var. Japonica thirty samples. For the PGW material twenty undamaged samples were measured (Table 7).

TABLE 7

Dimensions of husked rice of three sub-species of Oryza and P.G.W. cereal lot 'A'

Husked Oryza Sativa L.	Var. Indica			Var. Japonica			Var. Javanica			P.G.W. Cereal Lot. 'A'		
	(i)			(ii)			(iii)			(iv)		
	L	T	B	L	T	B	L	T	B	L	T	B
Average	5.47	2.03	1.49	4.89	3.67	1.75	7.10	2.42	1.74	4.12	1.96	1.32
Maximum	6.60	2.60	1.70	5.25	3.00	2.00	7.85	2.65	1.95	5.10	2.45	1.60
Minimum	4.00	1.40	1.20	4.50	2.35	1.55	6.10	2.30	1.60	3.55	2.10	0.90

The rice from Atranjikhera does not completely fit into any of the sub-species. It, however, comes nearest to the var. Japonica in length, and to var. indica in both breadth and thickness. Such variations are possible to occur during a state of evolution when the process of mutation is very active and the progenies are trying to adjust themselves to a fresh environment. It may be suggested that the PGW rice from Atranjikhera was passing through such a process, and that var. javanica was not at that time involved in the operation (Chowdhury, Saraswat and Buth 1977 : 378 ; Buth and Chowdhury 1971 : 280-3).

13. Hastinapur

Hastinapur in District Meerut, U.P. was the first site where the PGW culture was discovered in 1950-51. It has been dated to c. 1000-800 B.C. The plant remains have been investigated in detail by K.A. Chowdhury and S.S. Ghosh (in Lal 1954-55 : 120-124).

All the plant remains were found in a charred state. It was, however, possible to identify them all in spite of the fragile and delicate nature of the materials. In the case of the charred cereal every attempt was first made to obtain as much information as possible on the morphological features. For this, very careful dissections were often necessary. But it was a difficult task to isolate the spikelets and grains from the hard tar-like mass. Often the spikelets and grains came off in pieces. They were immediately stuck on to a piece of plasticine. The idea was to keep trace of the broken pieces for the reconstruction of the cereal.

For mud plaster a previously developed technique and Artschwager's peel method were used. At the outset only a few bits of plant remains were recovered and studied after maceration. An examination of a large number of slides made possible a successful reconstruction of the original material and its final identification. For charcoal, sections were cut according to the general procedure followed by Jeffrey and Maby with some modifications. No treatment with hydroflouric acid was possible. Repeated treatments with hot carbolic acid were given. The material was put through double embedding

Celloidin in clove oil gave better results than celloidin in alchohol ether. By the former method it was possible to cut a series of sections of charred grain on a rotary microtome.

The charred cereals embedded in the black mass show whole broken spikelets adhering to each other. There is no stalk nor any pedicel. In other words, there is no indication of inflorescence. Some scars showing attachment of the spikelets on the stalk are, however, noticeable. Spikelets vary in size from 5—7 mm in length and 2-2.7 mm in breadth, each containing one single grain. Sterile lemma are paired, rather minute (1.7mm ×5mm and 1.5mm ×.5mm), lancelote in shape and arranged alternately. The outer surface is smooth and shiny. Rachilla, in well preserved specimens, is expanded into an annular thickening appearing somewhat comma—shaped. Fertile lemma is boat shaped with convex side, five-nerved and pronged into an awn. Its outer surface looks like a chess board pattern. Palea is also boat shaped but three-nerved and less convex and slightly smaller than the fertile lemma. Apiculus is thick and straight but the tridendate nature of the apex of the fertile lemma is seldom distinct. Awn has been seen only in a few cases. It is slender, up to 3.5 mm in length. Lodicules are seen with difficulty due to charring. They disintegrate when dissected and are, therefore, better seen in serial cross sections of spikelet. Caryopsis or grain varies in shape and size, may be flattened or somewhat puffed, oblong or elliptical showing longitudinal ridges and grooves. The grains are 4.16—5.54 mm in length, 1.85—2.57 mm in breadth and 1.2—1.98mm in thickness. The ration L/(B×T) is 1.45. Embryo is not preserved but its position at the basal end of the grain is distinct.

Outer epidermis is very characteristic being an extremely thick walled, waxy or sinuous layer. Hypoderm is composed of several rows of cells of thick walled sclerenchymatous tissue. Spongy parenchyma cells are thin walled and somewhat rectangular in shape. Vascular bundles remain embedded in the spongy parenchyma and show concentric arrangement. Inner epidermis is not distinguishable except in some serial sections. Pericarp is recognisable but all the cells of the layer are not discernible. Epicarp is usually distinct and characteristic.

Endosperm occupies the major portion of the grain and consist of mainly thin walled Parenchymatous cells. Starch grains have not been observed. Aleurone layer, which completely encloses the starch parenchyma, is usually made up of large thin walled cells. Hair scars are often visible at several places on the epidermal walls.

These anatomical features, in addition to the general chess board pattern of the entire outer surface, indicate that the cereal belongs to the genus Oryza. It has not yet been possible to identify the particular sub-species to which the remains belong.

Fragments of husk or chaff of cereals were also noticed embedded in the mud plaster. Under a handlens these appeared yellowish in colour, and the the surface view indicated typical chees board pattern of the rice husk. Under the microscope, their rough surface appeared to be due to distinct ridges and grooves. The thick epidermal cells with characteristic zigzag wall running in parallel rows were also found. Here stout dagger-shaped hairs were present in a regular fashion. All these characteristics indicate that these are nothing but husks of rice.

14. Noh

Noh is in District Bharatpur, Rajasthan. Rice remains have been recovered from the Black-and—Red Ware, PGW strata at Noh. The rice record is in the form of charred grains (Vishnu-Mittre 1974 : 17, Vishnu-Mittre and Savithri 1974). A detailed analysis of the finds from this stratum is not available.

15. Hullar

Hallur is in District Dharwar, Karnataka. At this site, stratigraphically, the Megalithic phase overlaps with the earlier Neolithic one and the two radiocarbon dates give a date around 1000 B.C. (Agrawal and Kusumgar 1974 : 142). Rice finds which have been reported have been analysed by Vishnu-Mittre (in Nagaraja Rao 1971 : 125-132).

Plant remains are either carbonised or in the form of incrustations on rusted iron arrow heads. The sample containing rice belongs to the Iron Age. The incrustations (of rice)on the arrow heads were removed with the help of a needle, but being very fragile the spikelets crumbled to pieces. They were studied as such. Most of the spikelets were stuck vertically with only the cavities exposed. In the obliquely placed ones the kernel is partly seen. The incrustation from one of the arrowheads was removed with a needle, the fragile masses in which it came off did not reveal any better than on the arrow head. In one of the arrow heads three spikelets were noted horizontally sticking measuring 7-8mm × 22.5 mm. The chess board pattern of the spikelets can be made out in several fragments and in the complete ones. The incrustation, therefore, seems to be made up of spikelets of rice or the long grained variety (Table 7a).

TABLE 7a

Stratigraphical provenance of rice remains identified from Hallur

Sl. No.	Rec. No.	Tr. No.	Sub-sequence	Layer No.	Depth	Remarks	Identification
6	108	1	4	5	325 Cm. B.S.		Oryza Sativa Linn.

16. Gufkral

It is in Pulwama District, Jammu and Kashmir. No details are published, but Oryza Sativa Linn has been reported by Kajale in the Mesolithic levels 1000 B.C. In the same context should be mentioned the occurrence of Oryza Sativa L. in Period I (1000 B.C.) at Semthan in Kashmir (Buth, Bisht and Gaur 1982).

III. The Early Historic Levels

1. Atranjikhera

Earlier records of rice from this site have been studied. The plant remains from the Northern Black Polished Ware (NBP) period were recovered mostly from the floor and a few mud clods and wall plasters. The quantity or grains is many times more than that from the PGW period. The state in which these were found was more or less the same, i.e. there were husked and unhusked grains and some of them were embedded in tar-like mass. There are more husked than unhusked grains. The husked grains exhibit prominent ribs, two or four in number. The point to note is that though there is some variation in the size and shape of the grains, yet they show common morphological characteristics. The grains which have husk on them show characteristic chess-board pattern of structure on their lemma and palea, indicating their affinity to the genus *Oryza*. Bits of leaf and stem recovered from mud plaster also show anatomical similarity with that found in the extant Oryza. In fact, morphologically and anatomically these remains show no difference from those of the earlier periods. It may, therefore, be stated that this lot of cereals belongs to *Oryza Sativa* L.

It was thought that a study of remains from this period which consists of hundreds of undamaged husked grains, is more likely to show more accurate affinity with recognised sub-species than it was possible in earlier periods. Calibration of grains was therefore made (Table 8).

The average length of N.B.P. rice is 4.42 mm. i.e. it is shorter than var. Javanica and var. Indica and very much nearer to var. Japonica. The same tendency appears to be with the thickness. The breadth of the rice resembles most var. Indica. These data show that the dimensions of NBP rice are different from those of PGW period. Not only this, the var. Javanica seems still out of this picture. What it means is difficult to explain. It is possible that the environment of the North Indian region did not play an active part in the evolution of var. Javanica. Furthermore, a general impression that one gathers from the study of rice from Period I to IV at Atranjikhera is that between 2000—50 B.C. this important food plant under the pressure of the environment was going through different stages of evolution. In these circumstances, it is not advisable to pin-point the sub-species which it resembles most (Chowdhury, Saraswat and Buth 1977 : 47-8).

In this period rice was more than 98% of the entire cereals (45% more than period III). Given this fact it may be suggested that rice production had increased manifold in the N.B.P. period.

TABLE 8

Dimensions of husked rice on three sub species of Oryza in the N.B.P. level, Cereal Lot 'A'

Husked Oryza Sativa L.	Var. Indica				Var. Japonica				Var. Javanica				N.B.P. Cereal Lot 'A'		
	(i)				(ii)				(iii)				(iv)		
	L	T	B		L	T	B		L	T	B		L	T	B
Average	5.47	2.03	1.49	0	4.89	2.67	1.75	0	7.10	2.42	1.74	0	4.42	2.54	1.30
Maximum	6.60	2.60	1.70	0	5.25	3.00	2.00	0	7.85	2.65	1.95	0	5.00	3.00	2.05
Minimum	4.00	1.40	1.20	0	4.50	2.35	1.55	0	6.10	2.30	1.60	0	3.90	1.30	1.00

2. Pataliputra

It lies in District Patna, Bihar. The NBP stratum here is dated to the period from the early seventh to the early second century B.C. (Sinha and Narain 1970 : 14). The only information we have regarding its rice finds is mentioned in Vishnu-Mittre's (1974 : 16) and Kajale's (1974 : 63) general surveys. A discussion of its plant remains is not available in the excavation report of the site (Sinha and Narain 1970). Vishnu-Mittre mentions that the rice record is in the form of charred spikelets and grains. The measurements he gives are as follows: Length 4.95 mm ; breath—2.66mm, thickness 1.82 mm ; L/(B×T) index—1.03mm. He dates the remains to 405-115 B.C. as does Kajale. The latter briefly identifies them as Oryza sp.

3. Rajghat

Rajghat lies in District Varanasi, U.P. It represents parts of the ancient settlements of Varanasi. The only information we have regarding the rice finds is found in Vishnu-Mittre's general survey (1974 : 16). The detailed excavation report which has been published does not have a section where plant remains are analysed (Narain and Roy 1976, 1977). The details of rice remains are not available.

4. Rajgir

Rajgir lies in District Patna Bihar. It is one of the most ancient capital sites of India. Vishnu-Mittre (1974 : 16), stating that data for analysis is not available, merely mentions the date for the rice finds at Rajgir, i.e. 200 B.C.

5. Noh

It is at Noh (Rajasthan), mentioned earlier in connection with PGW rice finds that rice occurs again in the NBP levels. Vishnu-Mittre and Savithri have provided an analysis of these finds (1974 : 77-80). The material consists of carbonised lumps of spikelets and kernels. The carbonised lumps, being partially tarred, it was possible to release as many as sixty kernels of rice. The typical chess board pattern of the rice spikelet is well preserved. The individual kernels are narrowly oblong, laterally flattened, longer than broader and strongly ribbed.

The grains are variable in size ranging from 4—6mm in length, 2-3mm in breadth and 1-2mm in thickness. The long hilum is preserved in many kernels. The dimensions of small medium and large sized grains and their average dimensions and L/(B×T) indices are given below (Table 9).

TABLE 9

Dimensions of rice kernels from Mauryan levels, Noh

	L	B	T	L/(B+T) Index
			Small Grains	
	4.00	2.00	1.00	2.00
	4.00	2.00	1.50	1.30
	4.50	2.50	2.00	0.90
	4.80	2.50	2.00	0.90
	4.80	2.50	1.50	1.30
	4.80	2.80	1.50	1.16
Average	4.50	2.40	1.60	1.25
			Medium Grains	
	5.00	2.50	1.50	1.30
	5.00	2.00	1.80	1.40
	5.00	2.00	2.00	1.20
	5.00	2.80	1.50	1.20
	5.00	2.50	2.00	1.00
	5.00	2.80	2.00	0.90
	5.00	3.00	1.50	1.10
	5.00	3.00	2.00	0.80
	5.50	2.80	2.00	1.00
	5.50	3.00	1.50	1.20
Average	5.10	2.64	1.78	1.11
			Large Grains	
	6.00	2.80	2.00	1.07
	6.00	3.00	2.00	1 00
	6.00	3.00	1.50	1.40
Average	6.00	2.90	1.80	1.16

The morphological characters viz. the shape, the size and the chess board pattern of the carbonised grains and spikelets compare with those of rice (*Oryza* spp.) and more closely with grains and spikelets of *Oryza Sativa* sub-species *Indica* L., the cultivated long grained rice. The L/ (B × T) index of wild and cultivated rice is additional help in the specific identity of spikelets and kernels of rice : the wild rice usually have a ratio higher than 2 and the cultivated ones under 2, rather much under .80. The L/ (B × T) indices, as calculated for the Noh rice material, is much under 1.80, hence their reference to Oryza sativa based on morphological characters is amply supported by the L/ (B × T) indices. The longer than broader grains suggest that they might have belonged to the long grained variety, of snb-species Indica of *Oryza sativa.*

What is striking about the above analysis is that the rice remains have been identified to a sub-species of the genus Oryza. Such an identification had not seemed possible for many earlier sites.

6. Ujjain

Ujjain in M.P. lies on the banks of the river Sipra. It represents the ruins of the eminently famous city of Ujjayini. According to Vishnu-Mittre (1974 : 16) the remains are in the form of charred spikelets and grains. The statistical measurements provided are as follows : length—4.73 mm ; breadth—2.49mm ; thickness—1.48mm ; L/(B × T) index—1.28mm. No further details are available.

7. Nagda

West of Ujjain, Nagda (also in M.P.) is situated on the west banks of the Chambal river. The N.B.P. rice remains consist of charred spikelets and grains. The measurements, are length—4.90 mm ; breadth—2.47 mm ; thickness—1.78 mm ; L/(B × T) index—1.76 mm (Vishnu-Mittre 1974 : 16). They have been identified as *Oryza* sp. by Kajale (1974 : 63). It is interesting to note the differences between the measurements of Ujjain and Nagda grains for this period. The differences in the two L/(B × T)indices is noticeable.

8. Kaundinyapur

This site also is in M.P. The rice record for the NBP period dates from 500-200 B.C. A scientific analysis of the remains has been provided by Vishnu-Mittre (1966 : 152-154). The grains from D4 layer 7 are more or less oblong and strongly ribbed (usually three ribbed) and are made up of two varieties, one comprising comparatively longer seeds than in the other. The kernels of the long seeded variety are 65 in number while those of the short seeded variety are comparatively broader than those of the long seeded variety (Table 10).

TABLE 10

Oryza Sativa var Sativa

	Average	Minimum	Miximum
Length (mm)	3.2	3.0	3.5
Breadth (mm)	2.7	2.0	3.0
Thickness (mm)	1.3	1.2	1.5
L : B	1.1	0.70	0.88
T : B	0.40	0.60	0.50
		Longer Grains	
	4.0	3.0	4.8
	2.0	1.5	2.2
	1.1	1.0	1.5
	2.0	2.0	2.1
	0.55	0.66	0.68

In some grains a part of the fertile lemma showing the chess board pattern is also preserved. The spikelets in the hard tarlike mass were very fragile. Several attempts to recover complete spikelets from the mass proved in vain, consequently it has not been possible to know the size of the spikelets and such other morphological details. Rachilla has been seen in some grains. The fragements of the fertile lemma, however, show the outer surface made up of a chess board pattern but the hairs of their scars have not been noted. From the fragments still sticking to some grains it appears that the fertile lemma was probably five-nerved. The palea, as far as could be made out, is less convex and closely adhering to the grains. It is three-nerved.

The spikelets are invariably single grained with the exception of a few which approach the long grains, the rest have exactly the same shape and dimensions as those of the short seeded variety.

The carbonised grains of rice are referred to as the variety *sativa* of *Oryza sativa.* As for the short grains, such short grained rice has hitherto not been reported. If the Kaundinyapur grains belong to the African species, *O. glaberrima steud* to which it may be compared, then it would imply African contacts with Kaundinypur, but this is not borne out by archaeological finds at the site. A different variety of rice thus appears to be involved at Kaundinyapur.

9. Ter

This site is in District Osmanabad, Maharashtra. It is situated on the banks of the Terna. The finds date from the second century B.C. to the third century A.D. According to Vishnu-Mittre (1974 : 16, 1972 : 170-177) the rice remains are in the form of charred grains and spikelets. The following measurements have been given : length—3.00—5.00 ; 6.00—6.50 mm ; breadth—2.50—2.75 ; 2.50—3.00 mm ; thickness—1.00—2.25 ; 1.50—2.50 mm ; L/(B × T) index—1.30 ; 1.60mm.

10. Pauni

The site is in District Bhandara, Maharashtra. It has yielded rice remains from its NBP layer dated to 200 B.C. Vishnu-Mittre mentions that the rice remains are in the from of impressions of which the length is 6.00—7.00 mm and breadth, 2.25—2.50 mm(1974 : 16). Its plant remains have not been analysed in the excavation report (Deo and Joshi 1972). There are no further details.

11. Rupar

The site is in District Ambala, Haryana. Rice occurs in the NEP level but the details are not available.

12. Tripuri

Taipuri is in District Tripuri M.P. (Dikshit 1955). Rice

occurs in the NBP level (3rd century B.C. at this site). The details do not exist.

13. **Nagara**

This site in the Kaira District, Gujarat and rice has been put here between the third century B.C. and the first century A.D. (Mehta 1968 : 9). The details are not available.

14. **Kannatur**

This site is in the Chingleput District, Tamil Nadu. It is a Megalithic site which has yielded rice records. Vishnu-Mittre (1974 : 16) dates the remains to 400 B.C. They are in the form of spikelets, measuring 7.00 × 2.00 cm. No further details are available.

15. **Khokrakot**

This site in Punjab has been associated with the Yaudheyas who have a very long history in ancient India. B. Sahni (1936 : 799) has published a brief account of the plant economy at the site. A presumed mint has been exposed at the site. It seems that either the matrices where baked over a slow fire of paddy and wheat or barley, or that they were packed in these matrices while the molten metal was poured into them. Well preserved impressions of paddy husk, as well as entire, though charged grains of a cereal (wheat or barley) have been found sticking to the rims of some discs and to the bottom of the basal discs of a pile in the form of a more or less thick carbonised crust. Recognisable impressions of paddy, clearly showing the cell structure of the palace, have also been found in the substance or on the surface of many pieces of brown pottery. Husk appears sometimes to have been rather freely mixed with the potters' clay. Vishnu-Mittre (1974 : 16) dates the finds to 100 B.C. but it possibly had a more continuous history stretching into the Christian era. Evidence of matrices being packed with paddy has not been encountered at any site so far.

15. **Bhokardan**

This site in Maharashtra is a Sātavāhana site situated on the bank of the Khelna river. It ranges in date from the second century B.C. to the third century A.D. The botanical remains have been analysed by Kajale (in Deo and Gupte 1974: 217-23). They include seeds of cultivated and wild plants. Most of the grains are in charred condition. The grains studied critically under the binocular microscope were identified on the basis of external morphological features. Wherever necessary, grains were dissected to confirm the identification. As far as possible, only well preserved grains were selected for measurement. The occurrence of rice is represented in the Table below (Table 11).

TABLE 11

Provenance of rice remains at the Satavahana site, Bhokardan

Trench	Stratum	Site No.	Chronological Period	Rice
Al	3	2493	Ib	√
B4	1 & 5	585 & 2877	II & Ia	√
D	3	2494	Ib	√

The grains of rice are long and flat. The husk is not present verticle, ridges are present. The embryo is basal lateral. Not much variation is observed in shape and size. Twenty five grains were selected for measurements from sample B4 (5) (Period Ia) (Table 12).

TABLE 12

Dimensions of Rice Grains at the Satvahana site, Bhokardan

	Minimum	Maximum	Average
Length (mm)	5.0	5.7	5.50
Breadth (mm)	2.8	3.1	3.00
Thickness (mm)	1.7	1.9	1,80
L/B (mm)	—	—	3.50
T/B (mm)	—	—	0.60

16. Paunar

This site in District Wardha, Maharashtra, is supposed to be ancient Pravarapura, capital of the Vakataka dynasty. The sequence of culture at this site is spread over from c. 1000 B.C. to the medieval period. The rice records at this site come from Period II and III, belonging to the Sātavāhana and Vākātaka-Vishnukundin times.

Excavations brought out twenty four terracotta pieces comprising eight tile fragments and sixteen ring well fragments bearing impressions of food grains. They have been analysed by Vishnu-Mittre and Gupta (in Deo and Dhavalikar 1968 : 128-130). The terracotta pieces are of baked clay mixed with sand. Prior to turning terracotta figures and tiles, the clay was mixed with spikelets of rice and millet. The amount of organic material mixed with clay is variable. This differential mixing of organic matter with clay is not understandable. The black core in the fragments is of variable thickness. Those rich in organic matter have several impressions on the surface of the fragments.

The fragments were broken open along their length and the plant remains reduced to ash but still retaining the original anatomical structure, were studied. They study has been largely confined to to external features and no allowance has been made for the amount of reduction in size in the stated measurements. This microscopic sections of the fragments were also prepared but owing to ashy and fragile nature of the plant matter, only empty spaces would be in the sections.

Among the two kinds of impressions, the oblong have been identified as Oryza sativa Linn. The occurrence is presented in the Table below (Table 13).

The oblong impressions on the surface of the terracotta fragments still retain the impression of the chess board pattern characteristic of rice. More or less complete spikelets reduced to ash in the matrix also show similar anatomical details. In size, they range from 5—10+1—2 mm. Rachilla and lemina, however, could not be made out. Some of the impression show a distinct rib running all along the length of the grain. From the morphology and size of the spikelets, it is apparent that

TABLE 13

Showing stratigraphical details and nature of the terracotta pieces together with the identity, size range and frequencies of plant remains

Sl. No.	Period	Nature	Field No.	Impression	Size (mm)	Frequency	Remarks
1.		Ring Piece	PNR—I(4)—273	Rice	6—7X1.5—2	Frequent	Potsherd with 1—1.5 cm. thick Black core
2.		Ring Piece	PNR—I(5)—456	Rice	6—7X1 —2	Frequent	Potsherd with 1.5—2.5 cm. thick Black core
3.	III	Ring Piece	PNR—I(5)—457	Rice	6—7X2	Less Frequent	1.7 cm. thick Black core
4.		Ring Piece	PNR—I(5)—576	Rice	6—8X2	Abundant	.6—1. 5 cm. thick Black core
5.		Ring Piece	PNR—I(5)—580	Rice	5—8X1.2—2	Abundant	1.5—2.2 cm thick Black core

6.	III	Ring Piece	PNR—I(5)—583	Rice	5—7X1.2—5	Very Abundant	0.8—2 cm. tbick Black core
7.	III	Tile Piece	PNR—I(5)—587	Rice	5—10X1.5—3	Very Abundant	0.8—2 cm thick Black core
8.		Ring Piece	PNR—I(5)—588	Rice	6—7X2	Abundant	1.2—1.9 cm thick Blrck core
9.		Ring Piece	PNR—I(5)—588a	Rice	6—7X1—2	Abundant	2—2.5 cm thick Black core
10.		Tile Piece	PNR—I(5)—593	Rice	6—7X1—1.5	Rare	Black core absent
11.		Ring Piece	PNR—I(5)—594	Rice	5—7X1.5—2	Abundant	2—2.5 cm thick Black core
12.		Ring Piece	PNR—I(5)—595	Rice	5—7X2	Abundant	1.5—2 cm thick Black core

13.		Ring	PNR—I(5)—596	Rice	6—9X1.5—2.5	Abundant	1.4—2.2 cm thick Black core
14.		Ring Piece	PNR—I(5)—597	Rice	5—8X1.5—2.5	Abundant	1—1.6 cm thick Black core
15.		Ring Piece	PNR—I(5)—598	Rice	5—7X1.5—2	Less Frequent	1.2—2 cm thick Black core
16.		Ring Piece	PNR—I(5)—599	Rice	5—7X1—2	Less Frequent	1.5—2 cm thick Black core
17.		Ring Piece	PNR—I(5)—600	Rice	6.5—9X2	Frequent	0.8—2.5 cm thick Black core
18.		Ring Piece	PNR—I(5)—601	Rice	5—9X1.5—2.5	Less Frequent	2—2.8 cm thick Black core
19.		Tile Piece	PNR—I(5)—609	Rice	5—6X1—1.5	Rare	1.2 cm thick Black core
20.	IIb	Tile Piece	PNR—I(5)—605	Rice	5—6X1—1.5	Less Frequent	Black core absent

21.	1st cent. B.C. —3rd cent. A.D.	Tile Piece	PNR—I(5)—841	Rice	6—8X1.5—2.5	Less Frequent	1.5—2.5 cm thick Black core
22.	Late Satavahana	Tile Piece	PNR—I(5)—1000	Rice	5—7X1—1.5	Rare	Black core absent
23.		Tile Piece	PNR—I(5)—1000a	Rice	5—8X1—1.5	Rare	Black core absent
24.	IIa—4th—5th century A.D. Early Satava-hana	Tile Piece	PNR—I(5)—198	Rice	6—7X1.5	Rare	Black core absent

these impressions belong to the long seeded variety of Oryza sativa Linn. Var. Sativa Bor.

During the early Satavahana times, Period IIa (e. 5th century B.C. to 1st century B.C.) Sorghum was abundantly used over rice if the impressions could be relied upon for such a conclusion. The position more or less remained the same during Period IIB (Late Satavahana times, c. 1st century B.C. to 3rd century A.D.) although rice was more frequently used than before.

During Period III, the Vākātaka-Vishnukundin times, there was a change in plant economy. Rice was more abundantly used during this period and the use of Sorghum became rare.

17. Rangmahal

At Rangmahal along the now dry Ghaggar river, fragments of grains of rice, straw and chaff very found in almost every layer of the mound and were very especially plentiful in the topmost layers. Besides this information, the excavation report mentions rice having been recovered from a burial pit in Trench 1, stratum VII. A sacrificial meaning has been attached to these finds (Rhydh, 1959 : 33, 79). Occurrence of rice in burial pits is unique among the other reported finds.

18. Kolhapur

Kolhapur on the banks of the Panchganga river was under the occupation of the Sātavāhanas in the second century A.D. The excavation report has no discussion on plant remains (Sankalia and Dikshit 1952). Vishnu-Mittre (1974 : 76) has mentioned that the rice record is in the form of charred grains with the following measurements : length—3.80—5.40 mm ; breadth—2.30—2.60 mm.

19. Pariyapuram

This site is in Kerala. Remains of the husk have been reported by Vishnu-Mittre dated to the early Christian era (1974 : 16). However, there are no further details available.

20. Nevasa

This site is in Maharashtra. There is some controversy

regarding the date of the rice finds from Nevasa. Kajale (1974 : 63) dates them to the period from c. 150 B.C.—200 A.D. On the other hand, Vishnu-Mittre (1974 : 16) dates them from 1318—1759 A.D. It is difficult to resolve the discrepancy because the excavation report does not refer to rice remains (Sankalia, Deo, Ansari and Ehrardt, 1960) at all. Kajale identifies the remains as Oryza sp. and Vishnu-Mittre mentions that they are in the form of charred grains, with the following measurements. Length—4.38 mm ; breadth—2.18 mm ; thickness—1.38 mm ; L/(B×T) index—1.47 mm.

In addition to the above-mentioned sites notice should also be taken of the identification of rice in the Gandhara Grave culture of Swat in the northwest, although the details (chronological and morphological) of this identification are not yet available (Constantini 1979 : 705).

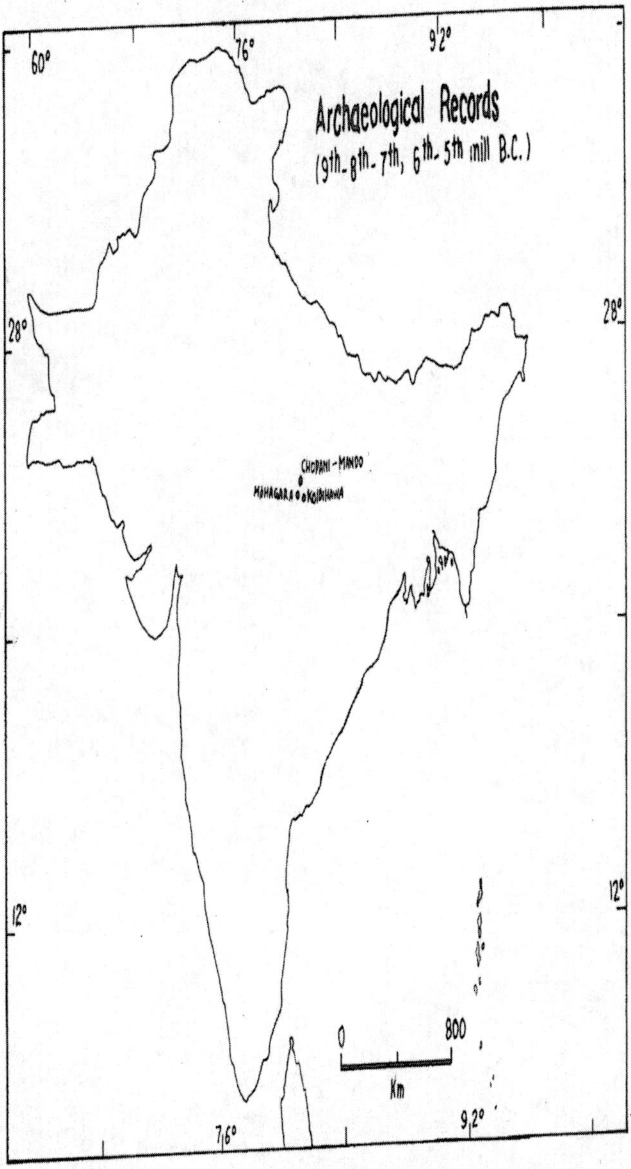

Archaeological Records
(9th-8th-7th, 6th-5th mill B.C.)
CHOPANI - MANDO
MAHAGARA
KOLDIHAWA
60°
76°
92°
28°
12°
0
800
Km

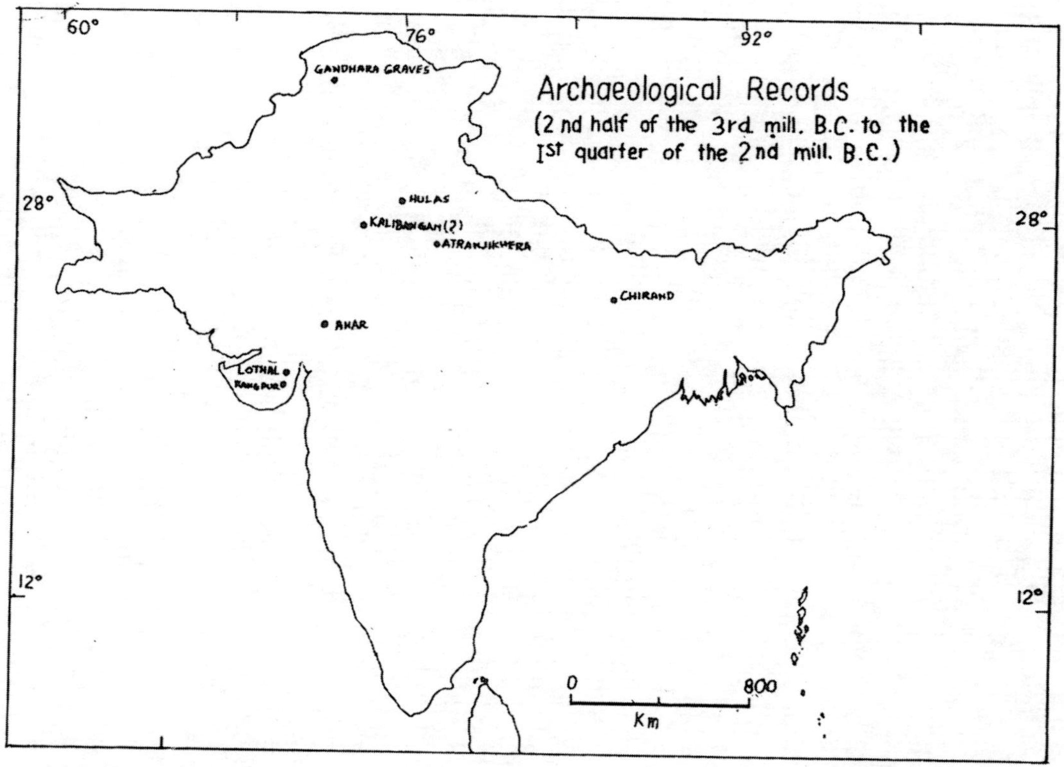
Archaeological Records
(2 nd half of the 3rd. mill. B.C. to the
Ist quarter of the 2nd mill. B.C.)
60°
76°
92°
28°
28°
12°
12°
GANDHARA GRAVES
HULAS
KALIBANGAN(?)
ATRANJIKHERA
CHIRAND
AHAR
LOTHAL
RANGPUR
0
800
Km

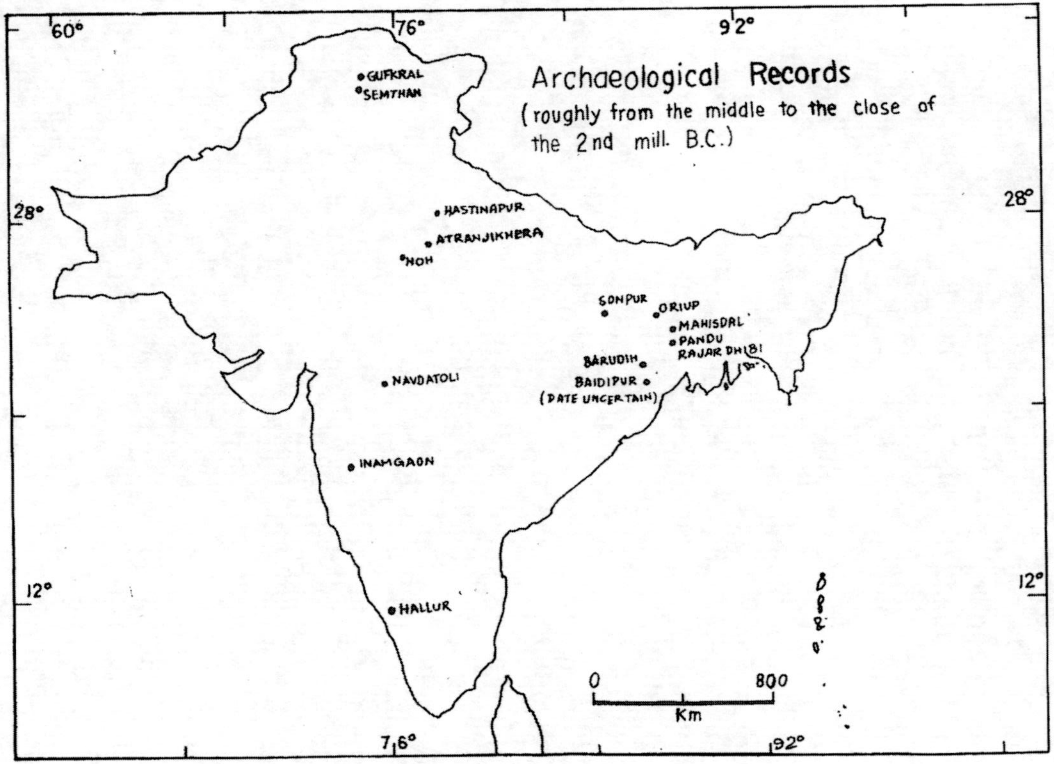
Archaeological Records
(roughly from the middle to the close of the 2nd mill. B.C.)
60°
76°
92°
28°
12°
GUFKRAL
SEMTHAN
HASTINAPUR
ATRANJIKHERA
NOH
SONPUR
ORIUP
MAHISDAL
PANDU
RAJAR DHIBI
BARUDIH
BAIDIPUR
(DATE UNCERTAIN)
NAVDATOLI
INAMGAON
HALLUR
0
800
Km

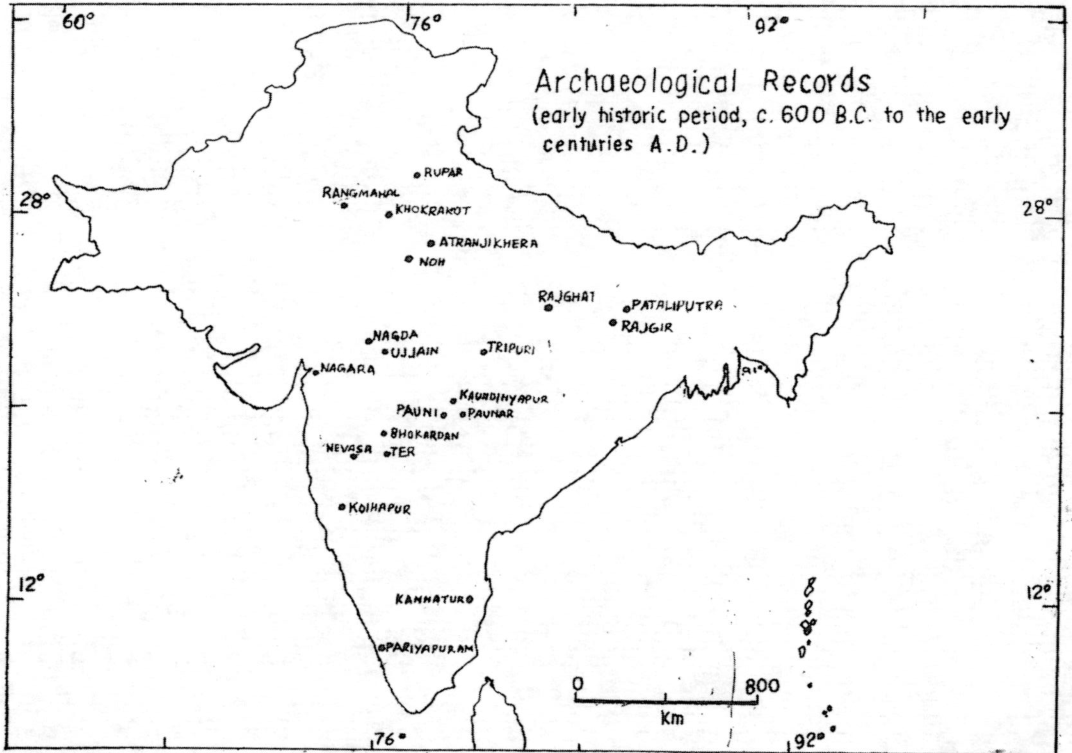
Archaeological Records
(early historic period, c. 600 B.C. to the early centuries A.D.)
60°
76°
92°
28°
12°
RUPAR
RANGMAHAL
KHOKRAKOT
ATRANJIKHERA
NOH
RAJGHAT
PATALIPUTRA
RAJGIR
NAGDA
UJJAIN
TRIPURI
NAGARA
KAUNDINYAPUR
PAUNI
PAUNAR
BHOKARDAN
NEVASA
TER
KOLHAPUR
KANNATUR
PARIYAPURAM
0
800
Km

4

The Botanical Issues

I. The Genus Oryza

Rice, *Oryza spp.*, belong to the tribe *Oryzeae* of the family *Gramineae*. The genus Oryza is itself small. Since the early part of the century, the taxonomy of this genus has been intensively studied. The first monographic treatment was done by Prodoehl (1922) and 17 species were then described. Subsequently the genus has been treated in full by Roschevicz (1931), Chevalier (1932), Sasaki (1935), Chatterjee (1948), S. Sampath (1961, 1962, 1964) and Tateoka (1962, 1963, 1964). Based on a recent examination of all the type specimens available in various herbaria, 23 species have been recognised as valid. However, it must be borne in mind that the taxonomy of the genus is still in a state of flux and at present only tentative conclusions may be drawn.

Of the species of Oryza, only two, viz. *O. sativa* and *O. glaberrima* are cultivated, the former including the common rice cultivated all over the world and the latter grown to a limited extent in Africa. Nevertheless, the existing cultivated varieties throughout the rice growing countries are enormously large in number. All other species are found wild in different parts of the world. Of these, only one, *O. perennis*, is of world wide distribution.

It should be pointed out that based on morphological,

cytogenetical and phytogeographical studies, the species of Oryza can be grouped into three sections viz. (1) *Sativa* including the two clutivated species, *O. sativa* and *O. glaberrima*, as well as the wild species related to them ; (2) *Officianalis* comprising species resembling *O. officianalis* in having large panicles, small, flattened, densely hairy seeds and (3) *Granulata* consisting of species of uncertain affinity, perennial in habit, and having partly or fully glabrous, terete seeds.

This classification not only clarifies the position regarding affinities within the genus but also proves useful in discussing the problem of evolution of the cultivated species.

We may turn our attention to the availability of species, both wild and cultivated, in the Indian subcontinent. Such an enumeration will provide a starting point from where one may begin asking questions and seeking answers.

II. The wild species of rice in India and their distribution

Of the wild species, five are endemic to India. These are *O. coarctata* Roxb., *O. meyeriana*, *O. officianalis*, *O. perennis* and *O. sativa var. fatua*. It must be stressed that there is little unanimity on the problems of taxonomy and nomenclature.

Roxburgh (1832) mentioned wild rice, called *newaree* by the *Telingas*, growing in abundance on the shores of the lakes in the country of the *Circars* (coastal belt of Andhra Pradesh). This has been quoted by de Candolle (1886). However, from a survey of the available literature it appears that the earliest to analyse the wild rices was by Watt (1908). His studies were based on field observation in the Deccan region and on herbarium studies at Saharanpur. Hooker (1897) and Prain (1903), too, discussed the distribution of wild species, though not in any detailed manner. In the period roughly between 1913 and 1934 we have what are in the nature of area surveys on rice species. Many of them throw some light on wild species (cf. Graham, 1913 ; Roy 1921 ; Bhide, 1925 ; Bhalerao, 1928 ; Sethi and Saxena, 1930 ; Mitra and Ganguli 1932 ; Kashiram and Saravayya, 1934; Hector and Sharangapam, 1934). Apart from the works of these botanists, notices of wild rice species appeared in various District Gazetteers compiled in the period (cf.

Allen 1912 ; O'Malley 1914 ; O'Malley 1933). India was considered by Roschevicz (1931) as the area of the greatest diversity of wild rice. Chatterjee (1947, 1948) based his analysis on the studies at the Royal Herbarium, Kew, England. It was only from around 1950 that cytogenetic work was undertaken on the subject of inter-relationships of species within the genus (Chatterjee 1951; Ramiah and Ghose 1951 ; Sampath and Rao 1951). These works brought to the fore more detailed and specific knowledge regarding the Indian wild species and set a trend for future investigative work. Intensive surveys of different regions by research teams have also contributed to supplementing the existing—and apparently limited—information on the subject (Sampath and Govindaswami 1958, Govindaswami and Krishnamurty 1959, Oka, Chang and Narise, 1959 ; Singh 1963 ; Nair, Nayar and Sahadevan 1964; Riccharia, Govindaswami and Ghosh 1966; Watabe 1972, 1974). However, in no recent work is a compilation of the up-to-date findings available. An attempt will be made here to achieve this end in a brief and succint manner.

Each of the available wild species will be treated separately.

1. **O. coarctata Roxb.**

It is a coarse stout grass with spinous-serrate leaves and is found in the lower Gangetic basis in the Sunderbans, in the estuaries of the Mahanadi in Orissa and in the Godavari delta in Andhra Pradesh. It has been recorded also from the Indus delta in west Pakistan and the Irrawady delta in Burma. It is essentially an aquatic plant, frequenting margins of rivers and tidal swamps and adapted to salinity in the soil. The grain resembles wheat and is said to be edible, the rice has a soft, chalky texture. In Bengali, this is referred to as *dhani* and *harakata*. (Roxburgh 1832, Hooker 1897, Prain 1903 ; Watt 1908; Thadani and Dutt 1921; Roschevicz 1931 cited in Nayar 1973 ; Gamble 1934 ; Chatterjee 1948, 1951; Ramiah and Rao 1953; Dept. of Ag., Orissa Govt. Publ., 1956 ; Nayar 1958 Nagai, 1959 ; Bor 1960 ; Sampath 1962 ; Alim and Hasanuzzaman 1962; Tateoka 1963: Nair, Nayar and Sahadevan 1964; Sharma and Shastry 1965; CSIR Pub. 1966).

2. **O. meyeriana**

A perennial grass, upto 1 m. high, with a compact and small root stock. it is found in the foothills of eastern India, the Khasi hills, Sikkim, Assam, Bengal and Bihar (Paresnath, Rajmahal and Chotanagpur hills), Orissa (extensively found in the eastern Ghat region of Koraput, Keonjhar and Kalahandi Districts), Madras, Madura, the Nilgiri Hills, Malabar and Courtallum. It bears short, erect panicles with awnless spikelets, 5-6.5 mmX2.5 mm and is glabrous, pale green or greyish in colour. This species is generally found in well-drained soils at altitudes up to 1000m or along streams under shade. The grains have a good flavour and the grass is eaten by cattle. (Hooker 1887; Prain 1903; Watt, 1908; Gamble 1934; Chatterjee 1948; Ramiah and Rao 1953; Dept. of Ag., Orissa Govt. Publ. 1956; Govindaswami and Krishnamurthy 1959; Nagai 1959; Bor 1960; Tateoka 1963; Nair, Nayar and Sahadevan 1964; CSIR Pub. 1966).

3. **O. officianalis**

It is a tall, annual or perennial grass with sub-woody roots occurring in the eastern Himalayas, Assam, (Gauhati, Cachar) Sikkim, Terai, Khasi Hills, Sylhet, Manipur, Bihar, Central India (Chanda), South India and Maharashtra. The culms are tufted, with broad, multi-nerved leaves and profusely branched panicles, the spikelets are elliptic, 3.5—5.5mm long and more than 2 mm broad, awns, when present, are less than 2.5 cm long.

This species was originally confused with *O. latifolia Desv.* which is purely tropical American. Some authors consider *O. officianalis* as conspecific with a species known at present only from the Philippines, but which is a tetraploid. Recent analysis of the two species, indicates that they cnn be separated by morphological, cytological and phyto-geographical standpoints.

A new tetraploid species (*O. malampuzhaensis* Krishnaswamy et Chandrasekharan) described from the Annamalai Hills, is similar to *O. officianalis* but can be separated from it by hairy ligules, longer spikelets as well as tetraploidy. It has been assigned to this species as a sub-species, since the morphological distinction between them is not marked, This grass is reported to be eaten by cattle. (Hooker 1897 ; Prain 1903; Watt 1908 ; Chatterjee 1948, 1951, Ramiah and Ghose 1951 ; Hamada 1956; Krishnaswamy and Chandrasekharan 1957; Bor 1960 ; Tateoka 1963 ; Nair, Nayar and Sahadevan 1964 ; CSIR Pub. 1966).

4. **O. perennis Moench**

This wild form has been described inearlier publications by several workers as Oryza sativa var. fatua. However, Ramiah and Ghose (1951) referred to it as perennis and distinguished it as an Asiatic form of perennis. Sampath and Govindaswami (1958) gave a more complete description and adopted the name Oryza perennis var. balunga. Accepting Watt's grouping, Sampath (1964) described *O. sativa* var. bengalensis as *O. perennis* Moench emend Sampath. Sharma and Shastry (1 965) and Chang (1976) characterise the from as *O. rufipogon.*

The habitat of *O. perennis* is in ponds and ditches, where the water depth is 10-50 cm. The plants are potentially perennial. They have creeping or bulbous rhizomes and erect or prostrate culms and are sometimes floating. The leaves are broad, 10-20 mm wide with pigmentation and long acute ligules. The panicle is medium sized, fully exerted and open. Spikelets are slender, rarely exceeding 3 mm in width. The anthers are very long, almost filling the spikelets. The awns are coloured, slender and 7-10 cm long. The ripening colour of the grain varies from typical straw to brown and black. A distinguishing trait is premature shattering of the grain. The form is asexually propagated. The grains are edible and are occasionally harvested.

As mentioned earlier, this species is considered polymorphic and widely distributed in tropical Africa, America and Asia. It is therefore considered by some to represent the common ancestral type from which all cultivated rices are derived.

In India, it has been reported from West Bengal (Durgapur, Asansol, Burdwan, 24 Parganas) ; Bihar (Darbhanga, Lauriya, Gaya, Ranchi) ; U.P. (Gorakhpur, Gonda, Faizabad, Lucknow, Rampur) ; M.P. (Raipur) ; Orissa (Balasore, Kalahandi and Koraput or the Jeypore tract) ; Manipur, Assam, the deltas of the Godavari and Mahanadi, Nagpur and Western India. The names are *Johl*, *Jara*, *Barunga*, *Balunga Wainuchara* etc. (Watt 1908 ; Chatterjee 1951 ; Ramiah and Ghose 1951 : Sampath and Rao 1951 ; Ramiah and Rao 1953 ; Dept. of Ag., Orissa Govt. Publ. 1956 ; Sampath and Govindaswami 1958 ; Govindaswami and Krishnamurthy 1959 ; Oka and Chang 1959 ; Kihara 1959 ; Nagai 1959 ; Riccharia 1960 ; Riccharia Govindaswami, 1960 ; Morishima, Oka and Chang 1961 ; Ghose, Ghatge and Subramanyan 1960 ; Yeh and Henderson 1961 ; Govindaswami and Krishnamurthy 1961 ; Sampath Chang 1962 ; Sampath 1962 ; Singh 1963 ; Henderson 1964 ; Sampath 1964 ; Tateoka 1964 ; Nair, Nayar and Sahadevan 1964 ; Chang 1964 ; Sharma and Shastry 1965 ; CSIR Pub. 1966 ; Govindaswami, Krishnamurthy and Shastry, 1966 ; Riccharia, Govindaswami, Ghosh 1966 ; Watabe 1972, 1974 ; Nayar 1973 ; Oka 1974, 1975 ; Chang 1976 ; Randhawa 1980).

5. O. rufipogon

It is a group of highly variable annual wild rices, closely resembling cultivated sativa. *O. rufipogon* has a wider distribution than *O. perennis*, growing in water or swampy places or appearing as weeds in cultivated fields. It is essentially seed propagated. There are long, erect culms, nearly 2 m long, and deciduous spikelets, nearly 7 mm long. The awns are rather rigid and coarser than in *O. perennis*. *O. rafipogon* carries many dominant primitive characters like awning, shattering, redness of rice and dark colour of husk. The baldness of grain, shortness of anthers and compactness of panicles give it the appearance of cultivated rice.

A prevalent opinion holds that the annual, bold seeded wild rice occurring as a weed in rice fields should be considered as of more recent hybrid origin, arising by introgressive hybridisation of the perennial Asiatic *O. perennis* with cultivated O. *sativa*. The characteristics of segregation for interspecific characters in the progeny, semi-sterility and heterozygosity are regarded as confirming this inference.

O. rufipogon occurs in abundance in India in the following regions : West Bengal (Sunderbans, Calcutta, Burdwan, Durgapur, Santiniketan and North Bengal) ; Bihar (Dumka, Patna,

Arrah, Buxar, Sasaram, Bhabua, Gaya, Nalanda and Rajgir) ; U.P. (Ghazipur, Gorakhpur, Gonda, Bareilly, Agra, Firozabad, Etawah, Kanpur, Fatehpur, Allahabad and Varanasi) ; Orissa (Balasore and the Jeypore Tract) ; M.P. (Jubbulpur, Raipur, Chanda ; Bilaspur, Balaghat, Seoni) ; the Surma Valley ; Eastern Himalayas ; Kangra Valley ; Punjab ; Nagpur ; Bombay ; the deltas of the Godavari and Mahanadi and the North Western Region.

The local names are *Uri*, *Jhara*, *Nivara*, *Tari Pashi Sada*, *Kala*, *Karanga*, *Karanga pashar*, *Parsad*, *Tinni*, *Passahi*, *Vari*, *Joadhan*, *Uli*, *Niai Bhatta*, *Karga* etc. (Roxburgh 1832 ; de Candolle, 1886 ; Prain 1908 ; Watt, 1908 ; Garham 1913 ; Roy 1921 ; Thadani and Durgadutt 1921 ; Bhide 1925 ; Bhalerao 1928 ; Sethi and Saxena 1930 ; Roschevicz 1931 ; Mitra and Ganguli 1983 ; Chatterjee 1951 ; Ramiah and Ghose 1951 ; Ramiah and Rao 1953 ; Dept. of Ag., Orissa Govt. Publ., 1956 ; Hamada 1956 ; Sampath and Govindaswami 1958 ; Nayar 1958; Oka and Chang 1959; Kihara 1959 ; Nagai 1959 ; Bor 1960 ; Riccharia 1960 ; Ghose, Ghatge and Subrahmanyan 1960 ; Morishima, Oka and Chang 1961 ; Yeh and Henderson 1961 ; Sampath 1962, 1964 ; Oka and Chang 1962 ; Tateoka 1963 ; Nair, Nayar and Sahadevan 1964 ; Chang 1964 ; Sampath 1964 ; Henderson 1964 ; Sharma and Sastry 1965 ; Riccharia, Govindaswami, Ghosh 1966 ; Govindaswami, Krishnamurthy and Shastry 1966 ; CSIR Pub. 1966 ; IRRI Pub. 1972 ; Watabe 1972, 1974 ; Nayar 1973 ; Oka 1974, 1975 : Chang 1976 ; Reed 1977 ; Randhawa 1980).

From the above it becomes clear that wild rices have an extensive sweep in India covering Sikkim, Manipur, Assam, the Eastern Himalayas, W. Bengal, Bihar, Orissa, M.P., U.P., Madras, Kerala, Punjab, H.P. and the North Western Region.

III. The cultivated variety of rice in India—O. sativa L.

We will next focus on the cultivated forms available in India. The progression from the wild to cultivated rices may be said to have been in the following external characters, from prostrate habit to an erect and compact one, from shedding to non-shedding character of grains, an increase in the number and length of panicles, from lax to compact panicles, increase in the weight and number of spikelets, reduction in awns, from black to straw lemma palea colour and lastly from red to white pericarp colour. These external differences are correlated with differences in the genetic system. Another very important point of difference between the two is the increase in seed weight.

1. The Species

O. sativa L. is an annual or perennial grass without a rhizome, leaves long and narrow, 30—50 cm x 1.2—2.5 cm ; slightly pubescent with spiny hairs on the margin ; a terminal panicle varying from close and compact in some to loose and spreading in others ; spikelets generally single, but in some clusters of 2—7, number of spikelets varying from 50—60 to 200—300, large number usually associated with smaller size and a densely packed arrangement; lemma and palea surrounding the kernel, variously coloured, golden yellow, red, purple brown or smoky black, becoming straw or light yellow when the grain ripens ; grain varying in size from 5—14.5 mm long and 1.9 to 3.7 mm broad, the length/breadth ratio defining size and shape of the grain ; kernel most commonly white, occasionally red, purple or brown.

2. The divisions of O. sativa L. and varieties of India

Because of the long period during which cultivated rice has been grown under varying conditions of environment, the species *O. sativa* L. is made up of a mass of complex forms showing large variations in morphological and physiological characters. Based on hybrid sterility, which is an important criterion in differentiation of species, *O. sativa* has been classified into two sub-species *Indica* and *Japonica*. While the former is grown all over the tropics, the latter is generally confined to temperate and sub-tropical regions beyond 30°N and S. The groups also differ in morphological and several physiological features, including response to temperature and day length. By continuing the work on hybrid sterility, some workers have shown that the Indica group of earlier workers includes a third group, *Javanica* consisting of rices which exhibit affinities of an intermediate nature between *Indica* and *Japonica*.

While the *Indica* group is rich in diversity of forms with

morphological and ecological variations, there is similar but less diversity in *Japonica* and comparatively little in *Javanica*.

Rice grown in India belongs to the *Indica* sub species. The varietal diversity of cultivated rices in India can be considered to be the richest in the world. The total number of named types of rices runs to 50,000 (Central Rice Research Institute Statistics). Rice cultivation in India extends from 8°—35°N. There are rices grown at sea level in the river deltas, in areas even below sea level with protective embankments as in Kerala, in 3-5 m of water as in Assam and West Bengal and at altitude of 1000-1500 m and even more in Kashmir and on the slopes of the Himalayas. The varieties exhibit wide diversity in their morphological as well as physiological characters. There are rices with grains varying in colour from yellow or straw to red, purple or brown, and in size from 5 mm to 15 mm in length and 1.9 mm to 3.5 mm in breadth. There are also scented and glutinuous varieties. It is, however, possible that there are duplication—the same rice variety growing under different names—and occasionally distinct rices growing under the same name in different areas. The remarkable number of varieties is associated with the fact that a single kind thrives only under very narrow limits of conditions to which it is perfectly adapted. It is this fitness of varieties to particular places (and uses) which explains their perpetuation.

The earliest attempt at classification of south Indian rices, particularly of the Andhra area, was by Roxburgh (1832) who based it only on the duration of the crop such a *punasa* (early) and peddapanta (late). Watt's (1908) classification covered the agricultural groups in Bengal, Assam, the United provinces, the Central Provinces and Berar, Kashmir, Mysore and Coorg, Madras, Bombay and Sind, Punjab and the Northwest Frontier. It took into account the duration as well as the cultural peculiarities of the different varieties. After him Graham (1913) made an attempt to classify the rices of the Central Provinces. Several other botanists have since dealt with the classification of the rices they were describing (Thadani and Dutt 1921 ; Sethi and Saxena 1930 ; Mitra and Ganguli 1932 ; Kashiram and Saravayya 1934 ; Hector and Sharangapam 1934 ; Kashiram and Ekbote, 1936). These classifications are based primarily on morphological features. This makes the classifications cumbersome, making it difficult to apply any uniform system to all the cultivated varieties.

Thereafter numerous cultivated varieties have been classified variously on the basis of such agricultural characters like the season of growth and period of maturity. There are three distinct seasons when rice is harvested. They are, "*Aus*" or autumn rice, "*Aman*" or winter rice and "*Boro*" which is spring or summer rice. Varieties of rice in India can be broadly divided into four main groups on the basis of the time required for ripening (i) very early: 110 days or less ; (ii)early :110 – 140 days ; (iii) late : 150—170 days ; and (iv) very late; about : 180 days. But it is known that season and maturation can be considerably modified by change in the environment. Classification on the basis of morphological traits, though it still persists, is often confusing, as mentioned earlier. One classification that has proved of some value is that based on size and shape of the grain. In 1980, the International Rice Research Institute and the International Board of Plant Genetic Resources published what purports to be a minimum list of descriptors-states for characterising the cultivars of rice. The Central Rice Research Institute of India has also prepared a "Rice Germplasm Collector's Data Sheet" wtth a view to facilitating orderly classification. Such Standardisation should go a long way in bringing order to this knotty problem.

3. The Distribution of Different varieties

95% of India's rice produce come from the following areas: Bihar (Gaya, Santhal Parganas, Shahabad, Purnea and Ranchi districts) ; West Bengal (Midnapore, 24 Parganas, Burdwan, Bankura districts); Uttar Pradesh (Basti, Gonda, Gorakhpur, Azamgarh, Bahraich and Deoria districts) ; Madhya Pradesh (Raipur, Bilaspur, Durg and Raigarh districts) ; Orissa (Cuttack, Sambalpur, Puri and Balasore districts) ; Andhra Pradesh (West Godavari, East Godavari, Krishna, Guntur, Srikakulam and Nellore districts; Tamil Nadu (Tanjavur, Chingleput, North Arcot, South Arcot and Tiruchchirapalli districts); Assam (Kamrup, Goalpara, Sibsagar and Darrang districts): Maharashtra (Ratnagiri, Thana, Kolaba, Bhandara and Chanda districts); Karnataka (South Kanara, North Kanara, Shimoga and Dharwar districts) ; Kerala (Palghat, Calicut, Trichur and Cannanore districts); Gujarat (Surat, Panch Mahals, Paroda and Kaira districts) : Punjab (Gurdaspur, Ferozepur and Amritsar districts); Haryana (Karnal district) and Himachal Pradesh (Kangra district).

As far as tne varietal distribution and associated special features are concerned, we may refer to some Government publications and area studies. Though mainly for commercial use, the Ministry of Food, Agriculture, Community Development and Co-operation, Government of India's report on the classification of rice may be utilised for our purpose. Local names have been recorded and the basis of classification adopted is the grain size and type.

Sole reliance cannot be placed on it as it includes some recently introduced improved varieties. However, it provides a roughly approximate overview. It also brings out the fact that a number of varieties are grown in different states with common names. On the other hand, varieties, though having same name, were seen to differ in quality.

The following picture emerges :

Orissa	—	349 varieties
Karnataka	—	230 varieties
Maharashtra	—	209 varieties
West Bengal	—	163 varieties
Madhya pradesh	—	119 varieties
Tamil Nadu	—	94 varieties
Andhra Pradesh	—	87 varieties
Bihar	—	86 varieties
Uttar Pradesh	—	77 varieties
Kerala	—	63 varieties
Assam	—	44 varieties

The various Disttrict Gazetteers are more useful as traditional types are clearly marked off from the more recent introductions. Besides giving an indication of the place of rice in economy, they also highlight the regional variations in a broad rice growing area.

The number of varieties supposedly available in various districts is indeed remarkable. Curiously enough, however, the details do not appear to tie in with those of the publication referred to above. To quote a few examples, in both Dhenkanal (Senapati and Tripathi 1972) and Sambalpur (King, 1932) districts of Orissa, 300 varieties of rice are said to be grown. In Bilaspur (Shrivastava 1978) and Raigarh (Guru 1976) (Madhya pradesh), the number of varieties are said to be 200 and 115 respectively. In Ramanathapuram (Ramaswami 1972) (Tamil Nadu) it is said to be 100. In Assam, in Sibsagar and Lakhimpur, (Hunter 1879) the '*Sali*' rice includes 74 and 87 different varieties respectively. The Shimoga District of Karnataka (Abhishankar 1975) grew more than 60 vaireties, prior to the introduction of High Yielding Varieties. Muzaffarpur, in Bihar, (Roychaudhuri 1958) grows 80 varieties.

A problem which surfaces at this point relates to the authenticity of these figures. Since the basis of differentiation is not clear in nearly all the cases (either the number or the names, alone or together, being mentioned) one should be cautious about drawing inferences. All that can be said is that these statistics underscore the diverse variability found in the Indian cultivars.

The area surveys referred to bring out some interesting facts. For example, a study of the rices in Nizamabad (Andhra Pradesh) (Pawar and Rajagopalan 1956) points out that a survey conducted in 1942-43 revealed 127 different varieties. In yet another survey in 1950-52 of the same area, it was observed that only 62 varieties were cultivated. Of these, less than a dozen were commonly cultivated. It is difficult to find an explanation for the reduction in the number of varieties. However, this survey does, in a way, help us interpret the data available in the foregoing statistics i. e. that numbers alone are not enough to bring out the existing cultivation patterns.

That the northeast region has a rice store of varieties has been amply shown by such area studies. Most importantly, some of the varieties show marked affinities with those occurring in different South East Asian regions. Such types are rare in other rice growing areas of India. Glabrous types have been collected from Manipur, Nagaland and Arunachal pradesh. Glutinous types appear in Upper Assam. *Japonica* type rices have been described from some higher elevations of Arunachal Pradesh and Sikkim (Sharma, Vellanki, Hakim and Singh, 1971; Riccharia and Govindaswami 1960 ; Kihara and Nakao 1960 ; Krishnamurthy, Ved Prakash and Sharma 1967).

Some questions arise from the foregoing account of cultivated rices in India. For example, (a) within the group of traditional varieties is it possible to distinguish older cultivars ? and (b) which regions appear to have a greater number of varieties and why so ?

So far as the first point goes, though it is possible to establish a demarcation between traditional local varieties and High Yielding Varieties, it is only historical evidence which will enable us to interpret the situation in the earlier periods. If a correlation is worked out between the two i. e.—varieties gleaned from historical sources and the traditional varities, it would be of great help. As things stand, we have to be content with the analysis that the more primitive a variety, the more coarse it is. Of course, it must be borne in mind that this is not to be mistaken for a rule which has uniform applicability.

As for the second point, it would appear that the rices are adapted to very narrow ecological niches. The diversity index will therefore tend to be greater in those tracts with marked ecological variations. According to Dr. J. K. Roy, Senior Scientist at the Central Rice Research Institute, Cuttack (personal communication), field work in Orissa has revealed that for every acre a farmer has at least 5-6 varieties. He also maintains that in areas of more primitive cultivation there is little of what is known as "gene erosion". Indeed, the existing forms can be regarded as ecovarieties being established in different regions by the the efforts of man and the work of nature. It may be noted in passing that the number of cultivated varieties of rice probably exceeds tnat of all the grains combined (Copeland, 1924).

IV. The Issues of Origin

Having completed a survey of the wild and cultivated

species, we are led to the very crucial and complex question relating to the domestication of the latter. The origin, evolution, cultivation, dispersal and diversification of the cultivated species are interesting not only to biological scientists but also to geographers, archaeologists, anthropologists, philologists, historians and other social scientists. However, the importance of the botanical analysis and interpretation cannot be minimised.

A comprehensive study of origin involves three aspects, the species from which originated, the mode of origin and the place of origin.

1. The Proposed Progenitors of Cultivated Rice

The following species have been proposed by various authors as having been the progenitor of cultivated rice.

(a) *O. coarctata* Roxb.
(b) *O minuta* Presl.
(c) *O. officianalis* Wall.
(d) *O. perennis* Moench.
(e) *O. sativa Lin. Var. fatua* Prain.

(a) Watt (1908) proposed that *O. coarctata* Roxb. occurring in the river estuaries and salt marshes of India might have given rise to some of the brackish and deep water varieties *O. coarctata* is a tetraploid species, and is so different both morphologically and ecologically from the other species of this genus, that it could not have been an ancestor of cultivated species. Attempts at crossing this species with *O. sativa* and with some other species of the genus have, so far, been unsuccessful. It is no longer considered to have contributed to the origin of rice.

(b) That *O. minuta* might probably have given rise to some small fruited paddy varieties was first proposed by Roschevicz (1931). It was supported by Chevalier (1932) and Gutschin (1938). *O. minuta* is also a tetraploid species, and as such it could not have been a progenitor of cultivated rice. It has the genome constitution BBCC. In addition, the hybrids between *O. sativa* and *O. minuta* are highly sterile.

(c) *O. officinalis* has been suggested to have contributed to the origin of cultivated rice by Watt (1908), Roschevicz (1931), Gutschin (1938), Chatterjee (1951) and Anderson (1951). It is a diploid and its area of distribution corresponds more or less to the areas of varietal diversity of *O. sativa.* The two speci s have some panicle characters also in common. *O. sativa* and *officinalis* have been crossed with difficulty and the F_1s were completely sterile with highly irregular meiosis. The total length of chromosomes of the latter are said to be about 1/3 longer than that of *O. sativa.* The natural back-crosses of the F_1 hybrids gave sterile allotriploids with two genomes of *O. sativa.* These pieces of evidence tend to preclude the possibility of *O.officinalis* having contributed directly to the origin of cultivated rice. Ramiah and Ghose (1951) have also opposed Roschevicz's proposition on the basis of chromosome size differences.

(d) In Chatterjee's (1948) revision of the genus, *Oryza*, he recognised the presence of perennial wild rices in Asia. This fact apparently made it easier to recognise soon after (Chatterjee 1951 ; Ramiah and Ghose 1951 ; Sampath and Rao 1951) its widespread occurrence in Asia. Then Sampath and Rao (1951) proposed that *O. perennis* is the progenitor of all cultivated riccs, both *sativa* and *glaberrima.* Ramiah and Ghose (1951) and Kihara (1959) conceded only a collateral role to this taxon. It was then proposed that *sativa* originated from the Asian perennial floating rice (Sampath and Govindaswami 1958 ; Riccharia 1960). The detailed studies conducted by Oka, Morishima and their co-workers have amply confirmed that *sativa* has directly evolved from this taxon (Morishima et al, 1961 ; 1963 ; Hinata and Oka 1962 ; Oka and Chang 1962 ; Oka 1964 : Oka and Morishima 1971 ; Oka 1974, 1975). Their main postulate is that the perennial type is more likely to be the ancestor of *sativa* because it stores up in its populations a large amount of genetic variability. Accordingly, it may have larger evolutionary potential than other likely progenitors. Considerable supporting evidence has bcen presented by other workers also (Nayar 1958 ; Riccharia 1960 ; Yeh and Henderson 1961 ; Nair et al 1964). These are : (a) its widespread occurrence in Asia ; (b) it is also a diploid species like cultivated rice (2n=24). It produces semi-fertile hybrids and shows normal F_2 segregation ; (c) its chromosome morphology is simllar to that of *sativa* ; (d) hybrids between geographical races of *O. perennis* produce by recombination, the various characteristics of *sativa* and (e) the actual process of evolution can be observed in some areas even today, Thus all evidence overwhelmingly indicates the evolution of the Asian cultivated rice *sativa* from the Asian perennial rice, *O. perennis* Moench.

(e) *O. sativa* L. *var. fatua* has been held to be the progenitor of *sativa* by Roschevicz (1931), Chevalier (1932), Gutschin (1938), Hamada (1949), Zurovskij (1950), Chatterjee (1951), Ramiah and Ghose (1951) and Porteres (1956) in view of their similarity in various characters. Great variability is present in this group. There are neither precise morphological differences to separate them from the cultivated form or genetic barriers to gene exchange between the two populations. A large volume of evidence is available to demonstrate the hybrid origin of most, if not all, annual wild rices (Sampath and Govindaswami, 1958 ; Nayar 1958 ; Oka and Chang 1959, 1961, 1962 ; Yeh and Henderson, 1961 ; Henderson 1964 ; Govindaswami et al 1966). Oka, Morishima and co-workers, who have made detailed and extensive studies on the nature of wild rices (Hinata and Oka 1962 ; Morishima et al 1961 ; 1963; Oka 1964, 1974, 1975) have also shown that these forms do not possess the potentialities to have been the ancestral form *O. sativa.* The annual wild rices are, however , very ubiquitous and, in their role as companion weeds of rice, they may serve, as reservoirs of germplasm for cultivated rices. According to Chang (1976), judging from the recent findings on the evolutionary processes of the grasses and of crop plants, it is more reasonable to visualise the general process as : wild perennial wild(prototype) annual cultivated annal. The annual weed race is a conglomerate of natural hybrids of all intergrade among the above three.

What is amply clear from the foregoing is that the polyphyletic origin os *O. sativa* —or its derivation from a number of species within the section—should be discounted. Recent evidence from cytogenetical studies of interspecific hybrids indicates that *O. sativa* had a monophyletic origin. Not only has the number of possible putative ancestors thus been narrowed, controversy veers around only two of the wild types, *O. perennis* and *O. sativa var. fatua.* It must also be added however, that the current opinion appears to be in favour of supporting *O. perennis* as the progenitor. This marks a great advance from Roxburgh's (1832) statement that wild rices present in India were probably the ancestors of cultivatcd rice.

A fruitful line of enquiry would be to trace the parallels between the evolution of the two cultivated species of the genus, *O. sativa*, discussed above, and *O. glaberrima*. Chevalier (1932), Chatterjee (1948), Sampath and Rao (1951), Richharia (1960), Sampath (1962) and Oka (1964) considered that *O. perennis* Moench was the common progenitor of both the Asian and African cultivated rices. One reason underlying this postulate was that *O. perennis* was the only wild species occurring over widespread areas.

However, the parallel and independent trends in the evolution of the two have been pointed out by Porteres (1956) and Morishima et al, (1963). *O. longistaminata* is said to be the perennial race from which *O. glaberrima* is descended. *O. barthii* represents the wild annual progenitor. Thus a parallel can be drawn between the two above mentioned species and *O perennis* and *O. sativa var. fatua* respectively. Chang (1976) proposed that both the wild perennials from which *O. sativa* and *O. glaberrima* were derived, had a common ancestor. However, such a conclusion must await further substantiation. For it to be accepted as valid a few questions have to be answered viz. relating to the details of the common progenitor, its differentiation in to two distinct perennial species as also an analysis of the species deriving from them. Till such time, the question remains an open one.

We may enquire as to whether any similarity exists between the evolution of *O. sativa*, on the one hand, and other major cereals on the other. The complex nature of species alone renders it difficult to attribute the ancestry of various cultivated species to simple and precise origins. Nevertheless, it must be stressed that studies on the origin of a number of cereal crops have indicated that all of them have followed essentially the same pathways from wild grasses to cultivated plants i. e.

they have arisen from rather restricted plant families. Besides, the domestication of cereals, in particular, have many features in common. Comparable with rice are the following:

(i) The wild and cultivated races interact ; genes from cultivated races flow into spontaneous races and vice versa ;

(ii) The geneflow is always across barriers of some sort, but the barriers are not of the kind that separate species ;

(iii) The differences between wild and cultivated races are likely to be linked and

(iv) The differences between wild and cultivated rices are relatively simple genetically (*Harlan, de Wet and Price*, 1973).

2. The Mechanism of Transformation from the Wild to the Domesticated varieties

From the complex problem of the progenitor species, we move to the process of evolution from the wild to the domesticated species. Here is involved not only the historical problem just mentioned, but also the evolutionary genetic problem, dealing with the cause-effect relationships in the origin of a cultivated species. From the former standpoint, an event is not repeatable, while from the latter what has happened many years ago can be repeated again if the necessary conditions are provided.

The genetic basis of evolution has been outlined as follows: The particular nature of the genetic material, the organisation of the material in a complement of chromosomes and the existence of a diverse gene pool preserved from selective elimination by the variability and changeability of the environment, replenished by mutation (Hutchinson 1970). This is not to discount selection pressures which have been very strong. These pressures have been biologically capricious and often in diverse directions. The end result is an enormous amount of conspicuous variation among very closely related forms.

Several authors have observed that wild rices show a continuous variation to cultivated froms (Watt, 1908 ; Roy 1921 ;

Ramiah and Ghose 1951 ; Sampath and Govindaswami 1958 ; Nayar 1958 ; Oka and Chang 1961, 1962). Now the progenitor species is more definitely known, viz. *O. perennis*. According to the majority view of the cytogeneticists, it may be recapitulated, *O. perennis* is able to accumulate genetic variations supplied by mutations and hybridisations. On approaching cultivated forms these variations are released. It was olso noted that in rice there is a three tier system of wild species—weed—and cultivated species complex. According to Chang (1976) the evolutionary pathway rr ay be described as wild perennial-wild (prototype) annual—cultivated annual. However, the role of the wild annual weeds in the process of evolution is still a matter of controversy.

Some elaboration of this dispute will note be out of place not so much because it will help to clarify the picture of the evolutionary process—which it probably will not, but mainly because it will help underline the tentative nature of the hypotheses regarding the origin of rice. Sampath and Govindaswami (1958), working on the wild rice of Orissa, concluded that some of the wild annual rices have originated by natural crossing between *G. perennis* and *O. sativa*, and are thus later in origin than cultivated rice. Sampath put forward the same view in 1962 and 1964. Oka and his co-workers, on the other hand, postulate that cultivated rice might have evolved from the wild species passing through a series of intergrades as evidenced in the Jeypore Tract of Orissa (Oka and Chang 1959, 1961, 1962 ; Morishima, Oka and Chang 1961). Nayar (1973) holds that intermediates occurred transiently in man's cultivated fields during the course of domestication. Chang (1976) points out that in weed races considerable introgressive hybridisation takes place and that gene flow has been largely from the cultivated rices to the wild forms.

What stand out is that the problem of the evolutionary pathway, as distinct from that of the progenitor species, is far from being easy of solution. For it has to be realised that any assumption regarding alternate pathways is difficult to prove.

Treatment of the cause-and-effect problem of evolution of cultivated rice has been based on different hypotheses. A detailed appraisal of them is not being attempted because this falls outside the scope of our historical investigation. However, a brief and generalised account will be outlined.

Regarding the first establishment of the cultivated from in rice, it may be only conjectured on limited evidence that it might be due to the presence of potential genetic variability in wild populations, which through hybridisation could produce genotypes with a selective advantage in a niche disturbed by man. If such a primitive cultivated form was once established, hybridisation would have created diverse genotypes adaptive under different intensities of cultivation pressure, and with the impact of increasing cultivation pressure, genotypes more closely resembling the present cultivated varieties might have been established. If a genotype become a "desired weed" some selection might have been practised by man through harvesting and seeding. Such a selection may be, in a sense, considered to be part of cultivation pressure. The flow of genes from cultivated to wild forms is more vigorous than that in the opposite direction, so that cultivated genotypes once established may be maintained surrounded by wild plants.

It is clear that inter and intra specific hybridisation, followed by natural and artificial selection may have been the primary methods of evolution of cultivated rice. Morphological and physiological changes brought about by mutations would appear to have mediated the different stages of evolution. A combination of these forces has led to the great ecological diversity now found in *O. sativa*.

A few interesting related facts are worth noting. With domestication, populations become homogenous and the sensitivity to minor environmental factors is reduced. More importantly, there is a marked contrast between the restricted flow of genes among different eco-geographic races of *O. sativa* and the relatively free flow among *O. sativa* and its wild relatives. This indicates not only the large number of sites where cultivation and domestication took place, but also the antiquity of the process of genetic differentiation.

3. The Probable Centres of Origin

Owing to its ancient origin, the problem of determining the native place of origin of *O. sativa* is rather complicated.

Though exact locations have not been pinpointed, it is possible to know the origin of eultivation within definite regions. These regions may be very wide. Various criteria have been adopted in order to delineate the region.

de Candolle (1886) mentions a ceremony instituted by the Chinese Emperor, Chin-nong, 2800 years B.C. in which rice played the principal part. Rice was considered by the Chinese as indigenous. On this basis, he postulates that cultivation of rice in China was prior to that of other regions.

Watt (1908) advances considerable philological evidence to suggest that rice cultivation originated in South India wherefrom it spread to the North. Vavilov (1951) believes that India is undoubtedly the birth place of rice and that it was a later introduction to China. He bases his conclusions on the following grounds : (a) occurrence of a number of wild rice species, common rices growing wild as a weed and intermediate forms connecting wild and cultivated rices ; (b) the great varietal diversity, particularly of the coarse grained ones (According to him the longer a group has been established in a given area, the larger the number of species that are to be found there) ; (c) prevalence of dominant genes, which are absent in other areas.

Roschevicz (1931) considers that India, China and Indo-China are the regions of antiquity of rice cultivation. He regards China as the centre form where cultivation spread to other countries. Africa, on the other hand, he considers the centre of origin of the section sativa on the basis of natural distribution of the different species included in this section.

Gutschin (1938) considers the area bounded by the southern slopes of the Himalayas and certain mountain ranges of China as the probable centre of origin of rice. Chatterjee (1947, 1948, 1951) believes that rice originated in India. In support of the Indian origin, he mentions the existence of an extensive terminology for various rice and rice products in the Indian languages. Hamada (1949) and Burkill (1953) consider Indo-China to be the centre of origin of rice. Hamada bases his proposition on the observation that rice shows widest taxonomic differentiation in South East Asia.

Ting (1949, 1957, 1958) believes that rice originated in China. According to him, rice was first mentioned in the Chinese classical literature of the time of Shen-nung (300 B.C.) and also during the periods of Hwangti, Yu and Chi (2600-2000 B.C.). Rice cultivation was finally established at the time of the Chou dynasty (1122-247 B.C.). A phonetic eonsideration for the character of rice as used during the Chou dynasty indicated to him that it was related to certain dialects of the south eastern coasts of China, Indo-China and Siam. From these and also from the presence of certain wild forms of rice, he concludes that rice originated in China.

Ramiah and Ghose (1951) support Watt's theory that rice evolved in peninsular India. They mention the antiquity of Dravidian culture and the designation of separate ricc varieties for use at specific religious occasions in ancient Tamil.

In his paper, Chatterjee (1951) refers to a philological work in which the author had argued that the generic name *Oryza*, the Greek word, Oruza and the Tamil word, *arise* had all originated from the word Ou-li-zz, meaning rice in the Nengpo dialect of Chinese. This, along with the story of the rice sowing ceremony performed in China (2800 B.C.) made him modify his earlier stand slightly. He now considered the whole region covering South and South East Asia as the area where rice originated.

Nayar (1958) concurs with the generally held view that cultivated rice arose in the region comprising Burma, Indo-China and South China, but adds that enough data is not available to locate the exact centre of origin. It is known that the wild species which are claimed to have given rise to *O. sativa*, occur throughout this region, that all these areas are centres of ancient agriculture and that there is great varietal diversity in cultivated rices throughout this region.

According to Riccharia (1960), rice must have originated in eastern or southern India, as in those regions the ancestral forms are common and climatic conditions favour rice cultivation. It may also have originated in some South Asian country.

Nair et al (1964) advance some phytogeographical evidence

in support of considering peninsular India and more particularly, the Malabar coast, as the centre of the origin of rice. The occurrence of as many as five wild taxa, including both perennial and annual, the presence of high varietal diversity, and also the wide occurrence of several dominant genes in local rice varieties such as red pericarp, colour, awning, bold grains, black husk colour, were given as supporting evidence. They also point out that the warm and humid tropical climate was unlikely to preserve cultural specimens in the area.

More recently, Sampath (1973) suggests that Thailand ought to be considered the centre of origin of cultivated rice. He based his postulate on an archaeological find from the region.

According to Chang (1976) the genus *Oryza* originated from the Gondwanaland continents. Based on recent palaeogeological and meteorological studies, he states that the prototype of *O. sativa* evolved primarily along the foothills of the Himalayas in South Asia and its associated mountain ranges in mainland South East Asia and South West China. The widespread distribution of the wild races in insular South East Asia, Sri Lanka and Taiwan was most probably facilitated by land bridges which existed as recently as the Pleistocene. The continuous and varied movements of people in Asia during prehistoric times was an important factor in the broad distribution of early *O. sativa* forms.

Huke (1976) postulates a more limited centre of orsgin, notably the inland valleys in northern Thailand, the Shan states of Burma and the adjacent areas of Laos. The dependable monsoonal rains of that area, its warm and humid environment, and the specific physiography of the valleys with their multitude of wet and seasonally shallowly flooded grassland depressions offer an ideal environment for the domestication of *O. sativa.*

Besides the primary centres of origin, suggesting wide geographical areas, secondary centres have also been suggested. The Jeypore Tract of Orissa is considered to be one such centre (Ramiah and Ghose, 1951). Uptil now, in a survey conducted by the Central Rice Research Institute, Cuttack, 1700 samples of rice varieties have been eollected. The grain types in this collection varied from very coarse to fine grain and included rounded pubescent *Japonica* type of grains. Rice varieties with long sterile lemma and with the glutinous endosperm have been collected. A variety, resembling the West African species, *O. glaberrima* has also been found. This area is also rich in the varieties of thc wild species, *O. perennis* and *O. sativa var. fatua*, The marked richness of rice varieties available in the region has led to its description as a secondary centre of the origin of rice.

On a similar basis, the North-West and North-East foothills of the Himalayas are considered important (Ramiah and Ghose 1951). Intensive surveys of the Eastern Himalayas, especially in Assam and Manipur, are being carried out by the Central Rice Research Institute, Cuttack. So far, 6000 and 400 samples of varieties have been collected from the two regions respectively. On completion, these surveys may be able to throw more light on centres of origin within a broad region.

From the above historiographical survey it is clear that there is little disagreement as far as the broad outlines of the region are concerned. This region would cover the broad sweep of territory from India to China. Differences of emphasis are present but they do not radically alter the picture. It is therefore clear that domestication could have occurred independently in different micro-areas within the region, and occasionally, even simultaneously so. Obviously, attempting to pinpoint a specific location of domestication will be a futile endeavour mainly because of the limited nature of evidence at our disposal on this subject. However, even such a general idea will enable us to draw some conclusions regarding the early centres of rice cultivation and its subsequent spread to other areas ontside the primary and secondary centres of origin.

The difference among scholars is to be traced more particularly to the criteria adopted for determining the region of origin. The different criteria which have been used are, broady speaking, philological, archaeological and phytogeographical. A few words may be mentioned regarding the utility of these different criteria.

To begin with, philology can at best provide evidence only of an indirect nature. Although it can be of help in determining the general nature of the antiquity of rice in a particular region, it may not be able to provide very precise clues as to the centre of origin. There is often a tendency to overlook this distinction.

Providing a rather sharp contrast, archaeology provldes a direct and precise kind of evidence ln outlining the region of origin. In fact, it is archaeology which can help us trace the centres of early cultivation in the broad region. However, identification and dating of the excavated plant remains have their own associated problems which detract from the intrinsic value of the tool. It should also be noted that new archaeological finds have the tendency to upset what may have been neat theories based on a similar kind of evidence.

Varietal richness and climatic suitability are other factors which have been used. Chang (1976) points out that when we compare the micro centres of diversity of the wild relatives with the most likely sites of early rice culture, cultivation and domestication appear to have occurred at the periphery of the belt of maximum diversity. This supports the contentions of Isaac (1970) that Vavilov's centre of variability is not necessarily the heart of domestication. Similarly, the area where the maximum diversity of wild relatives is found may not coincide with the magnitude of varietal diversity in that geographic region (Zohary 1970; Whyte 1972, 1974).

These criticisms bring out the fact that the basis on which regions of origin are outlined needs to be provided with great precision. More work is required in this field and also to narrow down, if possible, the known region of domesticaion.

The effort in this chapter has been to study the following—the available wild and cultivated species of rice and their related details ; the origin and evolution of *O. sativa* from the progenitor species and the region of origin.

The idea was to provide a comprehensive account of the botanical aspects of the early history of rice in India mainly to facilitate a well-rounded approach and understanding towards the topic.

5

The Terms in Indian Language Families

WHILE trying to reconstruct the history of a cultural item in a specific area an analysis of the related terms in different language families of that area may be considered a valid historical exercise. However, mainly because of their chronological uncertainties, the linguistic data can hardly be treated as a well-defined historical source. Such an analysis will establish, in the first place, the general significance of that cultural item in that area and secondly, may even lead through a study of the origin, the first documented literary use and the interrelationship of these terms to some historical understanding. The present chapter is based on this theoretical assumption.

I. Rice in the Indo-Aryan language family

There are five primary terms documented in ancient texts viz. *śāli, taṇḍula, dhānya, bhatta* and *vrīhi* for rice. On the basis of Turner (1966), one may draw up the following lists.

1.

Name of Language	*Term for Rice*	*Meaning of the term*
Sanskrit	Sali	Growing or unhusked Rice

Name of Language	*Term for Rice*	*Meaning of the term*
Pali	Sali	Rice
Prakrit	Sali	Rice
Ashkun (K)	Salima	Rice
Waigali (K)	Seli, Salima	Rice
Kati (K)	Seli	Rice
Prasun (K)	Sili	Rice
Bashgali (K)	Shali	Rice
Dameli (K)	Sali	Growing Rice
Pashai (D)	Sal	Rice
Woṭapuri (D)	Sole	Rice
Gawar-Bati (D)	Sali	Rice
Kalasha (D)	Sali	Unhusked Rice
Khowar (D)	Sali	Rice
Bashkarik (D)	Sel	Rice
Torwali (D)	Sal	Rice
Maiya (D)	Shayl	Rice
Phaluṛa (D)	Seli	Rice
Sindhi	Sari	Unhusked Rice
Lahnda	Saria	Rice
Assamese	Xali	Principal variety of transplated Rice
Bengali	Sal, Sai	A kind of Rice
Oṛiya	Sali	Unhusked Rice
Bihari	Sal, Sail	Rice
Hindi	Sal	Rice
Gujarati	Sal, Saliyu	Rice
Maraṭhi	Saḷ, Saḷi	Rice
Sinhalese	Hal, Al	Rice

(D=Dardic ; K=Kafiri)

Though the first occurrence of *śāli* is early, it is interesting to note that references to it become copious in the later Sanskrit texts. As the table shows, it has cognates in as many as twenty seven languages.

There is no very great difference of form amongst these languages as far as this term goes. However, the difference in meaning may be noted. The most common meaning attributed is that of growing of unhusked rice. It is among some of the vernaculars that it is mentioned as a particular variety of rice. The earlier meaning seems to be of a more general nature.

2.

Name of the Language	*Term for Rice*	*Meaning of the Term*
Sanskrit	Taṇḍula	Rice after threshing and winnowing
Pali	Tandula	Husked Rice
Prakrit	Tamḍula	Husked Rice
Waigali (K)	Tanulo, Taul	Husked Rice
Dameli (K-D)	Talun	Husked Rice
Tirahi (D)	Taṛun	Husked Rice
Ningalami (D)	To	Husked Rice
Woṭapuri (D)	Tanulo, Taṇul	Husked Rice
Gawar Baṭi (D)	Toṇḍul	Rice in the fields
Bashkarik (D)	Talun	Husked Rice
Shumasti (D)	Taṛul	Husked Rice
Torwali (D)	Ṭala	Husked Rice
Shina (D)	Tarun	Boiled Rice
Oṛiya	Taṇḍula	Husked Rice
Gujarati	Tadul̤, Tadal̤	Grains or Rice, Grains of some kind of corn
Maraṭhi	Tadul	Rice
Kashmiri	Tomul	Husked Rice
Old Bengali	Taula	Husked Rice
Old Maraṭhi	Tamdula	Husked Rice
Sinhalese	Saneḍla	Husked Rice

(K=Kafiri ; D=Dardic)

Unlike *śāli*, *taṇḍula* is among the earliest terms for rice. It however, has more precise connotation viz. grain, especially rice, after threshing and winnowing. It occurs abundantly in Sanskrit texts. According to the findings presented above, similar terminology occurs in about twenty languages. However, differences of meaning are apparent. In Gujarati, the term, besides denoting rice also conveys the meaning of grains of certain kind of corn. In one of the Dardic Languages, Gawar Bati, it stands for rice in the fields. In another, Shina, it means boiled rice.

3.

Name of Language	*Term for Rice*	*Meaning of the Term*
Sanskrit	Dhanya	Corn, grain especial parched grain
Prakrit	Dhaṇṇa	Corn, growing rice
Western Pahaṛi	Dhaṇ	Growing Rice
Panjabi	Dhaṇ	Rice before threshing
Kashmiri	Dane	Growing or unhusked Rice
Lahnda	Dhan, Dhanj, Dhaj	Rice, seedling rice before transplantation
Kumauni	Dhan	Growing or unhusked Rice
Oṛiya	Dhana	Growing Rice
Bihari	Dhan	Growing Rice
Maithili	Dhan	Growing Rice
Bhojpuri	Dhan	Growing Rice
Awadhi	Dhan	Growing Rice
Hindi	Dhan	Growing Rice
Gujarati	Dhan	Grain, Corn
Maraṭhi	Dhan	Growing Rice
Sinhalese	Dan	Growing Rice

The term, *dhāna* occurs in the earliest extant text, the Ṛgveda, as already mentioned. However, it cannot be taken to mean an unambiguous reference to rice as in the case of *śāli* and *taṇḍula*. Different meanings are apparent both in Sanskrit and Prakrit where it means grain and corn, besides specifically rice. The same meanings appear in Gujarati too. Most commonly, it stands for growing rice. However, in Lahnda, it denotes seedling rice before transplantation.

The different forms of *dhāna* in the various languages resemble each other more closely than either *śāli* or *taṇḍula*. It may also be noted that *dhāna* figures in the greatest number of modern day 'vernaculars'. The number is fourteen. For sali, the number is eight and for *taṇḍula*, six.

Curiously enough, the term has no affinities in Dardic and Kafiri. However, the affinity with Sinhalese is common to *śāli*, *taṇḍula* and *dhāna*.

4.

Name of Language	*Term for Rice*	*Meaning of the Term*
Sanskrit	Bhakta	Food boiled Rice
Pali	Bhatta	Meal, Food
Prakrit	Bhatta	Food Rice
Waigali (K)	Bot	Rice
Bashkarik (D)	Batt	Cooked Rice
Torwali (D)	Bat	Boiled Rice, Meal
Phaluṛa (D)	Bhat	Boiled Rice, Meal
Shina (D)	Bat	Boiled Rice, Meal
Kashmiri	Bata	Boiled Rice, Meal
Sindhi	Bhatu	Boiled Rice
Lahnda	Bhat	Boiled Rice
Panjabi	Bhappa	Boiled Rice
Western Pahaṛi	Bhatt	Boiled Rice
Oṛiya	Bhata	Boiled Rice
Bihari	Bhat	Boiled Rice
Bhojpuri	Bhat	Boiled Rice
Awadhi	Bhat	Boiled Rice
Hindi	Bhat	Boiled Rice
Old Marwari	Bhata	Boiled Rice
Konkaṇi	Bhata	Husk of Rice
Sinhalese	Bata	Cooked Rice
Maldivian Dialect of Sinhalese	Bat, Bai	Rice Meal

(K=Kafiri ; D=Dardic)

The term *bhatta* is found earliest in the Buddhist canonical texts. The meaning attributed to it in virtually all the languages, it appears is of cooked or boiled rice, the latter being more frequently used. A noteworthy point is that *bhata* is very often used interchangeably with food and meal and in these contexts they are obviously considered to be synonymous. We do not find this in the case of other terms. About the only instance of a divergence of meaning is to be found in *Konkaṇi.* Here it means not cooked or boiled rice but the husk of rice. The forms are, however, fairly similar.

5.

Name of the Language	*Term for Rice*	*Meaning of the Term*
Sanskrit	Vrīhi	Rice
Pali	Vihi	Rice
Prakrit	Vihi	Rice
Sinhalese	Viya	Growing Rice

Vrīhi, as will be recalled, is the earliest precise term for rice in extant Sanrkrit literature. It finds frequent mention in in later Sanskrit texts.

As the table shows, the term figures in both Pali and Prakrit. It has possible cognates in Gujarati and Marathi. The terms are *Vari* and *Vari*, meaning respectively, not rice, but a particular kind of grain and the grain, coix barbata. But apart from these,. the word is found in strangely restricted circulation in the 'vernaculars'. It has not been easy to account for the fact.

Vrīhi has cognates in Sinhalese though not in Dardic and Kafiri. In this respect we find a similarity between it and *dhāna.*

Concluding, we may say that a study of the terms above has indicated a great degree of similarity within Indo-Aryan family of languages as far as rice is concerned.

II. Rice in the Dravidian Language Family

The following tabulations are based on Burrow and Emeneau (1961).

1.

Name of Language	*Term for Rice*	*Meaning of the Term*
Tamil	Avi	A single grain of boiled Rice
Kannada	Avuḍu	A grain of anything
	Agalu	A grain of boiled Rice; A small lump of Rice Kneaded into a Ball

2.

Malayalam	Kuruva	A sort of black paddy
Tamil	Kuruvai	A dark species of paddy maturing in two months, An inferior reddish paddy maturing in three months

3.

Tamil	Campa	A superior kind of paddy
Malayalam	Campa	A superior kind of paddy
Kannada	Sambe Nellu	A superior kind of paddy
Telugu	Sàmbavu	A fine sort of rice

4.

Tamil	Navarai	A kind of paddy
Tamil	Nakarai	A kind of rice

Name of Language	*Term for Rice*	*Meaning of the Term*
Malayalam	Navira Niviri Nakara	A kind of rice that ripens within two or three months
Tulu	Navara Navare	A kind of grain A kind of rice
Telugu	Nivari	A kind of rice
5.		
Tamil	Nel	Rice, paddy, grain of paddy
Malayalam	Nel	Rice (as growing), rice in the husk, paddy
Kota	Nel	Paddy, unhusked rice
Kota	Nelaky	Husked rice
Toda	Nes	Rice in songs
Toda	Nesisky	Rice
Kannada	Nel	Paddy, rice in its husk, rice as growing, a grain of paddy
Kannada	Nellu	
Koḍagu	Nelli	Rice, paddy
6.		
Telugu	Pralu	Rice
Gondi	Paṛek	Husked rice
Konḍa	Per	Husked rice
Kuï	Prau	Rice, husked paddy
7.		
Gadba	Majik	Rice
Konḍa	Manji	Rice
Kurukh	Manji	Seed in general

Name of Language	Term for Rice	Meaning of the Term
8.		
Tamil	Vari	Paddy
Malayalam	Vari	A wild growing rice with rough beard
Telugu	Vari	Paddy
Gadba	Varsil	Paddy
Gondi	Wanji	Rice, Both growing and in the grain
9.		
Tamil	Viyam	Seed, rice
Kannada	Biya	Rice when cleaned from the husk, food
Telugu	Biyyamu	Seeds or grains of Oryza sativa without husks, paddy deprived of husks, rice
Kolami	Bi'Am	Rice
10.		
Tamil	Ari	Rice, paddy, ear of paddy
Tamil	Arici	Rice without husk, any husked grain
Malayalam	Ari	Grain of rice freed from chaff, seed, grain
Kota	Aky	Grain of any grain food when husked
Toda	Asky	Rice
Kannada	Akki	Rice deprived of husk, grain that resembles rice
Koḍagu	Akki	Husked rice
Tulu	Ari	Rice freed from

Name of Language	*Term for Rice*	*Meaning of the term*
		husk, any small grain
Tulu	Akki	Rice, grain
Telugu	Arise	A sweetmeat made of rice flour and Jaggery
11.		
Kurukh	Khess	Paddy, rice in the husk or standing in the field
Malto	Oesu	Paddy
12.		
Tamil	Valci	Paddy, husked rice boiled rice, food
Malayalam	Varru	Grain or boiled rice, from which water is strained off
Kannada	Batta Bhatta	Paddy rice in the husk
Telugu	Vadlu	Unhusked rice, paddy
Kolami	Val	Grain of unhusked rice
Kolami	Val Bi. Am	Husked rice
13.		
Tamil	Aval	Rice obtained from fried paddy by pestling it
Tamil	Avaiyal	Well husked rice
Malayalam	Avil	Rice bruised and dried
Malayalam	Avekka	To beat rice
Kota	Ofil	Puffed rice

Name of Language	*Term for Rice*	*Meaning of the term*
Kannada	Aval-Akki	Rice bruised and crushed
Koḍagu	Avl-Akki	Rice fried and each grain pounded flat
Tulu	Abeccunt	To beat of pound rice
14.		
Kurukh	Tlkhil	Rice, paddy cleansed of husk
Malto	Tigalu	Rice
15.		
Toda	Obely	Watery mass of rice
Kannada	Ambali	Porridge of rice with water milk
Tulu	Ambuli	Gruel of rice
Koliam	Amba	Cooked rice
16.		
Tamil	Uṇti	Boiled rice
Tamil	Uṇā	Boiled rice
Malayalam	Uṭṭu	Giving rice, esp. to Brahmans
Malayalam	Uṇ	Boiled rice
Kannada	Ummu	Boiled rice (used when talking to children)
Koḍagu	Uṇpu	Boiled rice
17.		
Tamil	Ecar	Water in a pot set over the fire for boiling rice

Name af Language	*Term for Rice*	*Meaning of the term*
Kui	Eju	Cooked riee, rice water
18.		
Tamil	Orai	Boiled rice, rice that is mixed with other edibles like sesamum etc.
Kannada	Ogara	Boiled rice
Telugu	Oremu	Boiled rice, food
19.		
Malayalam	Kuṟ	Boiled rice
Malayalam	Kuṛạm	Rice as eaten in temples
Kota	Ku	Cooked rice
Toda	Kuowiṟ	Cooked rice from which water has been drained
Kannaḍa	Kuṛ	Boiled rice, food
Kodagu	Ku.Li	Cooked rice
Tulu	Kuḷu	Boiled rice
Telugu	Kuḍu	Boiled rice, food
20.		
Tamil	Korru	Food, means of subsistence
Malayalam	Korru	Food, rice
21.		
Tamil	Coru	Boiled rice
Malayalam	Coru	Boiled rice

Name of Language	Term for Rice	Meaning of the term
22.		
Kannada	Buvva	Boiled rice (in children's language)
Telugu	Buvva	Food, rice
23.		
Tamil	Purukku	To boil paddy before husking
Tamil	Puṟukkal	Cooked rice
Kannada	Puggi	Rice boiled with pulse, salted or sweetened
Telugu	Pulagamu	Rice boiled with green dal
24.		
Tamil	Ponkal	Boiled rice seasoned with salt, pepper or cumin seeds and ghee
Kannada	Pongil	Rice boiled with pulse, salted or sweetened
Telugu	Pongali	Rice boiled in milk
25.		
Tamil	Mitavai	Boiled rice
Tamil	Vitavai	Boiled rice
Tamil	Metukku	Boiled rice
Tellugu	Meduku	A grain or boiled rice, boiled rice
Telugu	Metuku	A grain or boiled rice, boiled rice

Name of Language	*Term for Rice*	*Meaning of the term*
26.		
Tamil	Vakkal	Boiled rice from which conjee has been poured
Kannada	Bagu	To pour out water from boiled rice
27.		
Kui	Algu	Rice obtained from paddy without boiling it
Kurukh	Alkhṛa	Parched rice
28.		
Kannada	Puri	Parching, roasting, partly boiled and then parched rice
Kannada	Burugalu	Parched rice
Telugu	Boruvulu	Parched or fried rice
29.		
Malayalam	Nuccu	Broken rice
Toda	Nuc	Broken rice
Koḍagu	Nuri	Very small bits or broken rice
30.		
Tamil	Putitu	First sheaves of a rice crop offered to Lakshmi
Malayalam	Puttari	New rice used in ceremonies

Name of Language	*Term for Rice*	*Meaning of the term*
Kodagu	Putteri	Rice harvest festival
Tulu	Pudu Baṛu	New paddy
31.		
Tamil	Maṛakku Maṛukkal	To beat (as paddy) Husked rice with bran removed
32.		
Tamil	Avi Aviṛ	Boiled rice Boiled rice

One fact which stands out is the great abundance of references to rice in the Dravidian language. In *Tamil* alone, the references to rice, inclusive of cooked rice, number thirty two. For *Kannada*, *Telugu* and *Malayalam* the number are twenty two, twenty and sixteen respectively. For the other Dravidian languages, the picture is as follows :

Tulu and *Kodagu*	—	eight
Kurukh and *Toda*	—	six
Kota	—	five
Kui and *Kolani*	—	three
Malto, *Gondi*, *Konda* and *Gadba*	—	two

The position may be contrasted with the earliest representative Sangam texts which do not have as copious reference to rice.

We are not in a position to detect the older terms for rice among the various references and what changes, if any, have occurred in them over a certain period of time. However, an examination of our evidence brings out the following points :

(a) *Similarity of both form and meaning* : *e.g. campa, sambe nellu* and *sambavu* in *Tamil, Malalayam, Kannada* and *Telugu* all mean a superior or fine quality of rice.

(b) *Similarity of form, along with differences of meaning* : e.g. *Vari*, *Varsil* and *Wanji* in *Tamil*, *Teluug Gadba* and *Gondi* mean paddy while *Vari* in *Malayalam* means a wild growing rice with rough beards.

(c) *The occurrence of more than one term for something with similar meaning within one language itself* : e.g. in *Malayalam, navira, naviri, nakara* and *navara* all refer to a rice that ripens within two or three months.

(d) *The occurrence of different meanings for one term in one language itself* : e.g. in *Tamil, Kuruvai* refers to a dark species of paddy maturing in two months and also in inferior reddish paddy maturing in three months.

(e) *The existence of terms which mean both rice and something else* : e.g. in *Malayalam, Korru* stands for rice as well food in general. This obviously highlights the place of rice in the economy. This point differs from (a) above in that the other meaning is not directly related to rice and that this difference of meaning occurs in one language itself.

(f) *Specialised use of the terms for rice* : e.g. *Unnu in Kannada* is a term for boiled rice but it is used only when speaking to children.

(g) *The greatest number of cognates in the different languages is of the Tamil* term *'arici'*. This may be an indication of its antiquity. The other terms with wide affinities are the *Tamil, aval* and *nel* and the *Malayalam, Kur.*

(h) *The terms which have cognates in the Dravidian languages are, by and large, not restricted to the four, Tamil, Telugu, Kannada and Malayalam.* This may be taken to suggest either diffusion of the existence of a common source from which the terms have been drawn. We cannot be sure of either, however.

Summarising the above points, it may be briefly mentioned that the rice and rice related terminology is remarkably varied in Dravidian language.

III. Rice in the Muṇḍa language family

We will now turn our attention to a discussion of affinities within the *Muṇḍa* languages. Some comparative work on these languages has been done particularly in the present century. However, it must be borne in mind that the vocabulary of many of these languages is not particularly structured and a great deal of uncertainty will remain in semantic identification. The ethnobotany and folk plant taxonomies of even one of the *Munda* groups have yet to be closely analysed. Thc data is therefore restricted in comparison with the *Indo Aryan* and *Dravidian* languages.

Campbell (Macphail (Ed.), 1954) provides a useful guide to the terminology of rice in the Santali language.

1.

Term in Santali	*Meaning*
Horo, AN, Khorca	Rice
Daka	To cook rice
Ạiṭạu	To sift rice
Suṛe	To cook along with rice
Humạk Hōsēc	To clean rice
Caoie	Husked rice
Daka, Kak	Boiled rice
Daka, Mạṇḍl	Cooked rice
Biḍir	Well cooked rice
Manja	Insufficiently cooked rice
Kharca	Uncooked rice
Khạjạri, Taben, Khoi, Muc Ḍhol	Parched rice
Horo	Unhusked rice
Beṇḍer	Rice not well husked
Jojo Jhara	Cooked rice which becomes stale
Gēlē, Gāthni	An ear of rice
Dak Maṇḍi, Daka Mạṇḍi	Rice water
Khir	Rice cooked in milk
Datri	Rice cooked with flour
Usna	Rice boiled before husking
Caole Khode, Mạrkhu	Rice broken in husking
Cạḍi Caole	Given by bridegroom
Bạki	A rice post
Gạchiạu	To thin out rice

The following are different terms for a variety of rice fields.

2.

Term in Santali	*Meaning*
Khet	Rice field
Bheṭra Bhiṭri	High rice field
Buhi, Khet, Dabar, Dabar, Dabar, Khet Ḍhab, Gahḍa, Jạrhi	Rice field which is always moist
Karnạli	Rice field which is on a slope
Sokṛa, Songha	A valley of rice fields
Aṛe	Ridge around rice fields
Raksha	Wood uses to level rice fields

There is a number of terms which describe rice lands.

3.

Term in Santali	*Meaning*
Jạmin, Jạmi, Jumi, Ahar	Rice land
Goḍa, Bheṭra Bhiṭri	High rice land
Jumi Sagor	Large area of rice land
Hiṛ	Rice land reclaimed by Dam
Khạṇḍit, Khạṛti, Khut, Kaṭa	Rice land reclaimed at own expense
Loeya Khaṇḍi	Newly reclaimed rice land
Bohal, Jubhi	Rice land with plenty of water
State Sote	Rice land dependent of rain
Ṭopra	Small plot of rice land
Guṛha, Suṭia,	Strip of rice land
Maṇḍal Khe̱tko	Terraced rice land

Term in Santali	*Meaning*
Bạihạr	First class rice land
Bad	Third class rice land
Rekhja	To divide rice land

For the rice plant and its varities there occur the following terms.

4.

Term in Santali	*Meaning*
Hoṛo, Huṛu	Rice plant
Sisi	An ear of the rice plant
Dal, Uṛth	Wild rice
Hẹṇdẹ Koeya, Kurchih	Black rice
Ạgnisạr	
Ạṛhạia	
Bạd Kolma	
Bạdrạs	
Bag Aenọm	Varieties of rice plant
Bag Panjar	
Bajal	
Bana Koṛam	
Basmạti	
Benaphul	
Bhạdoe	
Bhasa	
Bhuṇḍi Kolma	
Boaṛdạl	
Boaṛi	
Bọrọh	
Candar Gạki	
Cingul	
Dạhar	
Dhusri	
Dubraj	
Dudhkani	
Ghisali	
Gitạ	

Term in Santali	*Meaning*
Goeṭ Hasar	
Gopal	
Gopal Bhog	
Guhmạ	
Guipha Rạngi	
Gurpạ	
Hemca	
Jagarnath	
Jạlth	
Jaṭah	
Jawae Lạḍu	
Jhagṛah	
Jhagṛih	
Jhaṛa	
Jhinga Sạl	
Kadolia	
Kajri	
Kạmaṇi	
Kanakcur	
Karhaṇi	
Kạribạnki	Varieties of rice plant
Kạrimṡạl	
Kạsiphul	
Kele	
Kehtorni	
Kodom Sar	
Koeyah	
Kolmah	
Koyah	
Lachman	
Lachman Bhog	
Loton	
Mac Nothor	
Mahadab	
Mahadab Jaṭa	
Matoli	
Mohan Mala	
Mohipala	
Moticur	

Term in Santali	Meaning
Mugdi	
Musur	
Nạgi	
Nanha	
Ṇarda	
Nona	
Parmonosal	
Pasa	
Paṭnai	
Puṭki	
Raebundi	
Raemundi	
Raja Muni	
Rajmohal	
Rajpol	
Ramsal	
Rạngi	
Rankih	
Rạtua	
Kaṇḍa	
Rọkọt Cọndọn	
Rudhin	
Sal Mungạr	
Samundar Phen	Varieties of rice plant
Saṭhih	
Sitạsạl	
Sundọr Mukhi	
Suraj Muni	
Ṭangabeṭ	
Tila	
Sar	
Til Kancan	
Tulsi Phul	
Tursi Phul	
Uṛih	

Liquor from rice is known as *haṇḍi*, *ạrika*, *boḍea soḍea*, *boḍoc*, *hạṇḍi*, *boḍoc mela*, *lạg hạṇḍi*, *nahel gaḍa dak*, *pocoe haṇḍi*, *ṭạgri haṇḍi* and *tapandak*.

From the foregoing, it is clear that rice is undoubtedly an integral part of the Santali culture. The extreme specalisation of terminology is proof enough of this. This feature may be taken to denote the antiquity of the plant in the particular culture.

Bhattacharya (1966) has drawn attention to inter-relationships within the Munda languages. They are as follows.

1.

Language	*Term*	*Meaning*
Birhor	here	Chaff
Muṇḍa	here	Chaff, husk of rice
Munda	heṛe	Husk, Chaff
Korku	Kere	Chaff
Korwa	heṛet	Skin

2.

Language	*Term*	*Meaning*
Kharia	Kunda	Husk of rice
	Bhu : RA :	Husk
Juang	Alonan	Husk

3.

Language	*Term*	*Meaning*
Korwa	Kosona	Rice beer
Koṛaku	Kosna	Rice beer

4.

Language	*Term*	*Meaning*
Kharia	Golan	Rice beer
Korwa	Gorra	Liquor
Koṛaku	Jhara	Rice beer

5.

Language	*Term*	*Meaning*
Bonda	ILI	Liquor
Gadba	ILI	Liquor
Parengi	ALI	Liquor
Sora	ALI-N	Liquor
Sora	LI :-N ALI :-N	Beer, Spirits etc.
Ho	ILI	Liquor
Ho	OTE-ILI	A part of the MA : GE Parab festival when rice is poured in the courtyard
Muṇḍa	ILI	Beer brewed from rice or grain
Koṛaku	ILLI	Liquor
Korku-Ko	ELA	Jungle Vine

The examples of inter-relationships focus mainly on a very limited range of rice-related terms. There are probably more such terms which have not been studied in depth. On its basis we cannot say more than that the affinities exist for items related to rice which are known to occupy an important place in the ethos of these linguistic groups.

Norman and Arlene Zide (1973) suggest that the bi-morphemic from composed of *run* and *kug* denotes husked, uncooked rice in *South Muṇḍa*. For *North Muṇḍa*, the form is *baba*. It may be likened to *Kharia ba a* and *Juang bua*. The *North Muṇḍa* form may possibly relate to forms for seed in some of the *Koraput Muṇḍa* (i.e. *South Munda*) languages e.g. *Sora, ba ay*, seed, to spawn ; *abay*, seed and *Gurum ba a*, to spawn. They have suggested other hypotheses, too, which on their own admission, are of a highly tentative character.

Taken together with the restricted nature of the existing data, this makes a fruitful discussion on inter-relationships within the *Munda* family, difficult. We are further handicapped by the fact that we cannot date these languages and this distinguish later accretions from earlier terms.

IV. Rice in Tibeto-Burman Family

Southworth (1976) refers to some relevant terms. *Garo*, a Tibeto-Burman languages of Assam, has two terms for rice. *Mero* stands for uncooked rice and *mi* for cooked rice. The *me* of the first term also occurs in *me-na-ku*, maize and *me-su*, vegetables. Thus one cannot be sure that it refers specifically to rice or to something more general like grain of food. He also refers to a number of *Tibeto-Burman* languages which contain forms of the type *ca* or *ja* meaning rice. There are, however, no accompanying details.

V. Some suggested interrelationships between different Language families in the Area of Rice terminology

Chatterji (1927) mentions *bīja* in the *Ṛgveda* as among the words of probable Dravidian origin. *Taṇḍula* and *Vrīhi*, terms for rice in the later Vedic texts, are said to be words of non-Aryan origin whose number steadily increases. No details are provided to explain this assumption.

Turner (1966) refers to the possibility of *taṇḍula* being of Dravidian origin. He draws a comparison between its *Sinhalese* cognate, *sanḍela* and *Tamil*, *cantikkar*, which denotes a kind of rice. No elaborations are provided.

Burrow (1968) describes what he considers to be, among others, rice-related Dravidian words in Sanskrit. They are as follows :

1.

Sanskrit	Kali, Sour rice gruel
Tamil	Kaḻi, Gruel, Conjee
Malayalam	Kaḻi, Gruel, Conjee
Telugu	Kaḻi, Gruel, Conjee

2.

Sanskrit	Kuru, boiled rice
Pali	Kura, boiled rice
Prakrit	Kura, boiled rice
Hindi	Kura mixture of flour ghee and sugar

Tamll	Kur, thick gruel, porridge
Malayalam	Kuŗ, boiled rice
Kannada	Kuŗ, boiled rice
Tulu	Kuṛu, Kulu, boiled rice
Telugu	Kuḍu, boiled rice

3.

Sanskrit	Nivara, wild rice
Pali	Nivara, raw rice, paddy
Tamil	Navarai, Nakarai, a kind of paddy
Malayalam	Navira, Niviri, Nakara, a kind of rice that ripens within two or three months
Tulu	Navare, a kind of rice

4.

Sanskrit	Kancika, Kaniika, Kanji, rice gruel
Tamil	Kanci, rice gruel
Malayalam	Kanni, rice gruel
Telugu Kannada Tulu	Ganji, rice gruel

5.

Sanskrit	Muṭa, basket or bundle
Tulu	Muḍi, a bundle of rice

6.

Sanskrit	Maṇḍa, the scum of boiled rice
Malto	Meṇḍi, rice water

Emeneau and Burrow (1962) have made a study of Dravidian borrowings from Indo-Aryan, and one may isolate those which relate to rice in some way.

7.

Kannada	Carige	A flat cake made of wheat or rice flour and jaggery and fried in ghee or oil
Sanskrit	Gharika	
Prakrit	Gharia	A kind of sweetmeat
Gujarati	Ghari	

8.

Tulu	Cakkuli	A cake made of rice, flour, salt etc. and fried in oil
Sanskrit	Saṣkuli	A large round cake of ground rice, sugar and Sesamum cooked in oil
Prakrit	Sakkuḷi	

9.

Kannada	Sajjige, Sajjaka Sojjige, Soji	Grits or roasted rice, a mess or dish made of grits of roasted rice
Telugu	Sojje, Sojji	Rice boiled after being roasted
Hindi	Suji	
Maraṭhi	Soji	

10.

Tamil	Catam	Boiled rice
Tamil	Cappiṭu	To eat, drink, consume
Tamil	Cappaṭu	Food, meal
Malayalam	Sappaṭu	A meal of Brahmans
Tulu	Prasadamu	Cooked rice
Telugu	Sadamu	Food, rice
Kannada	Pasadamu	Boiled rice
Sanskrit	Prasada	Food presented to God or a Guru

11.		
Parji	Cava	Rice gruel
Parji	Var Java	Water in which rice has been boiled
Sanskrit	Yavagu	Rice Gruel
Buddhist Hybrid	Yvagu	
Sanskrit	Yagu	Rice Gruel
Pali	Yagu	
Oriya	Jau	Overboiled rice

12.		
Malayalam	Piṭṭu, Puṭṭu	A thin meal cake, rice bread
Kolami	Pit	Rice, Ragi
Koḍagu	Puṭṭi	A preparation of rice
Sanskrit	Piṣṭa	Kneaded cake
	Piṣṭaka	Cake of anything made of flour
Buddhist Hybrid Sanskrit	Piṣṭaka	Cake

13.		
Tamil	Poṉakam	Food
	Ponam	Boiled rice
	Poṇam	
Kannada	Bona	Boiled rice
Telugu	Bonamu	Boiled rice
Sanskrit	Bhojana	Eating, meal, food
Prakrit	Bhona	Eating food

14.		
Tamil	Paṭai	To serve (as food to Guests) ; offer (as boiled ride) to Gods, manes
Malayalam	Patekka	To serve up, offer

		boiled rice to idols
Sanskrit	Vṛhd	To serve (the food of a meal)
Maraṭhi	Vaḍhṇe	

These borrowings relate mostly to different preparations of rice. It may be conjectured that these were probably later accretions. Until an approximate idea of the dates of these borrowings is available, they cannot be fitted into a historical perspective.

In the Dravidian Etymological Dictionary (1961) it is mentioned that *batta* or *bhatta* in *Kannada*, meaning rice in the husk, is derived from *Prakrit*, *bhatta*, meaning boiled rice. An influence in meaning is traceable to *Marathi*, *bhat*, boiled rice, rice in the husk.

Identification of borrowings from *Munda* into Indo-Aryan and Dravidian engaged several scholars in the twenties and thirties notably J. Przyluski and Suniti Kumar Chatterji. This was continued by publication in 1948 of F.B.J. Kuiper's Proto Munda Words in Sanskrit (cited in Emeneau, 1954). The work of Pinnow (1963) may also be quoted in this context.

A few borrowings have been described by these scholars. As these were not related to rice, they are not being mentioned here. The exception seems to be Chatterji's (1928) hypothesis that *haṛiya*, or rice beer, is a borrowed word into Bengali from Santali.

6

An Ethnographic Perspective

THE present chapter will try to isolate the basic features of pre-industrial rice cultivation and emphasise the nature of significance of rice in certain tribal or peasant rituals and customs. The range of data is understandably large and all that can be attempted in this context is to cover examples from different geographical areas and tribal and peasant groups. Such a treatment, however, limited, will bring out, in the first place, the diversity and common features of the pre-industrial methods of rice cultivation in different parts of the country, and secondly, will demonstrate through an analysis of the role of rice in different tribal and peasant rituals and customs, how the cultivation of rice went far beyond the level of mere agricultural trait and was integrated into the general Indian ethos. Theoretically, this falls in the domain of ethnobotany, and in the Indian context where a continuity between the past and the present is more than apparent in the areas of pre-industrial technology and beliefs, such an approach may impart a meaningful depth to any historical treatment of these issues.

Regional Modes of Cultivation

I. *Assam* (Imperial Gazetteer 1906)

Generally speaking, the land on either side of the Brahmaputra falls into four broad classes. The first is the *chapari* or land in the immediate neighbourhood of the river, which is heavily flooded in the rains. It is, as a rule, covered with high jungle grass which has to be cut down and burnt before it can be brought under cultivation but, when the floods do not rise too soon, it yields excellent crops of *ahu* or summer rice. The seed is sown in March or April and reaped in June—July and is followed by a crop of mustard or pulse, which is sown when the river falls in October and November and gathered about three months later. When the land is first cleared of jungle, it is free from weeds, but they spring up with great rapidity in the second and third year cropping, and it is then abandoned for from 8-10 years to allow thc jungle growth to kill them out. Behind the *chaparis* comes a belt of low lying land, in which *bao*, a long stemmed variety of rice is grown. It is usually sown in April—May and reaped in November—December. Summer rice is sometimes mixed with *bao* in the hope of getting a crop before the river rises. The water drains off slowly from this belt and the land is left too damp and cold for winter crops. The level of the country than gradually rises above the level of the ordinary floods and *śāli* or transplanted winter rice becomes the staple crop. The grain is sown in nursery beds, the seedlings are transplanted in June—July, when they are about two months old and the harvest is reaped in November. *Śāli* is divided into two main varieties, *bar* and *lahi*. The former gives a heavier yield and ripens later and requires more water than *lahi*. It is therefore usually planted on lower land. This belt of land is a broad one and contains most of the permanent cultivation area and the bulk of the agricultural population. Beyond this again comes the submontane tract. The level of the land is higher and the fields are often irrigated from the hill streams. The chief crop is *sali*, or a transplanted from of *ahu* known as *kharma*. This land is practically free from all risk of flood, and artificial irrigation renders the harvest particularly secure.

The majority of the hill tribes cultivate on the *jhum* system. A patch of land is cleared with axe and fire, the soil is hoed up, and the seeds of hill rice, chillies, cotton etc. are dibbled in among the ashes. The same plot is seldom cropped for more than two or three years in succession. After this the weeds sprout up in great profusion and further cultivation would destroy the roots of bamboo jungle upon the growth of which the land depends for its fertility. *Jhums* are left fallow for as long a time as possible. The shortest period is four years, but it is generally extended to 8-10 years. In the Khasi Hills (now in Meghalaya), rice is grown on terraced and well irrigated fields in the valleys. Terraced rice fields are built up with stone retaining walls at different levels and irrigated by channels, which dirstribute, the water over each step in the series.

II. West Bengal

1. *24 Parganas* (O'Malley 1914)

The cultivation of rice predominates almost to the exclusion of other crops ; it accounts for 88% of the cultivated area in this district.

Aman rice is cultivated on low land where water lies from one foot to three feet deep in the basins. The preparation of the land begins in the latter half of February or the beginning of March, the land being ploughed several times before sowing. In April or May after the first fall of rain, seed is scattered broadcast in a nursery. When the seedlings make their appearance, another field is prepared for trans-planting. After the rainy season has thoroughly set in, the field is repeatedly ploughed until the water becomes worked into the soil, and the whole is reduced to thick mud. The young rice is then taken from the nursery and transplanted in rows about nine inches apart. The crop is generally ready for harvesting in November or December.

Aman rice is also sown occasionally broadcast in marshy lands, e. g. in parts of the Sunderbans where land suitable for nurseries is not available. Sowing takes places in the early part of July, and the crop is ready for reaping in January, the soil easily retaining uptil that time all the moisture necessary for the growth of the grain. When the crop is sown in deep water, it is reaped by cutting off the heads, and the straw is subsequently burnt down when the land dries up.

Aus rice is generally sown on high land. The field is ploughed when the early rains set in, 10-12 times over, till the soil is nearly reduced to dust, and the seed is sown broadcast in April or May. As soon as the young plants reach six inches in height, the land is harrowed in order to thin the crop and clear it of weeds. The crop is harvested in August or September and a second crop of pulse or oilseed is generally taken off the land in the cold weather.

Boro rice is a comparatively unimportant variety sown on marshes which dry up in winter. The preparation of the land commences in the middle of November ; sowing takes place ten days later ; and reaping lasts from the middle of March till the middle of April. The land is hardly ploughed at all. The seed is scattered broadcast in the marshes or *bils* as they dry up, and the young shoots are transplanted when about a month old. There is another kind of *boro* paddy called *aus boro* which is sown during the months of April and May, and reaped in August or September.

An important feature of rice cultivation in the Sunderbans is the embankment of water inlets. It is a characteristic of deltaic formations that the banks of the rivers are higher than the lands further removed from them ; and the whole of the Sunderbans may be looked on as an aggregation of basins, where the higher level of the sides prevents the water coming in to overflow the interior. Many of these basins are so formed that, left to themselves, they would remain under flood, as they communicate with the surrounding channels by means of *Khais*, or small water courses which penetrate the bank.

In order to bring this land under cultivation, all the inlets from the surrounding channels are embanked and smaller channels called *poyans* opened around their ends. This embanking is usually done in November after the rivers have gone down. When the tide is low, the channels are opened and the water from the inside drains off. When it is high, the channels are closed. The effect of the rain is to partially destroy all the embankments that were used in the previous year and to flood the land. The rice that is sown has, however, attained sufficient hardihood to remain uninjured ; and when the waters again go down, the harvest may be reaped. But unless the embankments are again renewed in November, the floods will not have ceased to cover the low lands by sowing time; the land will remain unsown, and the jungle marshy reed will take the place of the paddy.

Malda (Lambourn 1918)

The area under winter rice in this district is estimated at 290,000 acres and that under *bhadoi* at 234,000 acres. The method of cultivation for *aghani* and *bhadoi* is practically the same. The land is ploughed and cross ploughed from 4-8 times according to its quality. A laddcr (*Moi*) or plank (*choma*) is used to break up the clods and cover the seed, which is sown broadcast. When the plants are about 4" high, a harrow (*bidia*) is used to thin them and the land is weeded : the use of the *bidia* makes the crop grow as regularly as if it had been transplanted. A second weeding is given to crops on high land.

The ordinary *bhadoi* rice is sown in May and reaped, as its name implies, in August—September, but a variety of 60 day rice known as *jethi* is sown in small quantities in April, in the Ganges *diara,* in the mud at the edge of the river, and reaped in June before the river begins to rise. There is some tendency for jute cultivation to encroach on the high land *bhadoi* area and for more extensive sowings of *bhadoi* rice to be made in the low lands. The outturn in such areas depends entirely on the rate of rise of the rivers, and in particular, the Ganges. If the main flood come before the crop is ripe there are heavy losses. *Bhadoi* rice does not keep and is mainly eaten by the poorer classes.

Aghani, thc non-transplanted winter rice, is grown mainly in the north of the district. It is reaped in November—December. It is sown in June—July. This rice, though it has keeping properties, is not so fine as the transplanted rice.

Haimantika or transplanted winter rice grows in the higher land of the *barind.* As soon as the rains commence, low lying plots of land, or plots near a tank which can be irrigated prepared and sown broadcast for seedlings. At the same time the fields are ploughed for from 4-6 times, the rain water being retained in each plot by low walls of mud or *ails*. On steeper slopes, the ground is terraced, and frequently there is a tank at the top of the slope from which the upper fields are irrigated as necessary. Before transplantation of the seedlings the soils in the fields is reduced to soft mud. Transplantation goes on from July to September acccrding to the rainfall. There are 20 varieties of *haimantik* rice. The crop is reaped in December—January.

The spring rice known as *boro*, is largely cultivated in the *bils* or swamps in which water remains throughout the cold weather. The land up to the edge of deep water is ploughed as for winter rice during the months of November—December and the surface of the fields, which are divided by *alis*, made into a soft batter of mud. Water is lifted from the *bil* by means of the *jat*, a trough closed at one end. By a series of *jats* a water can be lifted in large quantities to a considerable height. The seedlings are grown either in specially prepared piece of ground, or more frequently in the sort mud left on the banks of the rivers as they fall in October—November. Transplantation is done as for *haimantik* paddy, and the crop is cut in April—May, being kept watered by means of the *jat*.

East Bengal/Bangladesh

Dacca (Allen 1912) : The staple food of the district is rice, which falls into three main species—*boro* or spring rice, or *aus* or summer rice and *aman* or winter rice which is again subdivided into two distinct kinds—the long stemmed *aman* sown boradcast on the lower lands and the transplanted *aman* (*roa*) which is grown on the higher land in the north of the District.

Boro paddy is grown on the sides of bils and streams and on the *chars* and along the banks of the Meghna and to a less extent of the Padma and the Dhaleswari. At Mirpur, a little to the west of Dacca, there is a great expanse of *boro* land near the confluence of the Turag and Buri Ganga and much *boro* is grown along the banks of the Turag all the way from Mirpur to Kalia Koer. As soon as the rains are over, the seed is sown on a piece of soft land which has been worked into a puddle by treading it up, or, in exceptional cases, by from 3-5 ploughings. Before it is sown, the seed is moistened and hung up in a damp basket in the cultivator's house till it begins to germinate. When the plants are about 9" high they are moved from the nursery to the field, though on the banks of the Meghna and in other places where they are exposed to a strong tide they are often allowed to grow to double that height. The fields are, as a rule, not ploughed and the seedlings are simply planted in the soft mud left behind when the floods recede, but, unless the plants are exposed to the action of the river tides the fields have to be irrigated by water lifts. The seed is generally sown in November, transplanted in December or January and harvested in April or May. The grain is coarse, but the cost of cultivation is less as there is, as a rule, no ploughing to do. There is another system of *boro* cultivation, known as *lepi*, which really entails the minimum of time and and trouble. The seed is simply sown broadcast on soft mud flats near the big rivers and then the mud is smoothed over it to protect it from the action of the tides. There is no ploughing, harrowing, transplanting or weeding, simply the sowing of the seed and the reaping of the harvest. It must, however, be addmitted that the sowing is a little troublesome as the mud is so soft that the cultivator has to seek a precarious foothold on the trunk of a plantain tree or a couple of bamboos to prevent himself from sinking in.

Aus paddy is grown on high land and is usually found in more elevated parts of the Madhupur jungle and on high land near rivers. It can, however, be grown only on land on which the depth of water does not exceed two feet at the beginning of the rains, as the crop is only from 3—3½ ft. high and the stalk does not grow fast enough to keep pace with the rising of the flood. The date of sowing depends upon the time when the floods may be expected to rise in the locality. As soon as the tiny shoots appear, the field is harrowed with a ladder and when the plants are about 6" high the operation is repeated with a rake. Weeding is a troublesome process and hired labour is occassionally employed. Harvesting takes place between July and September, but in the *diaras* if the rivers rise too soon the cultivators have to cut the crop while it is still green and only fit for fodder. The principal varieties of *aus* are the *puki*, *gorfa*, *surjomukhi* and *shaita*, the last supposed to ripen in 60 days.

Long stemmed *aman* is grown in those parts of the district where from 5-15″ of water accumulate during the rainy season. It possesses the power of growing to keep pace with the rising of the flood to a remarkable degree and has been known to shoot up as much as 12″ in a day and night and to attain a total length of 20″, though the average length is from 10-12′. This is, however, prejudicial to the proper development of the plant, and if it has had too severe a struggle to surmount the rising flood, there is not enough strength left for the proper formation of the ear. At harvest time only about a foot and a half of the stalk is cut off with the ear and the remainder is gathered into heaps and burnt upon the field. The land is then ploughed two or three times and left till the middle of March when the clods are broken with the mallet and there are one or two more ploughings and harrowings. Sowing takes place in April and after the seeds have germinated, a ladder is dragged over the field. When the plants are four to five inches high the soil is loosened with a rake, and then all that remains to be done is to weed, and this is an operation which is often omitted. The principal danger to which this rice is exposed is too high and too sudden a rise of water which may either drown the plants altogether or wash them bodily away. *Aus* is sometimes sown in conjunction with long stemmed *aman* in the hope that if one crop fails, the other may prove successful. In these cases, the sowing takes place a few weeks earlier and the *aus* is reaped towards the end of July.

Transplanted *aman* is generally grown in the Madhupur jungle and in the higher land in the north east corner of the district. In April, a small plot of land is reduced by numerous ploughings to a fine tilth and is thickly sown with seed which has been soaked in water for 12 hours and kept till it has germinated. While the seed is growing the fields are ploughed up into a rich puddle and the embankments intended to retain the water are repaired. The plants are transplanted between August and October when they are from 1′ to 18″ high and harvested in December. Late transplantation often injures the crop as if the rain stops early it fails to obtain sufficient moisture and raiyats often allow it to be partly choked by weeds. *Śāli* paddy is sometimes sown after jute or *shaita aus* has been harvested but in such cases, seldom yields a good return

IV. Bihar

Santhal Parganas (O'Malley 1910)

The slopes of the long undulating ridges and the swampy ground in between these ridges supply the only land on which a riee crop can be raised. Rice accounts for about one half of the tolal cropped area, and the greater part of the crop consists of winter rice. Boro (or spring) rice is scarcely grown at all except in the Rajmahal subdivision, where it is raised on the edge of *jhils* (marshes).

In other areas, the soil is brought under cultivation by cutting level terraces out of the slopes, a small bank being left around each plot. The slopes thus present the appearance of a series of steps, varying from one to five feet in height. When the slopes are too steep for terracing, or the soil too stony for cultivation, the bed of the stream is banked up and made into one long, narrow rice field. The rice terraces are flooded as soon as possible after the rains set in, and the water is retained until the crop ripens in late autumn. After the crop has been reaped, the higher levels become dry and hard, but the lower fields often remain moist till February and March. The cultivable area which cannot be converted into rice fields is used for other crops requiring less moisture.

Artificial irrigation is necessary for the cultivation of rice except in the level tract adjoining the Ganges and at the bottom of inland depressions, where the soil is kept moist by perennial springs or is capable of retaining water draining off higher levels. Here heavy crops of rice are obtained, even though the rainfall is short or ceases prematurely ; but there is a danger of crop failure. If the surrounding slopes are too steep, for the rush of water often brings down with it drifts of sand which ruin the crop. To obviate this danger a small channel is often provided for the escape of sand-laden water.

Except in such localities, artificial irrigation is absolutely necessary and the undulating nature of the country affords great facilities for protective works.

The irrigation works generally take the form of embankments, constructed across ravines, hollows or other natural depressions or at the head of numerous valleys which impound the drainage water and also dam up any stream there may be in the bed of a valley or a ravine. They thus form reservoirs, from which the rice fields, stretching away each on a lower level than another and widening as they recede from the dam, are irrigated. These embankments, when small, are called *hirs* and when large *bandhs.* Their number is legion and no village is without one or two at least. The smaller ones dry up a month or two after the rains cease, but generally hold sufficient water to carry the fields below over the precarious months of October and November. The larger ones have frequently catchment basins large enough to ensure a continuous water supply from the end of one rainy season to the beginning of the next.

Gaya (Roychowdhury 1957)

Rice is the staple crop of the district. The *aghani* or winter rice forms a greater part of this crop. It is sown broadcast after the commencement of the rains in June or July on lands selected for seed nurseries, which have been previously ploughed 3-4 times. After 4-6 weeks, when the young plants are about a foot high, they are generally transplanted ; each plant is pulled out from the land, which is soft with standing water, and planted again in rows of flooded fields, in which the soil has been puddled. After this the rice is left to mature, with the aid of water, till towards the end of September. The water is then drained off and the fields are allowed to dry for 15 days, and at the end of that time they are again flooded. It is this pratice known as *nigar*, which makes the rainfall, or failing that, irrigation essential to successful harvest. These late rains (*Hathiya*) are the most important in the year, as not only are they required to bring the winter crops to maturity but also to provide moisture for the sowing of the rabi crops. The rice comes to maturity in November—December.

Some winter rice know as *baog* is not transplanted; it is sown broadcast on lowlands at the commencement of the rains, and also in years in which there has not been sufficient moisture to allow of transplantation at the proper time.

The *bhadoi* rice is also sown broadcast in June—July and not transplanted ; it is regardcd as a 60 days crop, and is generally harvested in August or September.

There is another kind of rice known as the *boro* or spring rice, which is sown in January, transplanted after a month and harvested in April. It is grown on marsh lands and in the beds of shallow streams, but the area cultivated with it is insignificant.

A not'ceable feature of the rice cultivation in this area is the way in which it is conducted religiously according to lunar asterisms.

V. Orissa

Koraput (Bell 1945)

About 300 varieties of paddy have been collected from the five *taluks* of the Koraput subdivision.

Rice fields, as a rule, never receive manure. Transplantation takes place in less than 10% of the rice lands and elsewhere the seed is sown broadcast.

There are three systems of rice cultivation: (i) the dry system on high lying or *dongara* lands, (ii) the partially wet system on medium lands and (iii) the wet system on lowlands. Under the dry system the lands are ploughed five or six times when the summer showers set in and are brought to a fine tilth. The seed is broadcast after the break of the southwest monsoon. They are covered up by ploughing or by a levelling board or a brush harrow. The crop is grown either pure or as a mixture crop. It ripens and is harvested earlier than the other rice crops. The partially wet system is adopted where rainfall and irrigation facilities are not sufficient to permit of cuitivation by the wet system. The land is tilled and puddled after the first showers and water is allowed to stand in it for some time. Then seeds which have been previously moistened are broadcast and after a few hours water is let out of the field. The young plants are able to survive dry conditions for some weeks until satisfactory rains fall and fields are swamped.

The wet system is adopted on low lying lands in those parts of the district where the rainfall is abundant. Lands are never ploughed in the dry state. But when the monsoon begins, the fields are ploughed and puddled. Before sowing, the water is let out of the fields. The seeds are soaked in warm water for a day and sown broadcast the next day. When transplantation is the practice, the seeds are first sown in a nursery which had received a basal dressing of cattle manure. After 30-40 days, they are pulled up and planted out in the fields in bunches about six inches apart. Once sowing or transplantation has taken place, the wet fields usually receive no attention except for regulation of the supply of water, until the harvest. The crop is not weeded under this system, later strains of paddy are cultivated, the period of growth being about six months, as against three months under the dry system.

Cuttack (O'Malley 1933)

The staple crop is rice which is grown on 77% of the cultivated area. The varieties grown are very numerous, but they all fall under one of the three heads according to the season in which they are sown and reaped, viz. *biali*, or early rice sown in May or June and reaped in August and September *sarad* or winter rice, sown in June and July and harvested between October and January, and *dalua* or spring rice, which is sown after the floods have subsided and is harvested in March and April.

The most important of all these crops, is the *sarad* or winter rice. It is divided according to the amount of water it requires into *guru* or heavy and *laghu* or light varieties, the *laghu* paddy being grown on moderately low lands which are wet or covered with 6"—1' of water from June to October, while the *guru* paddy is grown at a lower level. Rice fields are enclosed on all four sides by small ridges (*hira*) about a foot in height and breadth, in order that the rain water collected in these artificial shallows may keep the plants wet, otherwise, the land loosing its moisture, the plants would quickly wither and the crop be lost.

After the winter crop has been harvested in December, the cultivator is on the look-out for the first shower of rain to plough his land. The rainfall usually occurs in February. As a rule, 4-5 ploughings are considered sufficient. The soil after being turned up is exposed to the action of the sun and wind, and those lands which lie beyond the reach of the fertilising river silt are manured. With the onset of the monsoon, the seeds are sown in May or June. The seed germinates in three days and consequently, the earlier the seed can be sown and the stronger the young plants are when the rains set in, the better is the chance of a good crop. During the latter half of June and the first half of July the growth of the rice is helped by the monsoon rains. During the rest of July and August when the plants have attained a height of 9″-12″, there is the important operation called *beusen* (literally changing of place) to be performed. This consists of driving the plough through the young rice in order to thin the crop and aerate the soil, wherever this results in too severe a thinning, the gaps are filled up by transplantation from thicker parts of the field. The ridges enclosing the fields are then finally strengthened, the grass cleared away from them, and the weeds removed. For these operations an ample supply of water is necessary, and if this is available and there is sufficient rainfall in September and October, a good harvest is assured in November and December.

It will be clear that the times of sowing and reploughing are two important periods when the *sarad* crop requires water, but by far the most critical period is in the middle of October, when its fate depends entirely on there being enough water to mature it and to fill out the ear. At the first period, no artificial irrigation is possible, and the people depend on rain water. At the second and third periods lands commanded by the canals, or about ¼ of the cultivated area, can always get a plentiful supply of water, and under normal conditions, the other lands also get sufficient rain water, but in years of deficient or unevenly distributed rainfall the people are obliged to irrigate the crop from every available natural or artificial reservoir.

Nearly all the *sarad* rice is broadcast, transplantation

being an unpopular system of cultivation, as it involves more labour, and the transplanted seedlings are very delicate for the first month and liable to injury by flood and still more by drought. It is resorted to for fields, especially for those under irrigation, which grow a *sarad* crop after *biali*, to get rid of the wild paddy called *balunga*, to avoid the risk of early floods and to replace the loss of the broadcast crop, if it is destroyed before the end of July. The seeds are sown either wet or dry in a nursery which is generally a field near a village well-manured and fenced in to keep off cattle. The land is carefully watered, and when the seedlings are a month old they are transplanted into the rice field. The latter is prepared by manuring and ploughing in the same way as for broadcast rice, by puddling before the young plants are planted. The seedlings are arranged in bunches of three or four plants with a small space between each bunch, the roots are carefully embedded to the depth of a couple of inches, they are then left and require no further attention beyond a good weeding and a copious supply of water. The earlier the transplantation is done, the better the results and the proper time is considered to be from the middle of June to the middle of July.

The *biali* or early rice, which is always sown broadcast, ranks next to the *sarad* rice in importance. There are two main classes of biali, viz. the early variety, called *sathika* from the fact that it comes to maturity 60 days from the date of sowing and the *bara dhan*, ripening about a month later, which supplies the people with a food grain only second in importance to lowland paddy. Both varieties are grown on the higher lands of the villages, and preferably in a light loamy soil, they are sown and reaped in the rainy season. The whole crop is more precarious than the winter rice, being injuriously affected by drought in June and July, and being also liable to destruction by floods early in the season. A failure of this crop does not, however, affect the people very seriously, as loss can generally be recouped by a good harvest of winter rice. On the other hand, if the rain is well distributed in the early part of the season but fails at its close, a bumper crop of *biali* will in part at least compensate for the *sarad* crop getting spoilt. In rich soil under irrigation, or in favourable seasons, *laghu* paddy is transplanted to the lands from which the *biali* has been cut.

Dalua is a coarse variety of rice, which is grown in the Kharsua and Brahmani estuaries on low swampy grounds and on lands too heavily waterlogged to yield *sarad.* Clay lands subject to tidal inundation are commonly chosen for the purpose, as irrigation is easy and the crop is not affected by saline matter. It is sown in winter and reaped in the spring and therefore requires constant irrigation. Canal water is utilised for the purpose in the area commanded by the distributaries, but elsewhere it requires no artificial irrigation, as being planted along marshes and tidal waters a natural supply is generally available. The crop may be either transplanted or broadcast, but the former method is the more common. A nursery is selected in the corner of a field or tank in which the seedlings remain until they are about a foot high, they are then imbedded in the rice field which has been ploughed till it is a pulpy mass, and this is kept covered with water till the plant flowers. It ripens in March or April, and the crop is then cut. The area covered by it is not large, and it is only in the low-lying lands to the north of the district that it is a staple crop.

VI. Madhya Pradesh

Durg (Nelson 1910)

Rice is the most important crop of the district. It can be cropped year after year from the same land.

The total number of varieties found in this district is legion. But they resolve themselves into three classes viz. *haruna* or early rice, grown, on light soil such as *matasi* which is reaped within 90 days of its sowing, *majhola* (intermediate or medium), also called *ardhana*, grown on richer soils, and *mai* or mother crop which takes the longest time and is grown on heavy black soil and level land. The varieties most common in the district belong to the last class.

Rice is almost always grown alone as the conditions of its cultivation do not suit any other crop. But most of the embanked black soil in this district is double cropped, the first of them always being rice.

Transplantation is practically unknown in this district.

Broadcast rice naturally requires thinning. The method by which this is effected is peculiar to Chhatisgarh, and is termed *biasi*. The operation commences about the middle of July, when the plants are about 3″-6″ in height and consists in passing a plough through the field and uprooting many of the young shoots. The banks of the fields are carefully repaired beforehand, for the operation is quite fatal if the surface of the field is not covered with 2″-3″ of water. Heavy rain muat have fallen before *biasi* can be attempted.

The method of cultivation is otherwise simple. On the approach of the rains, the fields are covered wirh sweepings, ashes, cattle dung etc. However, as the supply of manure is short, some fields remain uncovered. When the soil has become sufficiently softened by the first few showers of the monsoon to admit of a plough being worked, the seed is scattered broadcast. The field is ploughed once immediately afterwards where the soil is black and the surface fairly clear of weeds. This method is locally called *batar* and is the ordinary method of sowing. If the soil is is *matasi*, the field requires one ploughing prior to the sowing of the seed and a cross ploughing to cover it up. This latter method is locally known as *hagdum*. There are two other methods of broadcast sowing, which are locally known as *lei* and *khurra*.

The *lei* method is followed when there is extensive rain which does not permit the sowing of the seed at the proper ttme. The seed is steeped in cold water and kept for four or five hours ; it is then placed in a heap, hot water is poured over it, and it is covered with straw for the night. Next morning it is spread out on the ground and germinates. As soon as there is a break in the weather, the sprouted seed is sown and when the plants grow sufficiently high, the *biasi* operation is effected.

The other method, *khurra* is resorted lo when the rains are late. The seed is simply scattered on the *kanhar* or *dorsa* land befor the rains, when the land is dusty and then it is ploughed. When the rain falls, the seed wlll germinate. It will not be harmed by being in the ground for a month so long as the rain, when it comes, is sufficient.

2. *Betul* (Shrivastava 1971)

Paddy was of minor importanee in the beginning of the century. It was generally sown as a cash crop in *sihar* (sandy loam found along banks of small streams) and *retari* (sandy soils poorer than sihar) before gram or some other pulse. However, now it has become an important kharif crop. Unlike the paddy bandhis (embanked fields) of paddy districts of Balaghat and Chhatisgarh, paddy is grown in open fields and is either broadcast or drilled. Before the paddy fields receive the seed, one summer ploughing is given to the field. One weeding operation is also done. Only early varieties are grown as a cash crop before gram or other rabi pulses as before.

VII. Andhra Pradesh

Cuddapah (Brackenbury 1915)

Paddy occupies the most prominent place among the crops grown on irrigated lands. Formerly, when indigo was more extensively cultivated this crop was used in rotation with paddy over large areas. Indigo refuse from the vats is a very good manure for paddy and the continued growth of this crop must be attributed to its restorative values. Formerly, the practice of sowing the paddy seed broadcast was almost universal. It is the prevailing system of the present day.

Other kinds of manure used are ordinary cattle manure and leaf manure, of which some 5-10 cartloads constitute the usual application for an acre. The manure is applied to the land after the soil has been reduced to a state of liquid mud puddle. The seed is sown broadcast immediately. After the seed is sown, the fields are generally allowed to dry until the sprouts are about 2″ high and from that time till the harvest, it is considered necessary to keep 2-3" of water on the land.

The uneven crop which usually results from broadcasting is usually remedied by crossing it with a rake when about 6″ high and removing the seedlings from the thicker to the thinner patches.

Paddy has two main seasons known as *Kartikam* and *Vaisakham,* these being the months in which the harvest is gathered. The most popular variety is *sanna vadlu,* and unless the soil is of an inferior quality no other sort is grown on single cropped land ; but it takes nearly five months to ripen. Some other variety immediately precedes or follows it where irrigation facilities render possible the cultivation of two paddy crops in a single year.

Nizamabad (Rajagopala 1973)

Paddy is cultivated in both the kharif (June—September) and rabi (October to February) seasons. The Kharif paddy is also known as the *Abi* crop and the Rabi paddy as *Tabi* crop in this region. Paddy, locally known as Vattivari, is also grown under semi-dry conditions by broadcasting the seed where water supply is limited.

The preliminary preparations of soils for kharif start after the summer showers in May and that of rabi during September. Paddy is first raised by growing nurseries and then by transplanting in the fields after 4-6 weeks.

In regard to crop rotation, no crop other than paddy is grown generally in the same land or two or more successive seasons. In some regions, paddy is rotated with sugarcane or turmeric and vice versa.

VIII. Tamil Nadu

North Arcot (Stuart 1895)

There are about a hundred different varieties of rice in the district. Almost all the irrigated land is under paddy. The land is prepared by ploughing after being flooded by rain or from a tank. The former process, *puludi*, is adopted when water is scarce, and the latter called *seru* is considered the better. Ploughing is continued, after short intervals for from 6-12 times during a month or six weeks, manure being applied in the shape of farm yard refuse or ashes. Leaves and the small boughs of various trees are also addded just before the sowing time and are trodden into the mire by men and women. In the case of saltish soil, oil cake is sometimes applied. When the surface has been levelled by means of a plank drawn by oxen, the field is ready to receive seeds. In the case of broadcast sowing the seeds are well trodden in by men. However, it is more usual to sow in a seed bed and transplant. Transplantation takes place when the plant is abont 10" or a foot in height and are planted by parties of women in the murky field at a distance of an inch or two from one another, depending on the richness of soil.

Before being sown, the seed grain is soaked in manure and water for several hours, and then, being put in a basket or pot, is covered with straw, upon which a heavy weight is placed. A little water is daily sprinkled upon it and it is occasionally exposed to the light, until on the fourth day it has sprouted and is ready for the field or seed bed. After being planted, water is allowed to stand on the soil for one day and is then drawn off for 4-5 days until the shoots have made a good start. From then, till the time of ripening, constant irrigation, is necessary; about a couple of inches water being made to stand upon the land, but not to stagnate, a regular flow from field to field is allowed once in two or three days. Oil cake is sometimes used as manure, powdered and thrown over when the crop is a month old. A few days latter, the first weeding takes place, and the plants are, if necessary, thinned out. Weeding is repeated two or three times as required.

There are two crops of rice, the hot and ihe cold weather crops called *Kar* and *Vaisakham*, after the months in which they usually ripen. The *Kar* crop is sown in June—July and being a 6 month crop, is harvested in December. It is quickly followed by the *Vaisakham*, or four month crop, which is off the ground by April—May. The only remarkable kind of paddy which needs separate remark is called *munagada* or submerged. It is grown only in a few localities, in the beds of tanks before they are covered with water. As soon as it has sprouted well, it is said to live, though submerged below as much as 3 feet of water. The stem is as thick and strong as a stalk of *cholum*, but the grain is coarser and not much prized.

IX. Kerala

Kozhikode (Menon 1962)

The first crop of paddy is the *Viruppu* and is purely rainfed. *Mundakan* is the second crop and it is only partly rainfed. The thired crop, *Punja* depends entirely on irrigation facilities. The major portion of the land is under *Viruppu.*

Viruppu is sown under dry conditions. With the pre-monsoon showers, the land is prepared by ploughing and paddy seeds dibbled behind the plough or sown broadcast and covered by ploughing and planting.

The is done in April—May. In the low lying *Viruppu* fields, transplantation takes place in June—July. When the plants are about one month old, weeding is done and sometimes a dose of manure is applied. Harvesting is in August—September.

Under the *mundakan* system, paddy is either broadcast or transplanted during August or September. In the heavy soils of the deltaic areas, the crop is invariably transplanted. Dry seed is sown in the puddle when swamp conditions exist. Direct broadcasting of paddy seed under swamp conditions is adopted only when necessitated by special local conditions. The usual practice is that as soon as the first crop is harvested, the land is ploughed six to eight times and manure applied. In certain areas, sprouted seeds are sown in well prepared fields. Weeding is done when plants are one month old. Harvests are in December—January.

Punja is restricted to small low level areas where water supply is abundant during the summer months between January and May. The out-turn is small.

Punam and *Modan* are special methods of rice cultivation.

Punam is the method of cultivation on the forest clad hills and on the slopes of the Ghats. A patch of forest is cleared and burnt. A crop of hill paddy is raised mixed with millets and plantains. The ground Is then left fallow for some years. The cultivators are generaily hillmen. They move from one forest to another and repeat the process. The seed is sown in April and beyond occasional weeding, the crop requires little attention. Fencing is often done to keep out wild animals. As the virgin soil is very rich, there is a bountiful harvest.

Modan is a from of dry rice cultivation. A well established rotation of crops is a noticeable feature of dry cultivation. *Modan* is grown on the low hills of the district or near the coast among the young coconut plants in new plantations. The rotation is usually *modan*, *gingelly* and *samai*, but on the best lands, a ginger crop frequently precedes the *modan.* The preparation of land for *modan* begins usually in August and between that month and the sowing of the crop in the following April. The land is ploughed well a number of times. The seed is sown with ashes and cattle dung and the crop is reaped in September. After the last *samai* crop, the land is allowed to lie fallow for 2-3 years.

X. **Karnataka** (Rao 1929)

Rice is the most important wet land crop of the State. In the western districts, it is grown to a great extent with the help of the south west monsoon. In the valleys of the Cauvery and its deltas, it is grown largely under canal irrigation. In the eastern districts, the large rainfed tanks supply the irrigation water : while in the cxtreme east and northeast, it is grown under well irrigation, In part of Chitaldurg district, quite a large part is under "dry land" paddy. In these areas, all low lying places, hollows and pockets of sandy soil, which collect and retain rain water, are put under this variety.

There is no kind of soil on which paddy is not grown in the state. The best crops are, however, obtained where there is an abundance of water and the soil is a clayey one with ample drainage.

The number of varieties in the state is truly remarkable. They may be divided into the *maidan* varieties and *malnad* varieties.

Rice is cultivated in different ways.

(i) The seed is sown dry, much the same as a dry crop and either broadcast or in drills.

(ii) The field is puddled and seeds previously sprouted are sown broadcast.

(iii) The field is puddled and then seedlings raised separately are transplanted into the field.

(i) The land is ploughed twice or thrice in the early rains about June when the ground is still moist after a rain. The seed grain is sown broadcast and harrowed in with the wooden *halube.* The crops receive no attention for two months when irrigation is commenced after the first flooding, the *halube* is again drawn over the standing crop in the soft mud, the field is then handweeded and the flooding is continued as in the case of the ordinary paddy cultivation till harvest.

(ii) The sowing of sprouted seed in puddled land called *mole* cultivation is followed more extensively in the case of summer paddy.

The method of cultivation is as follows. The field is watered and the soil is softened and then ploughed in puddle. The ploughing is repeated for four or five days till the stubble of the old crop rots well and the soil is thoroughly stirred up. The excess water is then drained. Leaves and twigs are spread on the field uniformly and then trampled in ; sprouted seed is then sown broadcast ; the seed sinks in the soft mud and the next day the field is drained thoroughly. For two weeks, water is let in carefully, for a few hours and drained, till the crop is well established. It is then irrigated, copiously ; after a month, harrowing is done both by the hand harrow and the bullock harrow ; this being repeated both cross wise and diagonally. Hand weeding follows and the crop requires no further attention till harvest.

The sprouting of the seed required for this as well as for raising seedlings for transplanting is effected by soaking the seed tied up in a bag or straw twist for a night in water : the bag is then taken out and the contents heaped in a cool place covered with straw and leaves ; the heap is kept moist for two days, after which the sprouts begin to appear. In some places it is usual to mix the leaves of *Tumbi* with the paddy in the heaps.

(iii) The method of transplanting seedlings is prevalent largely throughout the State. This practice has apparently displaced the other method in many parts. Land is ploughed soon after the harvest of the paddy as early as the condition of the soil will permit in the month of April. Provided there is rain, green manure, crops are sown. In June, water is let into the fields and the manure crops is trampled in the crop rots for a week, when the field is ploughed once again, the bounds are trimmed and the puddle is levelled. Into this puddle seedlings about 30-45 days old are transplanted in bunches. Water is let in scantily, till the yellow of the transplanted seedling changes into a deep green, after which the field is kept continuously irrigated till about 10 days prior to harvesting.

XI. Maharashtra

Kolaba (Campbell 1883)

Of the important crops ricc holds the first place. The twenty four chief sorts of rice belong to two main groups, red rice and white rice. Red rice is inferior and is grown only on salt low lying lands near creeks which are liable to be flooded by spring tides. White rice grows only on lands beyond the reach of salt water. Of the sixteen sorts of white or sweet soil rice, seven, known as *halve* or early, ripen about the middle of October, and nine, known as late or *garvi* about a month later.

During the cold weather months patches in the fields are covered with a thin layer of cowdung on which a second layer of brushwood and tree loppings is laid, and above this grass is spread to the depth of a foot. Earth is scattered on the grass and the whole set on fire early on some morning towards the end of the hot season. In June, just before the rains, the ground is strewn with seed, and then ploughed along with the wood and dung ashes. After a few heavy showers, the plants begin to shoot and are allowed to grow for three weeks or a month. When the soil is thoroughly softened, they are pulled up in little bunches of from six to eight seedlings and planted from eight to ten inches apart, in soil previously ploughed and cleared of weeds. The rice is weeded by hand about a month after planting. It is reaped in the end of October or the beginning of November. In lands near rivers, a second crop is grown.

In salt rice land, neither ploughing nor manure is required. When the ground is well soaked with rain, the seed is either thrown into mud, or, when the land is low, it is wetted and placed in a heap, until it sprouts when it is thrown into the mud or on the surface of the water. After the plants have grown a little, crowded patches are thinned and bare spaces planted. The chief labour and expense in growing salt rice is the making and mending of the banks. Every field is surrounded by a bank from two to four feet high according to its distance from a creek. This bank has to be renewed every year and kept in repair during the time the crop is on the ground. During spring tides it must be carefully watched day and night. If by any over-sight, the field is flooded with salt water, years pass before it again yields a good crop.

Ratnagiri (Rao 1962)

Rice occupies the first place among all the crops grown with an area of about 55% of that under cereals and 35% of the gross cropped area. In 1877-78, it held fourth place among all crops.

Rice is grown mainly on upland soil (*kuryat* soils) and on low lying lands (*mal* lands).

The practice of *rabbing* for preparing seed beds to raise seedlings is very common. Seed bed area is covered by a layer about 3" thick of dry leaves, dry cattle dung and other dry refuse and set fire to in April—May on the eastern end of the area, preferably in the evening to allow for the slow burning which is accomplished easily because the evening sea breeze blows from west to east and as such it takes some time for the fire to reach the western end. This process of burning the seed bed area is locally known as *rab* and is still followed probably with a view to destroying the weeds, weed seeds, harmful micro-organisms and insects and adding some manurial ingredients through the ash formed to give a better start to the young seedings. Since rains are due in the first week of June, after some operation with handtools, paddy seeds are sown, either in anticipation of the rains or immediately after rains. These seeds take about a month to come to the height suitable for transplanting and during this time the cultivators get busy in preparing land for transplating. The preparatory tillage of paddy consists of (a) *ukhalani* or light ploughing, (b) *chikhalani* or puddling and (c) *guta phiravine* or levelling. *Ukhalani* is done after first monsoon showers to break the hard crust of the surface soil so that penetration in the earth becomes easier for subsequent ploughings. Puddling is done by means of a light plough to prepare fine soft mud-beds for transplanting the seedlings. Puddling has to be done in all kinds of rice soils. A well-puddled field holds water longer and keeps the plant green. After puddling, a wooden plank is dragged by bullocks over the field to level the land.

As soon as the mud-beds get ready, seedlings are carefully uprooted from the seed bed, tied in small bundles and carried to *khachars* where they are finally transplanted. Transplanting is done by hand.

In the case of *kuryat* lands (low lands), transplanting is replaced by broadcasting of sprouted seeds in puddled fields. This method is locally known as *rahu* method. Paddy seeds are put in an oven-shaped vessel in which they are submerged in water. The lighter seeds, which float on water surface are rejected, as the heavy seeds give better stand and yield. After about 12-24 hours, water is allowed to drain away and the soaked seed is then filled in bamboo *Karandhas* (baskets) the inner side of which is covered by rice straw. Lukewarm water is then poured on the seed ; the baskets are then covered with teak leaves and rice straw and loaded with stones and pieces of logs so as to create warmth inside, required for sprouting. On each of the two consecutive days, water is sprinkled over the paddy straw to keep the seed moist.

In salt land, early coarse varieties of paddy are generally sown as sprouted seeds. These get very hard on drying and get very soft and stricky when wet. Farmers find it almost impossible to enter the field when wet and hence implements cannot be worked in such fields. This method of broadcasting sprouted seedlings is also followed in some parts where, after ploughing, the field remains inaccessible for sowing due to continuous torrential rain.

Dry sowing, which is known as *dhul-waf*, is also done in some places, in the months of May and June just before the rains. This method of sowing facilitates an early start for the seedlings.

In the low lying and retentive soils known as *shel* soils, seed is sown during March and April. Hand digging of seed beds precedes ploughing. Seeds are sown by broadcasting. The seed germinates and the seedlings remain on ground till monsoon starts. These seedlings are known as *tap-tarava* and survive on dew and on the moisture retained by the soil. They are supposed to resist pest incidence in a better way.

Though paddy is grown principally in the kharif season, it is also grown in an area of about 11,000 acres a year in the hot season wherever facilities of irrigation water from perennial nallahs or well exist. The paddy grown in the hot season is locally known as *waingan* crop. It is grown on upland soils and on low lying soils in the proximity of water facilities. In January—February paddy lands are artificially irrigated and immediatcly ploughed both length-wise and breadth-wise so that clods do not come up. Clods are then crushed by *gute-phali* on the third day and land is again ploughed both length-wise and breadth-wise after irrigation, followed by clod crushing. Bunds are then prepared in the rice fields and are plastered with mud so as not to allow any growth of weeds. Land is then puddled by a plough. Manure is applied before puddling. Application of more quantity is considered desirable as it helps the retention of soil moisture so badly required for the paddy crop in the hot season. When water is about 1—" high in the field, sprouted seeds of paddy called *rahu* are broadcast equally all over the field. Some days after broad-casting to the sprouted seeds in the fields, small quantities of water are given each day till all the seeds have germinated completely. Additional quantity of water is required when the crop reaches flowering stage. Water is withheld for about 8-10 days prior to harvesting.

XII. Himachal Pradesh

Kangra (Gazetteer of the Kangra District 1883-84)

Rice is the staple product of the upper Kangra valleys. The people recognise upwards of sixty varieties of rice. In districts dependent on rain, the seed is thrown into the ground as early as April and the later the season of sowing, the less chance of the crop reaching maturity. The harvest time is during the month of August.

There are three methods of cultivation. The first and simplest called *batar* is where the seed is sown broadcast in its natural state. On unirrigated lands, this is the universal method. In the second method, the seed is first steeped in water and forced under warm grass to germinate, and then thrown into the soil, which has been previously flooded to receive it. This method prevails wherever water is abundant and is called *mach* or *lurga*. The third system called *ur*, the young rice about a month old is planted out by hand at stated intervals in a well flooded field. The practice involves much labour and is seldom followed, except in heavy swamp ground where the plough cannot work. The yield, however, of transplanted rice is always greater than either of the other methods. The growth of weeds in the rice fields is very rapid, but the people have a simple and most effectual mode of ridding themselves of them. In July, the crop, weeds and all, is deliberately ploughed up. Imediately after the operation the whole appears utterly destroyed, but the weeds alone suffer, being effectually extirpated by this radical process, while the rice springs up again more luxuriantly than ever. This practice is called *holdna* and the crop is worthless which does not undergo it.

Rice is always sown by itself and never mixed. In Kangra it is seen as high as 5000 feet above the sea.

XIII. Haryana

Hissar (Fagan 1892)

The only flooded kharif crop is found in Tahsil Fatahabad and the principal one in Sirsa is rice (*dhān*). The great desideratum for the crop is a continuous but equable supply of water. The crop is grown in artificial reservoirs or *kunds* surrounded by earthen embankment at least two feet high. The different varieties of rice are *chun*, *munji*, *kharsu* and *santhi*. *Munji* is the commonest.

Of the first flood in June—July enough water is admitted into the rice kund to moisten the soil throughly and to leave a depth of water of some 2" on it. The soil is then ploughed and harrowed with the *Sohaggā*, which is supplied with some sharp points at the bottom which stir up the mud and silt. In Sirsa, the soil is occasionally manured with goat's dung. The crop is sown either by seed being scattered by the hand broadcast or by transplanting. With the latter method, the seed is put into earthen vessels (*chatis*) and is moistened with water. This causes the seed to sprout and it is then transplanted into the ground by being scattered with the hand. The process is called *chanta*. Another method is to transplant the seedlings. The sowing should be completed by the middle of August. The crop must grow in water, but care must be taken that it does not get submerged. The crop is reaped in November.

XIV. Jammu and Kashmir

(Gazetteer of Kashmir and Ladakh 1890)

The staple of cultivation in Kashmir is rice. There are around fourteen varieties available. Rice is sown both by broadcast and transplantation methods. In late March, the land is opened by one or more ploughing after which water is let in to convert the soil into a smooth, soft mud.

The seed grain, put into a sack of woven grass, is submerged in a running stream until it begins to sprout, which happens sooner or later, according to the temperature of the water and of the atmosphere, but ordinarily takes place in three or four days.

This precaution is adopted for the purpose of getting the young shoot as quickly as possible out of the way of a small snail which abounds in some of the watered lands of Kashmir. When the farmer suspects by the scanty appearance of the plants above the water in which the grain has been sown, and by the presence of the snail drawn up in the mud, that his hopes of a crop are likely to be turned into a disappointment he repeats the sowing, throwing into the water some fresh leaves of the *prangos* which either poison the snail or cause them to descend out of the reach of its influence. The seed is for the most part, sown broadcast into about four or five inches of water, which depth is endeavoured to be maintained. Manure consists of rice straw rejected by the cattle and mixed with cow dung.

The ground is prepared for shali by ploughing and, if necessary, applying manure, from the middle of March to the end of April or middle of May. Best lands do not require the application of manure or tury. Sowing continue during May and may last on through the first fortnight of June. The usual custom is to prepare seed beds and transplant a fortnight after transplanting, *Khustaba* or weeding and breaking the surface soil is done and the operation is repeated at intervals of about a fortnight to three weeks. The excellence of the crop largely depends on the care and the frequency with which this is done. Reaping goes on throughout October.

In Jammu, rice is grown between the Ravi and Ujh rivers, the irrigation being by channels let out of these rivers and from streams from the lower hills. In the hills themselves, wherever there is water, it is led over terraced fields, and elsewhere the fields are banked to retain the rain water. Rice lands in the Jammu districts are known as *pel.*

XV. Uttar Pradesh

Rae Bareli (District Gazetteers of the United Provinces of Agra and Oudh 1923)

Rice is by far the most important crop. This is due to the nature of the country, as the whole of the north of the district is situated in the claey tract in which rice thrives best. Beside this, rice is the main staple of the harvest in the southern lake belt. There are two kinds of rice, known as early rice or *dhān* and the late or transplanted rice commonly called *jarhan.* The latter comprises about one quarter of the whole crop.

Jarhan is sown after the commencement of the rains and when it reaches the height of 5-6 inches, it is transplanted, either in enclosures known as *jhatas* reclaimed from lakes and marshes, or in land, adjoining them for which irrigation is likely to be available late in the season. The crop is cut in November and the land is hardly ever cultivated for the ensuing rabi harvest.

Early rice, which is also known as *kuari* is sown in July and depends largely on the nature of the rainfall. When the plant is a fortnight old, weeding commences and then the standing crops are left to flourish till harvest time in the middle of September.

XVI. Gujarat

Panchmahals (Patel 1972)

During the last century paddy was not grown very extensively. None but *Sathi*, *Sutorsal* and other inferior and coarse varieties were grown. In embanked fields, the seed was sown in a nursery and the plants put out. In open fields the seed was sown broadcast and a careless tillage was adopted by Bhils and other cultivators. No second crop was ever raised from the fields. However, today, paddy is the second important cereal of the district. It requires good irrigation facilities. Preparatory tillage is done in April—May, sowing starts usually in June—July, and harvesting takes place in October—November.

Surat and Broach (Campbell 1877)

Rice holds the first place among the crops. Embanked salt marshes are increasingly used as rice land. Rice fields are either on black or red soil. They are usually located near some pool or hollow and well supplied with water.

XVII. Sind

(The Imperial Gazetteer of India XXII 1908)

The soil of Sind is plastic clay, deposited by the Indus with water, it develops into a rich mould, without water, it degenerates into a desert. There are two principal harvests, *rabi* and *kharif*. The latter crop is sown during the floods of the river from May to August, and reaped from October to December. It includes rice.

The method of cultivation still differs little from the primitive type. Rotation of crops is unknown and the implements belong to the coarsest pattern. The dry character of the soil and the almost complete absence of rain render irrigation a matter of prime importance. The supply of water from all canals is obtained in two ways, by flow and lift flow, which is due to the action of gravity. It leads to great waste of water and water logging.

Cultivation is carried on either within embankments, which are raised to impound the scanty rainfall or on water courses which distribute the water of the hill streams or *nais*.

XVIII. Baluchistan

(Imperial Gazetteer of India, VI, 1908)

The cultivable area of the country is necessarily small. The lands under irrigation are divided into lands which are permanently irrigated and those subject to flood cultivation.

There are two harvests, gathered in the spring and autum.

The latter known as *mane* in *Pashtu* and *Sanwanri* or aman elsewhere is important in the plains. The seed is everywhere sown broadcast after the ground has absorbed the flood moisture. Rice is a minor crop among the autumn crops. The implements of husbandry are primitive.

Rice requires more than a single flooding to reach maturity. The sources of permanent irrigation are canals, underground water channels (*karez*), springs and streams.

XIX. Discussion

Summing up, we may say that the following points emerge as far as patterns, parallels and divergence are concerned.

(i) More than one rice crop in these regions is a commonplace. This is an extremely important feature especially vis-a-vis other agricultural commodities.

(ii) Transplantation as a mode of cultivation is a late adoption when compared to the broadcast method. In many areas like Orissa, Madhya Pradesh and Andhra Pradesh, broadcasting is universal. In others like Karanataka, transplantation has only recently replaced broadcasting. However, in most regions, both modes are practised simultaneously.

(iii) Special kinds of topography and soil conditions demand special modes of rice cultivation. In this connection may by mentioned cultivation of the cereal in riverine basins, hills, creeks and marshy areas. This brings out the significance of adaptability of rice to different environments.

(iv) Special varieties of rice require different modes of cultivation. The submerged variety of rice of North Arcot can be taken to illustrate this feature.

(v) Wet cultivation of rice scores over dry cultivation both in terms of greater prevalence and increased yield. Irrigation methods vary in different areas.

(vi) Manuring of rice fields, though a common feature, has distinctive local characteristics.

(vii) The treatment of the rice seedlings prior to cultivation differ from place to place

(viii) Weeding and thinning of the rice crop, too, has distinct local patterns e. g. *biasi* of M. P.

(ix) Reaping practices are distinct as far as the deep water rices of the 24 Parganas and Dacca are concerned.

(x) Rice is usually grown as a single crop. However, where it is part of a double cropping pattern, rice is almost always the first and more important crop.

All the above mentioned parallels do not obscure the diversity of rice cultivation. Such a diversity is perhaps not in evidence in any other cereal. Broad regional pattern may be discerned, based primarily on geographical factors which impose a particular mode of cultivation. However, it is the diversity within broad similarities which is the outstanding feature of rice cultivation in the subcontinent.

Ritualistic and Customary use of Rice among Certain Tribal Groups

Much has been said about the extensive use of rice in rituals in the available literary texts. Its use still continues as such in the present period. In this section we undertake a survey of the ritualistic as well as customary use of rice and related festivals among certain tribes where there exists a close association between agriculture and religion. It is interesting to trace the connection between ceremonies and beliefs on the one hand and the bread and butter activities of daily life. This is important as subsistence techniques and strategies always adaptively interact with a whole range of institutional complexes.

Apart from this, the purpose is also to draw comparisons with the evidence from literary texts and arrive at a few general conclusions.

Only a few tribes will be studied in detail. The reason for this is that otherwise it would be difficult to handle the enormous amount of data which is essentially similar. The selected tribal groups are among the more populous and well known and are concentrated in important rice growing tracts. They are the Oraons, the Mundas, the Santhals, the Gonds, the Porojas and the Mikirs, Dimasa Kacharis and Zeoni Nagas.

The methodology adopted is as follows. The different groups will be taken up separately and the relevant data detailed. Relevant comments will be appended to each of them. A general discussion of the broader aspects of the problem will also be undertaken.

I. The Oraons (Roy 1928)

The principal agricultural festivals of the Oraons are the *Hariari* celebrated in June—July when the paddy seeds have just germinated and pushed out new shoots, the *Kadtota*, celebrated in the month of August when rice grains are forming in the stalks and *kharihari* when the paddy crops have been harvested.

Unless the public *Hariari* is celebrated, no one in the village may transplant his fields. When the rice grains have formed in the low lands and the upland rice crops are waiting to be harvested, the Oraon apprehends danger to the crops, not only from birds and beasts but also from the 'evil eye' and envious tongue of man and the mischief making propensities of evil spirits. In order to ward off these, the festival of Kadtota is celebrated. The Kharihari is the festival of the threshing floor held in November. No villager may thresh his paddy before the village priest has prepared his own threshing floor and performed the public Puja.

It is clear that these festivals, performed at important stages of the growth of the rice crop, are supposed to be instrumentally involved in farming success. In order to do this, they impose a regulatory control on farming operations and ensure collective endeavour towards a good crop. The subsistence crop, rice, occupies a significant place in the socio-economic set up.

Rice is associated with many other ceremonies and customs too.

(i) *Birth and childhood ceremonies* : Among the more significant, as far as the use of rice is concerned, one may cite the following ceremonies.

In the event of diffiicult labour one of the expedients tried is to fry a handful of rice on an earthen pan and distribute it among all those present.

The new born baby is bathed in rice-water which has been kept in an air tight container for over two or three years.

For her diet during the three days following the birth, the

mother is given rice boiled in water with a few pieces of turmeric.

The three colours, red (of the burnt clay of the hearth), white (of the rice flour) and black (of the coal dust) are believed to represent the rainbow--the largest and most powerful bow in heaven or earth—and therefore, most potential in warding off the evil eye and evil attentions of malignant spirits.

Rice which is not parboiled before husking but dried in the sun is used in some other related ceremonies.

It is obvious that of the customs outlined, some have a purely and clearly utilitarian value. In other cases, there is room for speculation. However, what stands out clearly is that the different properties of rice were recognised and also that it was considered particularly auspicious.

(ii) *Marriage Customs* : An interesting fact is that the Oraon celebrates the marriage ceremonies even of his paddy seedlings, otherwise, it is feared that the paddy seedlings will either rot or fail to germinate.

When going back to her husband's place, the bride takes with her as a present to her husband's family, a pot of rice beer (jhara) and a small basketful of rice flour. It is believed that unless this present is sent with the girl, she will become barren, or even if she has any issue, the children will be sickly and will otherwise suffer pain or some other trouble.

The connotation of fertility linked with marriage and cultivation emerges strongly in the above contexts.

(iii) *Death and its attendant ceremonies.* At the cremation ground, paddy is placed on the ground at the spot over which the head of the corpse rests. Usra rice (whice is parboiled before husking) is put in the mouth of the corpse by each relative and rice beer is dropped while putting in rice, women address the deceased, saying, "Take, eat. Now you have seen your way. Go, taking (with you) our sickness and sins."

If an Oraon dies after the sprouting of new paddy seedlings of the year in June—July, but before the harvest in November, the dead body is temporarily buried. After the harvest, the corpse is exhumed and burnt.

It is this latter practice which is more interesting than the former. The social customs of the Oraons obviously are determined to a large extent by the production pattern of the subsistence crop. Of course, it is the underlying theme of life and death as examplified in the agricultural cycle which more probably provides the cognitive underpinning of the unique practice.

The Oraons thus provide us with evidence of the varied and abundant use of rice in festivals, rituals and customs. This stem from its basic importance in the economy, the recognition of its diverse properties, its auspicious character and association with concepts of life and death.

II. **The Mundas** (Roy 1912)

The important agricultural festivals of the Mundas are as follows. *Hon-Ba-Parob* is celebrated in April—May, on the day preceding that on which the villagers commence sowing of paddy in their fields. *Batauli* is the sacrificial feast to celebrate the beginning of the transplantation of paddy seedlings in June. Rice beer is offered on the occasion. *Jon Nava* celebrates the eating of new rice in September. The *Kolon Sing Borga* is celebrated in November after the transplanted rice has been harvested. No villager will thresh his paddy before this festival is celebrated at the priest's threshing.

The earlier comments on Oraon agricultural festivals would be applicable here, too. Rice beer which is used is one of the above mentioned festivals is made of boiled rice which is fermented and mixed with certain kinds of vegetable roots. This liquid is stored in earthen jars and is ready for use in five days.

Rice figures in the following ceremonies and customs.

(i) *Birth and its ceremonies* : Rice beer, rice flour and arua rice are used in many of these ceremonies. The significant uses of rice are described below.

During confinement, the mother is not allowed to eat stale rice, but must eat hot rice. This is probably a recognition of the effect of different rice preparations on particular physical conditions.

An interesting custom is linked to the *Sakhi* or name giving ceremony. A brass plate is filled with water and a grain of rice is first dropped into it then another grain of rice is dropped into the water in the name of some chosen ancestor or other relative. If the second grain meets the first grain which represents the baby, it is named after this ancestor or relative. If, however, the second grain sinks to the bottom without meeting the first grain, another grain, of rice is dropped in the same way in the name of some other ancestor or relative. This process is repeaed till a grain of rice which is dropped in the same way meets the baby's grain. The baby is then named after this relative who becomes the baby's '*sakhi*'.

It is the auspicious quality of rice which is underlined in this custom.

(ii) *Marriage and its connected customs* : Paddy, rice, rice flour and rice beer are profusely used in the customs and ceremonies of marriage. Only one revealing custom will be quoted.

Before the marriage procession passes out of the bridegroom's village, it stops at the first mango tree on the way. Around the trunk of this tree, the bride-groom puts a mark of rice flour dissolved in water and ties up a piece of thread. The bridegroom's mother than sits down under the tree with the bridegroom on her knees. The mother asks her son, "Where are you going ?" The son replies, "I am going to bring someone who will take care of you and give you rice".

The reference is important as it shows how closely tied rice is to the well being of the community.

(iii) *Funeral ceremonies* : Rice, parched rice and rice beer are used in these ceremonies.

According to one of the customs, the female relatives place, outside the house of the deceased, a few leaf cups filled with rice. It is later scrutinised to find if any portion of the rice has been taken by the spirit of the deceased. The spirit—as a sign of its having partaken of the offering – is said to leave a grain or two of rice on the ground.

In the above, it is the auspicious character of rice which it is important to note.

The bone burial ceremony takes place after the winter rice is harvested. Relatives bring presents of rice, rice beer etc. Rice flour is sprinkled on the stone slab.

A similar custom is found among the Oraons. Together with the hypotheses offered earlier—which may apply as well in this case, too—it may be suggested that the matters related to subsistence demand prior attention and may be said to account for this practice.

It is interesting to observe that a little *arua* rice was customarily sprinkled on the victim in human sacrifices.

In the case of the Mundas, there are a few superstitious beliefs associated with rice.
For example, rheumatism of the lower limbs may be caused by an enemy getting hold of a little dust of one's feet and making offerings of *arua* rice over it.

Again, when a person fancies himself to be the victim of the wrath of some offended spirit, he goes with some *arua* rice. The ghost finder takes the oil and the rice, lights a small earthen lamp with this oil and places the rice on a winnower. He concentrates his gaze on the light of the lamp. Grains of rice are thrown in. As soon as the flame soars up at the name of a spirit, the particular spirit is said to have caused the affliction.

Ir is not clear as to what interpretation should be given to the above. More than its considered efficacy in occult matters, not much can be ventured with any assurance.

From the foregoing it may be concluded that the rhythm of Munda life bears a close connection with its subsistence base rice.

III. **The Santhals** (O'Malley 1910)

Rice is their staple food, in it wealth is reckoned and from it they obtain their drink.

Their agricultural festivals are as follows: *Horier-sin* is the feast of the sprouting of rice which is held in July-August. *Janthar-Puja* is held in November-December to celebrate the first fruits of the winter rice crop. *Sohrac* is the chief festival. It is celebrated after the rice crop of the year has been harvested. It used to be celebrated in Aśvin, for formerly they had gathered their principal crop by that time.

These festivals may by taken as part of a general pattern which was also observed among the Oraons and Mundas. Their significance will therefore not be repeated here.

The association of rice with birth, marriage and funeral

ceremonies are similar to those mentioned earlier. A superstitious belief has it that witches can be detected by putting a leaf with rice in a white ant hill and observing which grain is first touched by an ant.

The socio-economic significance of rice need hardly be stressed.

IV. **The Gonds** (Furer von Haimendorf 1979)

The life of the individual Gond and indeed of the whole tribal community is sustained almost entirely by the tillage of the soil and the whole nature of Gond culture can be understood best when seen against the background of the agricultural activities as is the case with the tribes described above. Similarly, in the eyes of the Gond,too, the material aspects of his work in the field is only one side of a process which involves also the action of supernatural forces.

The ritual eating of the new rice must always precede the Dassera. The rite is predominantly domestic in character. The village priest offers the new rice to *Aki Pen* and *Auwal* but no first fruits are offered in the rice fields. A few handsful of rice are reaped without any formality and cooked together with old rice. Any woman may do the cooking but the householder or a man of his clan offers the rice inside the kitchen to the *Persa Pen* and the ancestral spirits. With the ritual of the new rice, the rice harvest begins. The field owner cuts a little rice and clearing a small patch in the middle of the field, offers with the usual sweetened *dal* to Mother Earth, praying for continued favours.

Compared with the other tribes discussed, the significance of the agricultural festival related to rice, is less. This is accounted for by the fact that the quantities of rice grown are less in this region.

However, rice stands in a peculiar association with the cult of the clan deities. It is rice which should be offered to *Persa Pen* and rice which is used as ritual food during celebrations ; rice was said to have been planted by the hero, *Pahandi Kupar Lingal*, and was cooked by the divine ancestors of the Gonds at their mythical home, *Poropator Dhanegaon*, and it is rice which figures prom:nently in the famous myth of the river crossing.

The apparent contradiction implicit in the lesser degree of prominence in economic life and the reverse situation in social customs as far as rice is concerned is novel in ways. However, it becomes explicable in the light of the particularly sacred and auspicious character generally attributed to rice. The inclusion of rice in Gond myths and legends is indicative of its antiquity either in their earlier or present home.

V. The Porojas (Bell 1945)

They are the distinctive tribe of the three thousand foot plateau of Koraput in Orissa. Rice is extremely important in the region. Among the agricultural festivals may be mentioned the *Nua Khiya* feast on which new rice is first eaten.

Rice and rice beer are used widely in ceremonies and customs of the Porojas. Among the interesting rites relating to rice, a funeral rite may be described.

After the nightfall on the tenth day, the soul of the dead man is called upon by name and one of those that carried the corpse, who is supposed to be possessed with thc deceased's soul, comes out of the darkness sounding his *tangi* on a hoe. He is led to the house where the death had occurred.. In this house, three drawings have been made on the floor, representing Yama, Sani and a devil, three grains of rice placed between them and a pot placed over all. The possessed man enters house and picks away the pot, scattering the grains. The others then look to see on which of the drawings the grains lie, and from their position, the future of the soul after death is determined. If the grains lie on the picture of the devil, it is believed that the soul has become a devil.

The above is a variant of practices which we have come across earlier. Among the Porojas, unlike the Gonds, the economic importance and the ritualistic significance of rice are both observable.

VI. The Mikirs, Dimasa Kacharis and Zeni Nagas (Das 1978)

They are important tribes living in the forested regions of the Brahmaputra Valley, north, south and southeast Assam.

They are considered to be the earliest settlers of the region.

Rice is the staple food of the Mikirs. They attach more importance to the growth of paddy than to any other crop. The Mikirs are all addicted to a strong drink which is known as 'hor'. 'Hor' figures prominently in the observance of their ceremonies and festivals. This is a rice beer prepared by each household. It is mild compared to 'arak' (the strongest variety) and 'thap' (of medium strength). Gourds are used for preserving 'hor' and other rice beers.

Among the Dimasis, *Zu* or rice beer is an equally popular drink. It is made from a local variety of rice known as *Maizu*. *Zu* figures prominently in the observance of their ceremonies and festivals. Outsiders and strangers are also offered this drink.

Paddy is the main crop of the Zemi Nagas and similar details are available for it.

There are no further details available regarding either different specialised uses of rice in these ceremonies. The picture is therefore hazy in details in comparison with other tribes studied. Nonetheless, we are provided with a glimpse of what is, in all probability a greater and closer connection between rice and the existing ritualistic complex.

This brings us to the end of our survey. Admittedly, it is brief and leaves out of consideration many tribes. However, the broad patterns which come out of the study will now be found to be applicable on a more general plane. The important points relate to the importance of rice as a mode of subsistence. This in turn is related to public agricultural festivals in which collective involvement was essential (The exceptions are the Gonds and the north eastern tribes. For the latter the data at hand are insufficient). These festivals are events of socio-economic significanc for the tribes. The other details relate to the use of rice in a wide variety of ceremonies spanning birth to death. The rationale behind some of these uses is clear enough. However, in others, especially relating to occult matters, the exact significance is often obscured. The only fact which seems certain in all contexts is the auspicious and sacred character of rice which is generally recognised. The specific use of rice beer, for both secular and spiritual purposes is common to all the tribes studied. The details were mostly variants of these common features. What cannot be overlooked is the dynamic inter-relationship between the economy and the social structure. Its reciprocal nature must also be clearly mentioned.

The regions in which this close interaction was noted belonged roughly to south Bihar, Madhya Pradesh, Andhra Pradesh and Assam which are old and fairly important centres of rice growing. The tribes located in the region are basically agricultural. However, it was also brought to light that the auspicious quality of rice and its significance remain untarnished even in areas where rice is not the primary crop.

Tribes were chosen to illuminate modern day use of rice in spiritual practices for two reasons. Firstly, their practices would be somewhat divergent—though not completely—from that of Hindus who claim to follow the the ancient texts in this matter in toto. The other reason is that there would be relics of older indigenous tribal beliefs and cults in them. Though, of course, it remains a difficult task to delineate the older strata from newer and later accretions.

We may attempt a comparison with the data sifted from literary texts. As far as the agricultural festivals are concerned the communal aspect comes out strongly in the present kind of survey. Other details related to it are roughly similar in the two. The tribal rice—in—ritual motif is closely comparable to that in early literature. However, some differences are apparent. For example, there is no parallel for the unique tribal funeral rites governed by the agricultural cycle in the early texts. There is no parallel for the mainly occult practices involving rice. Neither is there found in early literature the immense popularity of rice beer in tribal festivals and ceremonies. However, in broad terms the resemblance is undeniable.

From whichever angle one looks at rice, its immense significance in the Indian ethos simply cannot be missed.

7

Summary and Conclusions

I. Introduction

THE history of research on ancient Indian agriculture may be traced back in a sense to the principally botanical writings of Roxburgh (1832), de Candolle (1886), Hooker, (1897) and Watt (1908). They were concerned with the botanical names of ancient plants, the distribution of their cultivated and wild (where applicable) varieties, their names in Sanskrit and regional languages and general speculations on the antiquity of their cultivation. The early textual data were mentioned only in passing. The relevant archaeological data were then non-existent and thus could not be considered at all.

Agriculture received only sporadic attention in the general works on ancient Indian economic history, published in the early years of the twentieth century (cf. Subbarao 1911, Iyengar 1912, Das 1925). The casual treatment of agricultural data is also apparent in Dutt's earlier economic history of India (Dutt 1891). Ancient Indian plant life first received systematic attention in the hands or Majumdar (1927). He drew upon ancient treatises and traditions and pointed out the abundance of scientific observations, classifications, generalizations, theories and applications relating to plants in these treatises and traditions. He was followed by Gangopadhyay (1932) and Raychaudhuri (1941). Among the economic historians of ancient India during this period mention may be made of Pran Nath (1929), Ghosal (1930) and Bose (1942-45) who, while discussing the general economic conditions in ancient India, discussed agricultural conditions as well. Their source was textual.

The consideration of excavated plant remains is a feature of comparatively recent period. A beginning was made with the identification of plant remains at Harappa but the archaeobotanical studies in the Indian context date by and large from the post-Independence period. This has been due to a number of factors. First there has been a growing awareness on the part of the archaeologists of the importance of plant remains in reconstructing the economic activities of the ancient periods. So a great deal of attention is given now-a-days to the recovery, identification and study of the plant remains found in archaeological excavations. Secondly, the botanists themselves are now more keen on knowing the antiquity of the crops they study. This has led to an increasing involvement on the part of the botanists in the identification of excavated plants and crops. In the Indian context this botanical participation is still limited but an important role has been played by Vishnu-Mittre who has now been joined by Buth, Kajale and others. Thirdly, the problem of agricultural origins is a burning issue in the modern archaeological research and one can think of a number of archaeological investigations specifically along this line. The impact of this thought-pattern on the Indian scene is still not particularly strong but the problem at least is well-recognized. Fourthlv, the awareness of the importance of agricultural history has been well-reflected in the publications of the Indian Council of Agriculture Research (1964), Bose, Sen and Subbarayappa (1971) and M.S. Randhawa (1980), among others.

The study of agricultural history has, however, many facets. One of the important facets is, of course, the history of agricultural technology which includes within its scope such features as the modes and implements of cultivation, systematic knowledge of plant life, soil, climate, etc. Another significant facet is the beginning and spread of agriculture and agricultural communities. Orthodox archaeological research and the archaeo-botanical analysis play the most important role in the reconstruction of this facet of agricultural history. The third, and perhaps the most significant, facet is the history of individual agricultural crops, including the determination of their probable centres of origin. The issue of the probable centres of origin is important because this throws a flood of light on the plant migrations and thus on the pattern of cultural dispersals as well.

The history of individual agricultural crops need not be dependent only on the archaeological, literary and botanical data. The approach is essentially multi-disciplinary and should cover, in addition to the archaeological, literary and botanical approaches mentioned above, linguistic and ethnographic data as well The terms used for different crops and activities related to these crops in various Indian language-families are likely to throw light on how a particular crop figured in the life of the people belonging to these language-families. The borrowals of some of these terms by a particular language-family from another language-family is often indicative of the primary association of that particular crop with that language family from which the relevant terms got disseminated to the another language-family. The ethnographic data on the regional modes of cultivation of an individual crop and the place of that crop in various peasant or tribal customs and rituals may reveal correspondence with the ancient historical sources and thus establish or suggest a pattern of continuity between the past and the pre-industrial present. In the Indian context this element of continuity is a significant issue.

This multi-disciplinary approach covering literary, archaeological, botanical, linguistic and ethnographic data has been applied to the early history of rice in the present work. In the previous chapter we have systematically put forward, in relation to rice, the textual and inscriptional evidence, excavated data, botanical facts and inferences, the terms used in various Indian language-families, the regional modes of cultivation and the use of rice in various tribal or peasant rituals and customs. It is now necessary to integrate these data and discuss the nature of evidence in each of these areas. In addition, the position of India as an early centre of rice agriculture may be considered vis-a-vis China and Southeast Asia, the two other early centres of rice agriculture.

II. The Nature of Textual and Inscriptional Evidence

The key-words in the *Rigveda*, the earliest literary record, are *yava*, *dhāna*, and *anna*. *Yava* (cf. 1. 53.2) has been translated as either any grain yielding flour or meal (Monier-Williams 1899, Macdonell and Keith 1958) or barley (Benfey 1866, Apte 1959). *Dhāna* (V. 53.13, IV. 24.7, I. 16.2) is taken to denote rice (Monier-Williams 1899), although this has been disputed (Macdonell and Keith 1958). The precise meaning of *anna* (VIII. 81.4) in this case is uncertain but may not extend beyond a generic name of staple cereals. The contexts in which these terms occur do not permit a precise identification in any case.

The primary agricultural terms used in the *Rigveda*, apart from the verb *kṛsh* (to cultivate, see Monier-Williams 1899 : 306) *śuna*, *śira* (both these terms in IV. 57.5), *sita* (IV. 57.6, IV. 57.7) and *phala* (IV. 57.8). *Sīra* may be a plough (Monier-Williams 1899: 1219, Macdonell and Keith 1958 : 451) whereas *śuna* may be a share. *Śuna* and *Sīra* may denote the deity personifications of the share and the plough as well. *Phala* means a share. Sita indicates a furrow and/or deity presiding over agriculture (Monier-Williams 1899 : 1218). The other important agricultural terms in this text are *ksetra* (V.62.7, IX. 85.4, IX. 91.6) or field and *dātra* (VIII. 78.10) or sickles. It is logical to deduce from the occurrence of the above-mentioned terms in the *Rigveda* that the element of pastoralism in this text has been overemphasized by scholars. We also suggest that the *Rigveda* was familiar with rice. It may be noted that rice was an important crop in the later Vedic literature and this suggests a long ancestry of rice cultivation, which should logically go back to the period of the *Rigveda*,

In the *Taittīriya Saṁhitā* of the *Black Yajurveda* the key-words are *vrīhi*, translated as rice, and *nīvāra*, translated as wild rice. The varieties of rice mentioned are black rice, swift-growing rice, large rice (I. 8.10) and white rice (II. 3.1). *Vrīhi* and *nivara* were offered to deities. The rice crop was harvested in autumn (VII. 2.10).

In the *Vājasaneyī Saṁhitā* of the *White Yajurveda* the preparation of rice cakes in rituals is described at length, from taking the rice grain from the cart, winnowing and pounding it and cooking on offering (I. 6-11).

Although the *Sāmaveda* does not specifically mention rice, the terms for rice in the *Atharvaveda* are *vrīhi* and *dhānyam* (III. 24.4). Rice (along with barley) was supposed to have possessed medicinal and recuperative powers (VIII. 7.20, VIII. 2.18) and was closely identified with *prāna* or breath (XI. 4.13) and prosperity (X. 6.24). Rice was offered to deities in the form of *odana* (XI. 3.1-49), *charu* (XVIII. 4.16) *purodāśa* (XII. 4.35) and *taṇḍula* (X. 9.26).

The *Aitareya Brāhmaṇa* mentions ritual rice offerings in the form of *charu* (I. 1.1), *purodāśa* (II. 1.9) and *pāyasa* (II. 3.23). Small-grained and large-grained rice are mentioned among the ritual items of a coronation ceremony.

In the *Śatapatha Brāhmana* two preparations of rice—rice cake, the preparation of which has been elaborately described (I. 1.2.5, I. 1.4.20, I. 1.4.23) and what has been called *anvāhārya* mess (I. 2.3.5)—were offered in rituals. Different varieties of rice were offered to different deities ; fast-grown rice (*plāśuka*) to *Savitri Satyaprasava* (V. 3.3.2), quick-grown rice (*asu*) to *Agni Grihapati* (V. 3.3.3), wild rice (*nivara*) to *Brihaspati Vak* (V. 3.3.5), red rice grains (*hāyāna*) to Indra (V. 3.3.6) and black rice grains to *Nirrīti* (V. 3.2.13). Malted rice also appears as part of the offerings in certain rituals (XII. 7.2.9). Rice was ascribed auspicious quality (XII. 7.1.9).

Rice is mentioned in the context of rituals in the *Panchaviṁśa, Jaiminiya* and *Gopatha Brāhmanas.* Rice (*vrīhi*) occurs in the philosophical analogies of the *Upaniṣads* (cf. *Brihadaraṇyaka Upaniṣad* V. 6.1). A couple's fertility was supposed to be enhanced after partaking of various rice preparations (*Brihadaraṇyaka Upaniṣad* VI. 4.13-14).

The *Sūtra* literature, particularly the *Śrauta, Grihya* and *Dharma* sutras, are full of references to rice in rituals, its varieties and preparations. The *Āpastamba Dharmasūtra* (I. 7.20.13) put restrictions on Brahmins regarding trade in rice. The *Vinaya Pitaka* mentions two varieties of rice—*vrīhi* and *sāli*. *Sali* is supposed to be a rice which is sown in rainy season and harvested in winter (Suryakanta 1975). The terms like *odana*, *bhatta* and *sukkhākura* denote different rice preparations. The size of the monk's bowl was measured by the amount of rice it could hold. Most of the references relate to how monks should collect and utilize the rice they receive. Stealing and coveting others' share are frowned upon as is wastage. Shortage of rice is spoken of when there would be a drop in alms-giving. There is also mention of wagon-loads of rice. There are references to some rice-growing areas—Champa, Sravasti, Rajagriha and Magadha in general. The extensive, terraced rice-fields of Magadha are described. There is also mention of liquor obtained from cooked rice. Rice was not considerd a suitable diet in certain ailments.

The following varieties of rice have been mentioned in the *Majjhima Nikāya* : hill paddy, wild rice, rice from which the black grains have been removed and large-grained rice. The preparations of rice mentioned are : boiled rice, rice cooked in milk, and gruel and powder of rice husks. There are references to the distribution of rice by the laity to the monks.

Ricc distribution as alms is also mentioned in the *Samyutta Nikāya* which also refers to a Brahmin offering a preparation of rice with *ghee* in a religious ceremony,

The *Jātakas* refer to the following varieties : hill paddy, wild rice (*nīvāra* and *sayamjātasāli*), red paddy, etc. Rice grains were known as *taṇḍula* and preparations of rice as *bhatta* and *pāyasa*. Rice growing areas such as *Gandhāra*, *Vārāṇasi*, *Srāvasti* and *Magadha* were mentioned. The lack of water brought a drop in rice yields. There is a reference to excess rain damaging the rice crop and also to draught. There is mention of the storage of rice in overflowing granaries. Wagon-loads of rice crossed the highways. Fresh, mature and scented rice were in common use. Rice given as alms is frequently mentioned and praised. Rice seems to have been a form of remuneration for both domestic and agricultural workers. The king probably received some tax in kind, specifically rice. Other uses of rice were as an ingredient of liquor and in religious offerings by the Brahmins. The medicinal use of rice is also mentioned.

The *Suttanipāta* mentions rice given as alms. In the *Thera* and *Therī Gāthā* there is mention of threshing, pounding and boiling of rice. Rice was offered to the Buddha and his followers. Wild rice seems to have been available in a forest glade near *Rājagrhia*. The term *kura* possibly denoted some kind of wild rice and it was found at *Śrāvastī*.

Red rice, hill paddy and wild rice are mentioned in the *Dhammapada*. There is also a detailed description of rice field. Women acted as keepers of rice fields. Storage of rice under famine conditions was possible for the better-off section of the society. The regions associated with rice cultivation are *Uttarakuru*, *Vāranasī*, *Śrāvastī*, the territories of the *Sakiyas* and *Koliyas* and *Kosala*. Rice was donated to the Buddhist congregation by all sections of the society. There is a reference to the fact that five hundred cart loads of rice, along with agricultural implements, were a part of a trousseau. Remuneration by way of rice is mentioned,

The *Aṣṭādhyāyi* of *Pāṇini* mentions *vrīhi*, *sāli*, *lohita śāli*, *hāyāna*, *mahāvrīhi* and *nīvāra*. Rice preparations (cf. *charu*, *purodāśa*) and the use of rice in religious offering are also mentioned.

In the *Arthaśāstra* of Kauṭilya the treatment of individual crops is not detailed but *śāli* and *vrīhi* are mentioned along with two new terms, *udaraka* and *varaka*, which, according to Om Prakash (1961), are two new varieties of rice perhaps introduced during this period. In Patanjali's *Mahabhāsya* there are references to *sali* and *vrīhi* and also to the use of rice in rituals. The use of rice in rituals is also mentioned by the *Arthaśāstra*. Rice figures as an important crop in the *Milinda Pānha*. Of the two types of red rice mentioned in this text, one (*parumbhaka*) is supposed to be unhealthy. In the *Mahābhārata* there are references to *śāli*, *nīvara*, use of rice in rituals and the auspicious character of sun-dried rice and fried paddy. In the *Rāmāyana* there are references to rice in different ceremonies : marriage, daily oblations, funeral ceremonies, etc. In the *Smriti* literature *vrīhi*, *śāli* and wild rice are mentioned. The most significant references relate to the use of rice in judicial proceedings, rituals and penances. In the *Purāṇas* the references to rice in rituals are overwhelming. The following varieties are mentioned : red rice (*Agṇi Puraṇa* XCIII), *śālī* (Agṇi Pur. CLXXV), *vrīhi* (*Matsya* Pur. II. CCLXVI), *aman* rice (*Mārkaṇḍeya* Pur. XV. 8), white rice (*Matsya* Pur. LXII) black rice (*Agni* Pur. CCXXX), *nīvāra* (*Visnu* Pur. III.XVI), *Samthi* rice (*Mārkaṇḍeya* Pur. XV. 8), plain rice (*Matsya* Pur. II. CCLXVIII), small-grained rice *Markaṇḍeya* (Pur. XXXII.2), *śyāmaka* rice (*Liṇga* Pur. LXXXIII. 23-26) and *ṣaṣtika* rice (*Śiva* Pur. XVIII. 43-46). The different parts of a rice plant are explicitly described in the course of a philosophical discourse (*Viṣṇu* Pur. VII). The medicinal properties of some varieties are listed. The use of rice in the cleansing of pearl-seeds is mentioned (*Garuḍa* Pur. LXIX). There are references to liquor distilled from rice (*Bhāgavata* Pur. I.XV.22-23) and to the hypothecation of paddy and the rules relating to it (*Agṇi* Pur. CCLIV).

In the lexical literature there are references to different varieties of rice (*vrīhi, śāli, nīvāra, kalama* and *ṣaṣtika*) and rice preparations (flattened rice (*pṛthuka*), boiled rice (*bhisma*) and rice gruel (*odana*) in the *Amarakoṣa*. In the medicinal literature the *Charaka* and *Śusruta* Samhitas mention the varieties of rice and the medicinal properties of these different varieties. The foreign accounts such as the *Periplus* and Hiuen-Tsang's *Si-Yu-Ki* do not provide much detail but according to the *Periplus* rice was exported from Barygaza to Egypt and Socotra.

The theoretical points which emerge out of the textual references are the following. First, whatever may be the opinion regarding the occurrence of the rice in the *Rigveda* (we have argued that rice was known to the Rigvedic people), rice is a well-established crop in the later Vedic literature, established enough to be identified with *prana* or breath and prosperity. The references to rice in the later Vedic literature involve three categories : (1) the mention of different varieties of rice beside the general references to *vrīhi* and *nīvāra*, (2) the use of different rice preparations as offerings in rituals and (3) the mention of medicinal and recuperative properties of rice. What makes these categories of references interesting is that these constitute the basic pattern of all the subsequent references to rice in the Sanskrit literature up to the early group of *Purāṇas*. The subsequent references are no doubt more elaborate—one has only to refer to the diverse ritualistic, judicial and medicinal uses of rice and the mention of its many varieties in the Sutra, *Smṛiti* and the medicinal literature to realize this—but the general pattern of references may be said to have remained unchanged throughout. Although there are some secular details in the Sanskrit literature, particularly of the later period, by and large it is the Buddhist literature which provides more secular details such as the giving of rice as alms, the description of a rice field, the mention of a few rice-growing areas, the use of rice as a remuneration in kind and also as royal tax etc.

Secondly, it is also possible to assert that the literary sources quite explicitly suggest a deeprooted antiquity of rice cultivation in India. The way in which rice figures in the later Vedic literature cannot but be the result of a long familiarity with, and the realization of the importance of, this crop.

Thirdly, although it is hardly possible to identify varieties of rice mentioned in the texts in botanical terms, one may safely claim that many of these varieties must be continuing in different regions of India. For instance, it is interesting to come across the varieties called *aman* and *saṃthi* in the *Mārkaṇḍeya Purāṇa* (XV.8) and the *Matsya Purāṇa* (II. CCXXXIX) respectively because these two varieties are commonly grown in modern times. The former is a winter crop while the latter is described as belonging to a race with short, strong stem, ear partially enclosed in the sheath and grain husk, dark-coloured or black (Watt 1908). Moreover, the point which needs emphasis is that the mention of different varieties of rice in the texts is unlikely to be an exaggeration. Even in recent times there are many regional varieties of rice, each with a distinct local name.

The inscriptional evidence which has been considered in the present context is no doubt late but this throws light on the payment of rice as revenue, the payment of allowance in rice, the payment of interest in rice and the use of rice for the procurement of articles for consumptian. Although the inscriptions relate primarily to the Chola kingdom, the general significance of rice in the economy was possibly the same in the earlier periods as well.

III. The Pattern of Archaeological Data

Attention should be first drawn to the occurrence of wild rice in the advanced Mesolithic context at Chopani-Mando (9th-8th millennia B.C.) and domesticated rice in the Neolithic context of Koldihawa and Mahagara (6th-5th millennia B.C.). All these sites are on the Belan and in a geographical area which may be said to constitute a plateau fringe to the central Gangetic valley.

The identification of rice grains, wild at Chopani-Mando and domesticated at Koldihawa and Mahagara, is the most significant archaeological record of rice in India, and the chronology of the contexts in which rice occurs at these three sites perhaps deserves some discussion.

The arguments in favour of the existence of an early mesolithic stage at Chopani-Mando are in two in number and quite positive in their implications. Chopani-Mando Mesolithic does not have any independent radiocarbon date, but two dates, one from the same area and the other from a contiguous region, are directly relevant to its dating. There is a date of 8080±115 B.C. (SUA 1421) from the pre-Neolithic context at Mahagara which like Chopani-Mando is on the Belan and about 3km. away from this site. Baghor II, a Mesolithic site in the upper reaches of Son, gives a date of 8380±220 B.P. (PRL—715) or 6480±220 B.C. Moreover, the Chopani-Mando sequence from its epi-Palaeolithic stage onward, closely corresponds to the sequence of the lithic industries found in the Belan section and in that section the uppper Palaeolithic deposit which precedes the epi-Palaeolithic one gives two dates of 23840 B.C. (PRL-86) and 17765 B.C. (TF-1245). It may also be noted that the Belan sequence offers a clear picture of the typological evolution of of the stone Age industries, and there is no apparent reason to doubt the existence of an early mesolithic stage on the Belan. According to the report published by Sharma *et al* (1980 : 72), "the entire occupational deposit of Chopani-Mando constituting the Epi-Palaeolithic, the early Mesolithic and the Advanced Mesolithic (Proto-Neolithic), may tentatively be placed within a time span of 17th-7th millennium B.C." This is a dating with which we would entirely agree. At one point Sharma (Sharma *et al* 1980 : 23) preferred the dating of 9th-

8th millennia B.C. for the advanced Mesolithic or what has been called proto-Neolithic level of Chopani-Mando. Even if this date is brought down to the 7th millennium B.C. it would not make any significant difference to the basic chronological picture of the site. The assemblage in which wild rice has been found in this level has been discussed by Sharma *et al* (1980 : 75) :

"The presence of carbonised rice/rice husk imbedded in clay lumps, looked in the context of grinding stones, both querns and mullers, suggests collection of wild edible grains, if not cultivation, during this period".

The chronological situation in the Neolithic level of Koldihawa and Mahagara is as follows : the Mahagara dates which, with one exception (2165 B.C.), falls in the second millennium B.C. (for the Mahagara dates, Sharma *et al* 1980 ; 199-200) do not agree with the three indisputably early dates from Koldihawa ——6570±210 B.C.(PRL—224), 5440±240 B.C. (PRL—100) and 4530±185 B.C. (PRL 101). One, however, notes that the site of Mahagara located on the top of the Belan cliff at that point suffers from gully erosions and hence the possibility of getting contaminated samples from this site is rather high. Moreover, there is a pre-neolithic date of 8080±115 B.C. from Mahagra itself. One would, in fact, think that the Koldihawa-Mahagara Neolithic complex with its domesticated rice safely belongs to the 6th-5th millennia B.C. horizon. Interestingly enough, the fact that rice husk was used as a tempering material in the clay for pots at these sites clearly suggests an easy familiarity with this crop at these two sites during this early period.

After this there is a remarkable gap in the archaeological record of rice in the subcontinent till about 2000 B.C. This, however, is merely a convenient chronological point. The actual span possibly falls somewhere in the second half of the third millennium B.C. on the one hand and continues up to the first quarter of second millennium B.C. on the other. The rice-bearing archaeological levels which are relevant to this time bracket are the Harappan levels at Lothal and Rangpur, the chalcolithic level at Ahar, the ochre coloured pottery level at Atranjikhera, the Neolithic level at Chirand, and the Gandhara

Grave culture. In view of the controversy about the identification of rice at the Harappan site of Kalibangan, this site should not be considered for the present list. The occurrence of rice in the Gandhara Grave culture in the northwest may also go back to c. 2000 B.C.

Rice husks and spikelets occur both at Lothal and Rangpur. At Ahar rice occurs in the first phase of the site (period Ia) and from the size of the spikelets and grains it appears that this represent the long-seeded strain of *Oryza sativa Lin var. Sativa Bor.* In the Ochre Coloured Pottery level of Atranjikhera (datable in the first quarter of the second millennium B.C.) the rice remains were recovered from mud clods and wall-plasters. The variety involved could not be determined. In the Neolithic context at Chirand, which begins perhaps around 2500 B.C. the carbonized rice grains are said to have been derived from both the cultivated and wild species of Oryza.

All these sites fall in three broad geographical clusters—— southeast Rajasthan (Ahar) and Gujarat (Lothal and Rangpur), the upper (Atranjikhera) and middle (Chirand) Gangetic valleys and the northwest (Gandhara Graves). The total evidence also suggests the deep rooted tradition of rice cultivation in each of these areas (cf. rice husks in wall-plasters, mud clods, etc.). It is almost obvious that by the second half of the third millennium B.C. the tradition of rice cultivation was well-established in disparate geographical areas, presupposing a long period of growth behind it. This fact itself makes the discoveries at Chopani-Mando, Koldihawa and Mahagara theoretically acceptable.

By the second half of the second millennium B.C. the evidence becomes more extensive. The rice-bearing sites falling in this time-range are Navdatoli (Period I, Phases II-IV) in Malwa, Inamgaon (right from the Malwa cultural level) in the Deccan, Hallur (Megalithic) in Karnataka Gufkral, Kashmir, east Indian Chalcolithic-Iron Age sites such as Pandu Rajar Dhibi, Mahisdal, Sonpur, etc. in West Bengal and Bihar, the Black-and-Red Ware level in Atranjikhera, the Painted Grey Ware levels at Hastinapur, Atranjikhera and Noh all in the upper Gangetic valley or its fringes and the late Harppan level at Hulas in Saharanpur, western U.P. The time-range of all these sites is in the second half of the second millennium B.C. roughly between 1500 and 1000 B.C.

The pattern of distribution does not, in fact, change significantly during the early historic period, and the available evidence suggests to us that by c. 1000 B.C. rice cultivation in India assumed its basic geographical character.

Another point to note is that on the basis of the archaeological records it has not been possible to establish the varietal diversities of the crop in different regions. For instance, it has been observed that the Navdatoli rice grains belong neither to the *Japonica* type nor to the *Indica* type but possess characteristics of both the types suggesting a hybrid nature of the Navdatoli rice grains. Almost the same thing has been said about the rice in the Painted Grey Ware level at Atranjikhera. This does not fit into any of the sub-species *Japonica* and *Indica*) and it has suggested that this was passing through a state of evolution when the process of mutation was very active.

IV. The Botanical Perspective

What seems to be the most significant in the botanical context is the wide distribution of a number of wild rice species in India. Of the five such species listed and discussed earlier (Chapter IV), *O. coarctata Roxb.* is said to bo confined to the Bhagirathi delta in West Bengal, the Mahanadi delta in Orissa, the Godavari delta in Andhra Pradesh and the Indus delta in Sind. The distribution of *O. meyerina* extends from Assam to Malabar through the Khasi hills (Meghalaya), Sikkim, the Chhotanagpur plateau region of West Bengal and Bihar, the Eastern Ghat region of Orissa, Tamil Nadu including the Nilgiri hills, etc. *O. officianalis* has more or less the same distribution, but is also found in Manipur, central India and Maharashtra. *O. perennis Moench* is found in Manipur, Assam, West Bengal (more or less in the western parts of the state and in the deltaic 24 Parganas as well), Bihar (both south Bihar——cf. Gaya, Ranchi——and north Bihar ——cf. Darbhanga, etc.), U.P. (apparently eastern U.P.—— Gonda, Gorakhpur, Faizabad, Lucknow, Rampur), Orissa (the Eastern Ghats region from Balasare to the Jeypore tract and the Mahanadi delta), M.P. (Raipur, Nagpur), the Godavari delta in Andhra Pradesh, and Keraal. *O. rufipogon* (also known as *O. sativa var. fatua*) has apparently the most extensive distribution——the Surma valley in Bangladesh, West Bengal (including north Bengal), Bihar, eastern U.P. including Allahabad and Varanasi districts, Orissa, M.P., Nagpur, Bombay, western India, the Godavari delta, the Kangra valley (Himachal Pradesh), Panjab and the northwestern region.

O. sativa is said to be derived from either *O. perennis* or *O. rufipogon*, although the general opinion seems to prefer *O. perennis* more. The distribution of both these species is strikingly extensive in India and takes in singularly large tracts of the country in a sweep. The most important loop of this distribution is from Assam to Kerala through West Bengal and Orissa. Two loops branch off this, one covering Bihar andU.P. and the other going to western India through Madhya Pradesh. A third (apparently detached) loop is spread over the Kangra valley, Panjab and the northwestern region.

It must be emphasizcd that the distribution of these five species, which has been enumerated on the basis of the published literature is not particularly precise. For instance, "western India" has been mentioned but the specific areas have not been given in detail. However, the broad outline of the distribution is clear enough.

The identification of the probable centres of origin of rice domestication and cultivation does not seem to be an easy and undisputed problem on botanical grounds. The archaeological discoveries of early rice-bearing contexts may play an important role in the solution of the problem. For instance, the archaeological evidence of wild rice at Chopani Mando and domesticated rice at Koldihawa and Mahagara decidedly makes this plateau fringe to the central Gangetic valley one of the earliest centres of rice cultivation, although this region does not figure in the relevant botanical region as a probable centre of origin. All that we know is that *O. rufipogon* has within its distribution zone the modern U.P. districts of Allahabad and Varanasi.

The distribution of *O. rufipogon* in Punjab and the northwest (including the Kangra valley in Himachal Pradesh) is interesting in the sense that rice has been found in early context at Gufkral in Kashmir and the Gandhara Grave culture in the northwest. Moreover, one notes that virtually all the rice-bearing archaeological sites which fall in the second and third orders of our chronological grouping of these sites (the second half of the third millennium B.C. and the second millennium B.C. as a whole)——Lothal, Rangpur, Ahar, Hulas, Atranjikhera, Noh, Hastinapur, Chirand, east Indian Chalcolithic sites, Navdatoli, Inamgaon, Hallur, etc.——are either within, or in the peripheries of, the distribution of *O. perennis* and *O. rufipogon*. We feel that in the ultimate analysis the direct archaeological discoveries will tell more about the centres of origin of rice domestication and cultivation than the background botanical hypotheses on the problem. The botanical research has, of course, delineated a numbcr of probable areas but the direct testimony will rest on archaeological research.

Finally, one may also add that there is no theoretical reason why the plateau fringe of the central Gangetie valley (the Belan valley) should be considered the only early centre of rice domestication and cultivation in India. The botanical opinion suggests an extensive belt in east and south India. But as things stand, our knowledge of the Mesolithic and the Neolithic in this belt is still inadequate.

V. The Linguistic Situation

The terms which are related to rice in the Indian language-families——the Indo-Aryan, Dravidian, Munda and Tibeto-Burman——bring out the following aspects. The five primary terms documented in ancient texts—*Śāli, taṇḍula, dhānya, bhatta* and *vrīhi*——occur extensively in the Indo-Aryan language family. *Śāli* has cognates in 27 languages, with no great difference in form and meaning (growing or, and rice in general). *Taṇḍula* occurs in about 20 languages. The main connotation is that of husked rice but occasionally it has meant some kind of corn (Gujarati), rice in the field (Gawar Baṭi) and boiled rice (Shina). *Dhāna* or *dhānya* occurs in about 16 languages and means in most cases unhusked rice or paddy. The form is more or less the same in all these languages. About 22 languages have *bhatta* or its cognates in the sense of boiled rice with the exception of Konkani where this means the husk of rice *Vrīhi* occurs only in 4 languages——Sanskrit, Pali, Prakrit and Sinhalese. In the first three this stands for rice. In Sinhalese this means "growing rice".

There is a great abundance of rice and rice-related terms in the Dravidian language family. Tamil alone has 32 such terms. The figures for the other relevant languages are: Kannada (22), Telugu (20), Malayalam (16), Tulu and Kodagu (8 each), Kurukh and Toda (6 each), Kota (5), Kui and Kolani (3 each), Malto, Gondi, Konda and Gadba (2 each). There is no doubt that the rice-related terminology is remarkable in the Dravidian language-family.

In the Munda language-family, the Santali has about 24 terms related to rice and activities associated with rice. In the Santali there is also an extensive set of terms for "rice fields" and "rice lands". What, however, is most interesting is that there are 102 terms for varieties of rice plant in the Santali. Terms for rice liquor, rice husk, etc. occur in other Munda languages as well.

The number of relevant terms in the Tibeto-Burman language-family is not extensive.

The linguistic data cited in this context may not be historically conclusive but the occurrence of 102 terms for varieties of rice plant in the Santali (Munda language family) and the extensive rice vocabulary in the Dravidian language family may indicate a broad sweep of concentration of rice-related terminology in east India (the Chhotanagpur plateau region which is the main distribution area of the Santali) and south India.

VI. The Ethnographic Data

The ethnographic data on the regional modes of cultivation from Assam on the east to Baluchistan on the west are intended to highlight the remarkable regional adaptation of rice cultivation in the Indian context. The theoretical point which may be put forward on the basis of these data is that this feature of regional adaptation is likely to be true of the early period as well. The basis of these preindustrial regional modes of cultivation possibly got laid down after the trait of rice cultivation spread to the major areas of the subcontinent. On the basis of the archaeological data it is possible to argue that by the time one reaches the early historic period the basis of rice cultivation was secure in all the major areas of the subcontinent and that in the early historic period itself there was possibly a considerable expansion of rice cultivation. The ethnographic data provide some insight into the different regional modes of rice cultivation during these periods.

The data on the place of rice in certain tribal rituals are intended to argue that the ritualistic role of rice mentioned in the corpus of early texts is not merely a feature of the ancient Indian literary tradition (which continues even now in Hindu society) but also a feature of those levels of Indian society, which lie on the fringe, or outside, of this tradition. Perhaps no specific historical inference can be drawn on this basis but this surely shows how deeply rice has been a part of the Indian ethos.

VII. The Early Occurrence of Rice in Southeast Asia and China

A critical and comprehensive review of the early occurrence of rice in the archaeological contexts of southeast Asia and China has been made by Glover (1979), and following him it is possible to identify the chronological points of the beginning of rice in the archaeological record of this region.

The earliest contexts in Thailand is marked by the carbonised grains and spikelets of rice embedded in pottery at Non Nok Tha and Ban Chieng in northeast Thailand. This material has been put in the late 4th millennium B.C. It seems that in the case of Non Nok Tha there is doubt about the cultivated status of rice but there is no such doubt about the Ban Chieng material and the clear emergence of cultivated rice in Thailand in the late 4th millennium B.C. is seemingly beyond dispute.

It Vietnam the first definitive remains of rice are in the middle second millennium B C. but it has been asserted, although without positive proof, that the "early Neolithic" Bac-son culture (c. 8000 B.C.) was familiar with the cultivation of hill rice. From the "late Neolithic" of about 4000 B.C. there is a list of cultivated plants including rice.

In China rice seems to be fairly common in the third millennium B.C. sites. The earliest contexts which Glover (1979) reports are : the Sung-tse site of Ch'ingpu, Shanghai (3395± 105 B.C.) and the Lungshanoid-type site of Ho-mo-tu, Chekiang province (3945±115 B.C. and 4360± 100 B.C.). The evidence appears to be indisputable.

The chronological picture of the beginning of rice in China, southeast Asia and the Indian subcontinent is thus varied and clearly underlines the multiple origins of this crop over a wide area.

Select References

Abhishankar, K. (Ed.) 1975. *Karnataka District Gazetteer, Shimoga*. Bangalore.

Agrawal, D.P. and Kusumgar, S. 1974. *Pre-Historic Chronology and Radio-carbon Dating in India*. Delhi.

Agrawal, V.S. 1953. *India as known to Panini*. Lucknow.

Akhtar, J.D. (Ed.) 1972. *The Matsya Puranam*. Delhi.

Alim, A., and Hasanuzzaman, S.M. 1962. Rice in East Pakistan, *Rice News Letter* 10(4). pp. 71-73.

Allen, B.C. (Ed.) 1912. *East Bengal District Gazetteers, Dacca District*. Allahabad.

Allchin, F.R. 1969. Early cultivated plants in India and Pakistan, in, Ucko, P.J. and Dimbleby, G.W. (Ed.). *The Domestication and Exploitation of Plants and Animals*. London. pp. 323-329.

Apte, V.S. 1959. The Practical Sanskrit-English Dictionary. Poona.

Beal, S. 1885. *Buddhist Records of the Western World* (2 Vols.). Boston.

Bell, R.C.S. (Ed.) 1945. *Orissa District Gazetteers, Koraput*. Cuttack.

Benfey, T. 1866. *Sanskrit-English Dictionary*. London,

Bhalerao, S.G. 1928. The wild rice of the Bombay Presidency, *Poona Agr. Coll. Mag*. 20(2). pp. 23-25.

Bhatt, G.H. (Ed.) 1960. *Bala Kaṇḍa*. Baroda.

Bhattacharya, S. 1966. Some Munda etymologies, in Zide, N.H. (Ed.) *Studies in Comparative Austro-Asiatic Linguistics*. The Hague. pp. 28-40.

Bhide, R.K. 1925. Wild rice, in *Poona Agr. Coll. Mag*. 17(1). pp. 41-44.

Bhisagratna, K.K. 1963. *Susruta Saṃhita.* Varanasi.

Bodewitz, H.W. 1973. *Jaiminiya Brahmana.* Leiden.

Bor, N.L. 1960. *The Grasses of Burma, Ceylon, India, and Pakistan.* London.

Bose, A.N. 1942-45. *Social and Rural Economy in Northern India (600 B.C. – 200 A.D.)* 2 vols. Calcutta.

Bose, D.M. Sen, S.N. and Subbarayappa, R. 1971. *A Concise History of Science In India.* INSA. Delhi.

Brackenbury, C.F. (Ed.) 1915. *Madras District Gazetteers, Cudappah.* Madras.

Brock, J.C. and others 1961. *Technical Reports on Archaeological Remains.* Poona.

Buhler, G. 1964. *The Laws of Manu.* Delhi.

Buhler, G. 1965. *The Sacred Law of the Aryas a Taught by the Schools of Apastamba, Gautama Vasishta and Baudhayana* (2 vols.). Delhi.

Burgess, J.A.S. (Ed.) 1892. *Epigraphica Indica.* Vol. I. Calcutta.

Burgess, J.A.S. (Ed.) 1894. *Epigraphica Indica.* Vol. II. Calcutta.

Burkill, I.H. 1953, Habits of men and the origin of cultivated species of the Old World, *in, Proc. Linn. Soc.* London, 164. pp. 12-41.

Burlingame, E.W. 1969. *Buddhist Legends,* (3 Parts) London.

Burrow, T. 1968. *Collected Papers on Dravidian Linguistics.* Annamalainagar.

Burrow, T. and Emeneau, M.B. 1962. *Dravidian Borrowings from Indo-Aryan.* Los-Angeles.

Buth, G.M. and Chowdhury, K.A. 1971. Plant Remains from Atranjikhera, Phase III. *The Palaeobotanist.* 20(1) pp. 280-287.

Buth, G.M., Bisht, R.S. and Gaur, G.S. 1982. Investigation of palaeoethnobotanical remains from Semthan, Kashmir. *Man and Environment* 6 : 41-45.

Caland, W. 1931. *Panchavimse Brahmanam.* Calcutta.

Campbell. J.M. (Ed.) 1877. *Gazetteer of the Bombay Presidency, Surat and Broach.* Bombay.

Campbell, J.M. (Ed.) 1983. *Gazetteer of the Bombay Presidency, Kolaba and Janjira.* Bombay.

Chalmers, R. 1932. *Buddha's Teachings, Sutta Nipata*, Harvard Univ. Press.

Chang, T.T. 1964. Present Knowledge of Rice genetics and cytogenetics, *International Rice Research Institute, Tech. Bull.* 1. Los. Banos.

Chang, T.T. 1976. The origin, evolution, cultivation, dissemination of Asian and African rices, *Euphytica* 25(2). pp. 425-441.

Chatterjee, D. 1947. Botany of wild and cultivated rices. *Nature*, 160. pp. 234-237.

Chatterjee, D. 1948. A modified key and enumeration of the species of Oryza Linn. *Indian J. Agr. Sci.* 18, pp. 185-192.

Chatterjee, D. 1951. Note on the origin and distribution of wild and cultivated rices. *Indian J. Genet, Pl. Breed.* 11, pp. 18-22.

Chatterjee, S.K. 1926. *The Origin and Development of the Bengali Language*. Part I. Calcutta.

Chevalier, A. 1932. Nouvele contribution a L'etude systematique des Oryza Linn. *Indian J. Agr. Sci.* 18, pp. 185-192.

Chowdhury, K.A. and Ghosh, S.S. 1954-55. Plant remains, in, Lal, B.B., Excavations at Hastinapur and other exploration in the Upper Ganga and Sutlej basins. *Ancient India*, Nos. 10 & 11, pp. 120-135.

Chowdhury, K.A., Saraswat, K.S., and Buth, G.M. 1977. *Ancient Agriculture and Forestry in North India*. Delhi.

Chowkhumba Sanskrit Series, 1964. *Srisuklayajurveda Satapatha Brahmaṇa*. Varanasi.

Constantini, L. 1979. Notes on Palaeoethnobotany of protohistorical Swat, in, Taddel, M. (Ed.), *South Asian Archaeology*. Naples. pp. 703-708.

Copeland, E.B. 1924. *Rice*. London.

Cowell, E.B. (Ed.) 1957. *The Jatakas* (six vols.). London.

Das, S.K. 1925. *Economic History of Ancient India*. Calcutta.

Das, S.T. 1978. *The People of the Eastern Himalayas*. Delhi.

Dandekar, R.N. (Ed.) 1962, 1973. *Srautakosa*, (2 Vols.). Poona.

Dasgupta, P.C., 1964. *Excavations at Pandu Rajar Dhibi*. Calcutta.

Davids, R. 1964. *The Sisters and the Brethren*. London.

Davids, R., and Woodward, F.L. 1950-56. *The Book of the Kindred Sayings, Samyutta Nikaya* (5 vols.). London.

De, S.K. (Ed.) 1936. *Virata Parvan.* Poona.

De, S.K. (Ed.) 1940. *Udyoga Parvan.* Poona.

De, S.K. (Ed.) 1958. *Drona Parvan.* Poona.

de-Candolle, A. 1886. *Origin of Cultivated Plants.* New York.

Deo. S.B. and Joshi, J.P. 1972. *Pauni Excavation, 1969-70.* Nagpur.

Deo, S.B. and Gupta, R.S. 1974. *Excavations at Bhokardan,* Nagpur.

District Gazetteers of the United Provinces of Agra and Oudh, 1923. Lucknow.

Dhavalikar, M.K. 1977. Inamgaon-the pattern of settlement. *Man and Environment.* 1, pp. 46-51.

Dikshit, M.G. 1955. *Tripuri, 1952, Being an Account of the Excavations at Triputi.* Nagpur.

Durgadutt, H.V. and Thadani, K.I. 1921. Studies on rice in Sind, Part I. *Mem. Dept. Agr. India, Bot. Series,* Vol. XV, no. 6, pp. 113-159.

Dutt, R.C. 1891. *A History of Utilization in Ancient India.* London.

Eggeling, J. 1966. *The Satapatha Brahmana,* (5 vols.). Delhi.

Emeneau, M.B. 1954. Linguistic prehistory of India. *Proceedings of the American Philosophical Society,* vol. 98, no. 4, pp. 282-292.

Emeneau, M.B. and Burrow, T. 1961. *A Dravidian Etymological Dictionary,* Oxford.

Fagan, P.J. (Ed.) 1892. *Gazetteer of Hissar District.* Lahore.

Fausboll, V. 1877-97. *The Jatakas* (6 vols.). London.

Fleet, J.P. (Ed.). 1963. *Corpus Inscriptionum Indicarum, Vol. III, Inscriptions of the Early Gupta Kings and their Successors.* Varanasi.

Furer-Haimendorf, C.V. 1979. *The Gonds of Andhra Pradesh.* Delhi.

Gamble, E. 1934. *Flora of the Madras Presidency, Bot. Survey of India.* Calcutta.

Gangopadhyay, R. 1932. *Some Materials for the Study of Agriculture and Agriculturists in Ancient India.* Serampore.

Gazetteer of the Kangra Dtstrict, 1883-84. Calcutta.

Gazetteer of Kashmir and Ladakh. 1890. Calcutta.

Ghose, R.L.M., Ghatge, M.B., and Subramanyan, V. 1960. *Rice in India*. Delhi.

Ghosh, S.S. and Lal, K. 1962-3. Plant remains from Rangpur, in, Rao, S.R., Excavations at Rangpur and other exploration at Gujarat, in, *Ancient India*, Nos. 18 & 19, p. 1(8.

Ghoshal, U.N. 1930. *Agrarian System in Ancient India*. London.

Glover, I.C. 1979. Prehistoric plant remains from southeast Asia, with special reference to rice. *South Asian Archaeology 1977*. pp. 7-37.

Govindaswami, S. and Krishnamurti, A. 1959. On the occurence of a Granulata in Jeypore tract. *Rice News Letter*, 7(1), pp. 9-10.

Govindaswami, S. and Krishnamurti, A. 1961. A pigmented variety of Oryza perennis Moench. *Rice News Letter*. 9(2), p. 21.

Govindaswami, S., Krishnamurti, A., and Shastry, N.S. 1966. The role of introgression in the varietal variability of rice in the Jeypore tract of Orissa. *Oryza*, 3(1), pp. 74-85.

Graham, R.J.D. 1913. Preliminary note on the classification of rice in the Central Provinces. *Mem. Dept. Agr. India, Bot. Series*, Vol. VII, No. 7, pp. 209-239.

Griffith, R.T.H. 1916-17. *The Hymns of the Atharvaveda*, (2. vols.). Benaras.

Griffith, R.T.H. 1957. *The Texts of the White Yajurveda*. Benaras.

Griffith, R.T.H. 1963. *The Texts af the Samaveda*. Varanasi.

Griffith, R.T.H. 1963. *The Hymns of the Rig Veda*. (2 Vols.). Varanasi.

Guru, S.D. (Ed.) 1976. *Madhya Pradesh District Gazetteers; Raigarh*, Bhopal.

Gutschin, G.G. 1938, Le Riz, Origin at Histoire de sa Culture, in *Riz Rizicult.*, 12, p. 61-96, *Cited in Nayar*, 1973, p. 269.

Hamada, H. 1949. Considerations on the Origin of Rice Cultivation, in, *Nippon Sakumutsu Gakkai Kiji*, 18, p. 106, (in Jap.). *Cited in Nayar, N.M. 1973*, pp. 158-269.

Hamada, H. 1956. Ecotypes of rice, in Kihara, H. (Ed.), *Land and Crops of Nepal Himalayas*, Vol. II, Kyoto, pp. 263-312.

Harlan, J.R., Dewat, J.M.J. and Price, E.G. 1973. Comparative Evolution of Cereals. *Evolution*, 27, pp. 311-325.

Haug, M. 1977. *The Aitareya Brahmaṇa af the Rig Veda.* Vol. II. Delhi.

Hector, G.P. and Sharangapam, S.G. 1934. Varietal characters and classification of the rice varieties in East Bengal, *Indian J. Agr. Sci.* 4, pp. 1-80.

Henderson, M.T. 1964. Cytogenetical studies at the Louisiana Agr. Experiment Station of species relationships in Oryza, in, *Rice Genetics and Cytogenetics, Proc. Symp. Los Banos,* 1963. Elsevier, Amsterdam, pp. 103-110.

Hinata, K., and Oka., H.I. 1962. Some considerations on the evolutionary dynamics of cultivated rice, *Nippon Idengaku Zasshi*, 37, pp. 329-42.

Hinata, K., and Oka., H.I. 1962. A survey of the hybrid sterility relationships in the Asian forms of O. perennis and O. sativa, *Nippon Idengaku Zasshi*, 37, pp. 314-28.

Hooker, J.D. 1897. *Flora of British India,* Vol. VII. Kent.

Horner, I.B. 1940, 1942, 1949, 1950, 1951. *Vinaya Pitaka,* (5 vols.). London.

Horner, I.B. 1954, 1957, 1959. *Majjhima Nikaya,* (3 Vols.), London.

Horner, I.B. 1963, 1964. *Milinda's Questions,* (2 Vols.), London.

Huke, R.E. 1976. Geography and climate of rice, in, *Climate, and Rice,* Los Banos, pp. 37-50.

Hultzsch, E. (Ed.) 1890. *South Indian Inscriptions,* Vol. I. Madras.

Hultzsch, E. (Ed.) 1891. *South Indian Inscriptions,* Vol. II. Part I, Madras.

Hultzsch, E. (Ed.) 1892. *South Indian Inscriptions,* Vol. II, Part II, Madras.

Hultzsch, E. (Ed.) 1895. *South Indian Inscriptions,* Vol. II, Part III, Madras.

Hultzsch, E. (Ed.) 1897. *Epigraphica Indica,* Vol. III, Calcutta.

Hultzsch, E. (Ed.) 1925. *Corpus Inscriptionum Indicarum,* Vol. I, Oxford.

Hunter, W.W. 1897. *A Statistical Account of Assam,* Vols. I & II, London.

Hutchinson, J.(Ed.)1974. *Evolutionary Studies in World Crops—Diversity and Change in the Indian Subcontinent.* Cambridge.

I.C.A.R. 1964. *Agriculture in Ancient India.* Delhi.

Imperial Gazetteer of India 1906, Assam. Shillong.

Imperial Gazetteer of India 1908, Sind. Oxford.

IRRI-IBPGR 1980. *Minimum List of Descriptors and Descriptor States for characterising cultivars of Rice.* Los Banos.

Isaac, E. 1970. *Geography of Domestication,* London.

Iyengar, P.T.S. 1912. *Site in Ancient India.* London.

Jolly, J. 1965. *Institutes of Vishnu.* Delhi.

Jolly, J. 1965. *The Minor Law Books.* Delhi.

Kajale, M.D. 1974. Ancient grains from India. *Bulletin of the Deccan College Research Institute,* Vol. XXXIV, no. 1-4, pp. 55-75.

Kajale, M.D. 1974. Plant economy at Bhokardan, in, Deo, S.B., and Gupta, R.S., *Excavation at Bhokardan.* Nagpur. pp. 217-223.

Kajale, M.D. 1977. Plant economy at Inamgaon, *Man and Environment,* 1. pp. 54-56.

Kajale, M.D. N.D. Paper read in the seminar on Kashmir Palaeoclimate, Physical Research Laboratory, Ahmedabad, Nov. 1983.

Kangle, R.P. 1963, 1965, 1966. *The Kauṭiliya Arthasastra,* (3 Parts). Bombay.

Kashiram, and Ekbote, R.E. 1936. The classification of the autumn rices of the Punjab and the Western United Provinces, *Indian J. Agr. Sci.,* 6(4), p. 930.

Kashiram and Saravayya, C.V. 1934. Classification of rices of Bihar and Orissa, *Indian J. Agr. Sci.,* 4, p. 537.

Keith, A.B. 1967. *Veda of the Black Yajus School Taittiriya Saṃhita,* (2 Vols.). Delhi.

Kihara, H. 1959. Considerations on the origin of cultivated rice, *Seiken Ziho,* 10, pp. 68-83.

Kihara, H. and Nakao, S. 1960. The Rice plant in Sikkim, *Seiken Ziho,* 11, pp. 46-54.

King, F.C. (Ed.) 1932. *Bihar and Orissa District Gazetteers, Sambalpur.* Patna.

Konow, S. 1929. *Corpus Inscriptionum Indicarum,* Vol.II, Part I, Calcutta.

Krishnamurti, A., Ved Prakash and Sharma, A.C. 1967. Glabrous Varieties of Cultivated Rice in Manipur, *Oryza*, 4(1), pp. 74, 152.

Krishnaswamy, N. and Chandrasekharan, 1957, notes. *Sci. and Cult*. 23, p. 307.

Krsnayajurvediya Taittiriya Samhita Padpathayuta. 1972. Vedic Sanshodhan Mandala, Poona.

Lambourn, G.E. (Ed.), 1918. *Bengal District Gazetteers, Malda*, Calcutta.

Macdonell, A.A., and Keith, A.B., 1958. *Vedic Index of Names and subjects*, (2 Vols.). Varanasi.

Macphail, R.M. (Ed.) 1954. *Campbell's English-Santali Dictionary*. Benagaria.

Majumdar, G.P. 1972. *Vanaspati : Plants and Plant Life as in in Indian Treatises and Traditions*. Calcutta.

Max-Muller, P., 1965. *The Upanisad*. Delhi.

Mehta, R.N. 1968. *Excavation at Nagara*. Baroda.

Menon, A.S. (Ed.) 1962. *Kerala District Gazetteers, Kozhikode*. Trivandrum.

Mirashi, V.V. (Ed.) 1955. *Corpus Inscriptionum Indicarum*, Vol. IV, Part I, Ootacamund.

Mirashi, V.V. (Ed.) 1963. *Corpus Inscriptionum Indicarum*, Vol. V, Ootacamund.

Misra, V.D. 1977. Excavations at Koldihawa, in, *Some Aspects af Indian Archaeology*. Allahabad. pp. 107-121.

Mitra, R.L. 1972. *The Gopatha Brahmana*. Delhi.

Mitra, S.K. and Ganguli, P.M. 1932. *Studies in the Surma valley rices and their classification*, *Indian J. Agr. Sci.*, 2(6), pp. 571-606.

Monier-Williams, M., 1899. *Sanskrit-English Dictionary* Oxford.

Morishima, M., Hinata, H. and Oka, H.I. 1963. Comparison of modes of evolution of cultivated forms from two wild rice species, Oryza breviligulata and Oryza perennis. *Evolution*, 17, pp. 170-81.

Morishima, M., Oka, H.I. and Chang, W.T. 1961. Directions of differentiation in populations of wild rice, Oryza perennis and O. sativa f. spontanaea, *Evolution*, 15, pp. 326-339.

Nagai, I. 1959. *Japonica Rice : Its Breeding and Culture.* Yokedo, Tokyo.

Nair, N.P., Nayar, N.M., and Sahadevan, P.C. 1964. On the occurrence of the Oryza species in south western India and its significance, *Curr. Sci.* 33, pp. 515-17.

Narain, A.K., and Roy, T.N., 1976, 1977. *Excavations at Rajghat*, (3 Parts), Benaras.

Narain, L.A., 1970. The neolithic settlement at Chirand, *The Journal of the Bihar Research Society*, Vol. LVI, (Parts I-IV), pp. 16-35.

Nath, Pran. 1929. *A Study at the Economic Conditions of India.* London.

Nayar, N.M. 1958. *Studies on the origin of cultivated rice, Oryza Sativa, L.*, Indian Agricultural Research Institute, Ph.D. thesis, Delhi.

Nayar, N.M. 1973. Origin and Cytogenetics of rice. *Adv. Genet.*, 17, pp. 153-292.

Nelson, A.F., (Ed.), 1910. *Central Provinces District Gazetteers, Drug.* Calcutta.

Oka, H.I., Chang, W.T., and Narise, T., 1959. A preliminary note on the wild and cultivated rice strains collected from the mountain region of Orissa state, in, *Ann. Rep. Nat. Inst. Genet,, Japan*, 9, cited in Oka, H.I. and Morishima, H., 1959. The pattern of interspecific variation in the Genus Oryza, *Evolutian* 14, 1960, p. 1964.

Oka, H.I. and Chang, W.T., 1959. The impact of cultivation on the populations of wild rice, Oryza Sativa f. spontanea, *Phyton*, 13, pp. 105-117.

Oka, H.I. and Chang, W.T. 1961. Hybrid swarms between wild and cultivated rice species, O. sativa, *Evolution*, 15, pp. 418-30.

Oka, H.I. and Chang, W.T. 1962. Rice varieties intermediate between wild and cultivated forms and the origin of the Japonica type, *Bot, Bull, Acad, Sin.*, 3, pp. 109-131.

Oka, H.I. and Chang, W.T. 1962. Responses to various growing conditions of wild and cultivated rice forms, *Ann. Rpt. Natl. Inst. Genet.*, Japan, 12 p. 61.

Oka, H.I. 1964. Patterns of interspecific relationships and

evolutionary dynamics in Oryza, *Rice Genetics and Cytogenetics*, Elsevier, Amsterdam, pp. 71-90

Oka, H.I. and Morishima, M. 1971. The dynamics of plant domestication. Cultivation experiments with Oryza perennis and its hybrid with O. Sativa, *Evolution*, 25, pp. 356-64.

Oka, H.I. 1974. Experimental studies on the origin of cultivated rice. *Procs. 13th Intl. Congr. Genet.*, 1, pp. 475-86.

Oka, H.I. 1975. The origin of cultivated rice and its adaptive selection, *Assoc. of Jap. Agr. Sci. Socs. (Ed.), Rice in Asia.* Tokyo, pp. 21-34.

Oldenberg, H. 1964. *Grihya Sutras*, (2 Vols.). Delhi.

O'Malley, L.S.S. (Ed,) 1910. *Bengal District Gazetteers, Santhal Parganas*, Calcutta.

O'Malley, L.S.S. (Ed.) 1914. *Bengal District Gazetters, 24 Parganas*. Calcutta.

O'Malley, L.S.S. (Ed.), 1933. *Bihar and Orissa District Gazetteers, Cuttack*. Patna.

Om Prakash, 1961. *Food and Drinks in Ancient India.* Delhi.

Pargiter, P.F. 1904. *The Markandeya Purana.* Calcutta.

Patel, G.D. (Ed.) 1972. *Gujarat District Gazetteers, Panchmahals.* Ahmedabad.

Pawar, M.S. and Rajagopalan, K. 1956. Rice varieties of Nizambad, *Rice News Letter*, 4(3-4), pp. 10-12.

Pinnow, H.J., 1963. *Cited in Sebeok, T.A., (Ed.)*, 1969, Current *Trends in Linguistics*, Vol. V. The Hague, p. 413.

Porteres, R., 1956. Taxonomic Agrobotanique des riz cultives O. Sativa et O. Glaberrima, in, *J. Agr. Trop. Bot.* 3. pp. 343-84, 541-80, 627-701, 821-56, *Cited in Nayar, N.M. 1958.* p. 85.

Prain, D. 1903. *Bengal Plants*, Vol. II, Calcutta.

Prodoehl, A., 1922. Oryza Monographice Describunture, in, Bot. Arch., 1, pp. 211-24, 231-255, *Cited in, Nayar, N.M., 1973*, pp. 154-284.

Puri, B.N. 1957. *India in the time of Patanjali.* Bombay.

Rajagopala, M.V. (Ed.), 1973. *Anddra Pradesh District Gazetteers, Nizmabad.* Hyderabad.

Ramaswami, A. (Ed.) 1972. *Tamil Nadu District Gazetteers, Ramanathapuram.* Madras.

Ramiah, K. and Ghose, R.L.M. 1951. Origin and distribution of rice, *Indian J. Genet. Pl. Breed.*, 11. pp. 7-13.

Ramiah, K. and Rao, M.B.V.N. 1953. *Rice Breeding and Genetics*. ICAR, Delhi.

Randhawa, M.S. 1980. *The History of Indian Agriculture*, Delhi.

Rao, C.H. 1929. *Mysore Gazetteer*. Bangalore.

Rao, P.S.M. (Ed.) 1962. *Maharashtra State Gazetteers; Ratnagiri*. Bombay.

Rao, S.R. 1973. *Lothal and the Indus Civilisation*. Bombay.

Ray, P.C. 1955. *The Mahabharata of Krishna Dwaipayana Vyasa*, (12 Vols.), Calcutta.

Ray, P.N. and Gupta, H.N. 1965. *Charaka, Samhita*, Delhi.

Raychaudhuri, S.P. 1941. *Agriculture in Ancient India*. Dacca.

Reed, C.A, (Ed.). 1977. *Origins oj Agriculture*. The Hague.

Report on the classification of Rice, 1968. Pub. by the Ministry of Food, Agriculture, Community Development and Co-operation, Govt. of India, Delhi.

Riccharia, R.H. 1960. Origins of cultivated rices, *Indian J. Genet. Pl. Breed*. 20. pp. 1-14.

Riccharia, R.H. and Govindaswamy, S. 1960. Glabrousness in cultivated rice, *Rice News Letter*, 8(4), pp. 5-6.

Riccharia, R.H. and Govindaswamy, S. 1960. Flowering and photosensitiveness in O. perennis. *Rice News Letter*, 8(1), pp. 3-4.

Riccharia, R.H., Govindaswamy, S., and Ghosh, A.K., 1966. Introgression between O. perennis and O. sativa, a cause of variation in O. sativa var. spontanea of Assam, India, in, *Riso*, 15, pp. 183-91, *Cited in Nayar, N.M. 1973*, pp. 160, 170, 285.

Rice Breeding, 1972. IRRI. Los Banos.

Rice in Orissa. 1956. Dept. of Agr., Govt. of Orissa, Bhubaneshwar.

Roschevicz, R.J. 1931. A Contribution to the Study of Rice., Tr., Priki. Bot. Genet. Selek., 27(4), pp. 3-133 (in Russ.), *cited in Nayar, N.M., 1973*, pp. 154, 157, 158, 167, 169, 170, 284.

Roy, S.C. 1912. *The Mundas and Their Country*, Calcutta.

Roy, S.C. 1921. Preliminary classification of the wild rices of the Central Provinces and Berar, *Agr. J. of India*, Vol. XIV, p. 365.

Roy, S.C., 1928. *Oraon Religion and Customs*, Calcutta.

Roychowdhury, P.C. (Ed.) 1957. *Bihar District Gazetteers,* Gaya, Patna.

Roychowdhury, P.C. (Ed.) 1958. *Bihar District Gazetteers, Muzaffarpur.* Patna.

Roxburgh, W. 1832. *Flora Indica.* Agra.

Rydh, H. 1959. Rangmahal, *The Swedish Archaeological Expedition to India 1952-54.* Lund.

Sahni, B. 1936. Antiquities from the Khokrakot mound at Rohtak in the Jumna valley; *Curr. Sci.*, (May), pp. 796-801.

Sampath, S. 1961. Notes on the taxonomy of the Genus Oryza, in, Shokubutsugaku Zasshi, 74, pp. 269-70, *cited in Nayar, N.M., 1973.* pp. 154, 286.

Sampath, S. 1962. The Genus Oryza : its taxonomy and species relationships. *Oryza*, 1(1), pp. 1-29.

Sampath, S. 1964. Suggestions for a revision of the Genus Oryza, in, *Rice Genetics and Cytogenetics*, Elsevier, Amsterdam, pp. 22-3.

Sampath, S. 1973. Origins of cultivated rice, in, *Indian J. Genet. and Pl. Breed.*, 33(2), pp. 157-61.

Sampath, S. and Govindaswamy, S., 1958. Wild rices of Orissa-their relationship to the cultivated varieties, *Rice News Letter*, 6(3), pp. 17-20.

Sampath, S. and Rao, M.B.V.N., 1951. Interrelationships between species in Genus Oryza, *Indian J. Genet. Pl. Breed.* II, pp. 14-17.

Sankalia, H.D., Deo, S.B. and Ansari, Z.D., 1969, *Excavations at Ahar, 1961-2.* Poona.

Sankalia, H.D., Deo, S.B., Ansari, Z.D. and Ehrardt, S. 1960. *From History to Prehistory at Nevasa.* Poona.

Sankalia, H.D. and Dikshit, M.G. 1952. *Excavations at Brahmapuri (Kolhapuri)*, 1945-46. Poona.

Sardesai, N.G. and Padhye, D.G. (Ed.). 1960, *Amara's Namlinganusasanam.* Poona.

Sardesai, N.G. and Sharma, H.D. (Ed.) 1941. *Amarakosa, with the Commentary of Bhatta Ksirasvamin.* Poona.

Sasaki, T. 1935. On the Distribution of Species in Genus Oryza, in, Papers in Crop Science Commemorating

Prof. S. Kikkawa's 25 years of Services, pp.63-75, (in Jap.), *cited in Nayar N.M., 1973*, pp. 154, 284.

Schoff, W.H. 1912. *The Periplus of the Erythraean Sea*, London.

Senapati, N. and Tripathi, P. (Ed.), 1972. *Orissa District Gazetteers, Dhenkanal*. Cuttack.

Sethi, R. L. and Saxena, B. P. 1930. Classification and study of characters of cultivated rices in United Provinces, *Mem. Dept. Agr., India, Bot. Series*, 18, pp. 149-210.

Sharma, G. R. 1960. *The Excavations at Kausambi, 1957-9* Allahabad.

Sharma, G.R., Misra, V. D., Mandal, D., Misra, B.B. and Pal, J. N. 1980. *The Beginnings of Agriculture (Epi-Palaeolithic to Neolithic Excavations an Chopani-Mando, Mahadaha and Mahagara)*, Allahabad,

Sharma, R. S. 1968. *Aspects of Political Ideas and Institutions in Ancient India*, Delhi.

Sharma, S. D. and Shastry, S. V. S. 1965. Taxonomic studies in Genus Oryza L. 111, O. RuffipogonGriff., Sensu Stricto and O. Nivara Sharma et Shastry nom nov. *Indian J. Gcnet* 25, pp. 157-67.

Sharma, S.D., and Shrstry, S.V.S. 1965. Taxonomic Studies in Genus Oryza I. Asiatic Types of Oryza Sativa complex, *Indian J. Genet. Pl. Breed.* 25, pp. 245-259.

Sharma, S.D., Vellanki, J.M.R. Hakim, K.L. and Singh, R.K. 1971. Primitive and current cultivars of rice in Assam—a rich source of valuable Genes, *Curr. Sci*,, 40, pp. 126-8.

Shastri, H.P. 1952, 1957. *The Ramayana of Valmiki*, (3 Vols) London.

Shastri, J.L. (Ed) 1969, 1970. *The Siva Purana*, (4 Vols) Delhi.

Shastri, J.L. (Ed.) 1973. *The Linga Puraṇa* (2 Parts), Delhi.

Shastri, M.N.D. 1967. *The Agni Puraṇam*, (2 Vols.), Varanasi.

Shastri, M.N.D, 1968. *The Garuda Puraṇam*. Varanasi.

Shrivastava, P.N. (Ed.) 1971. *Madhya Pradesh District Gazetteers, Betul*, Bhopal,

Shrivastava, P.N. (Ed.) 1978. *Madhya Pradesh District Gazetteers, Bilaspur*, Bhopal.

Singh, K.D. 1963. Wild rices in Manipur, *Rice News Letter*, 11 (1), p. 3.

Sinha, B.P. and Narain, L.A. 1970. *Pataliputra Excavation, 1955-6*, Patna.

Southworth, F.C. 1976. Cereals in South Asian Prehistory: The linguistic evidence, in, Possehl, G.L. and Kennedy, K.A.R. (Ed.), *Ecological Backgrounds of South Asian Prehistory*. The Hague, pp. 52-75.

Stuart, H.A. (Rev. Ed.) 1895. *Madras District Manuals, North Arcot*. Madras.

Subbarao, N.S. 1911. *Economic and Political Conditions in Ancient India*. Mysore

Suryakanta, 1975. *Sanskrit-Hindi-English Dictionary*. Delhi.

Swahananda, S. 1956. *Chandyoga Upanisad*. Madras.

Tagore, G.V. 1976, 1978. *The Bhagvata Purana*, (5 Parts), Delhi.

Tateoka, T. 1962. Species of the Genus Oryza, in, Nat. Sci. Mus., Tokyo, 29 (5/6), pp. 73-84, *cited in Nayar, N.M., 1973*, p. 289.

Tateoka, T. 1962. Taxonomic studies of the Genus Oryza 11. Several species complexes, *Bot. Mag., Tokyo*, 76, pp. 455-61.

Tateoka, T. 1963. Taxonomic studies of oryza 111. Key to the species and their enumeration, *Bot. Mag., Tokyo*. 76, pp. 165-73.

Takeoka, T. 1964. Taxonomic studies of the Genus Oryza, *Rice Genetics and Cytogenetics*, Elsevier, Amsterdam, pp. 15-21.

Thapar, B.K. 1974. Problems of the neolithic cultures in India: A retrospect, *Purattatva*, 7, pp. 61-2.

Ting, Y, 1949. Origin (ation) of the Rice Cultivation in China, in, Coll. Agr. Sun Yat Sen Univ. Agron. Bull. Ser., 111, No. 7, (in Chin.), *cited in Nayar, N.M., 1973*, pp. 159-290.

Ting, Y. 1957. The Origin and Differentiation of cultivated Rices in China, in, Nung Yeh Hsueh Pao, 8, pp. 243-60. (in Chin.), *cited in Nayar, N.M., 1973*, pp. 159, 290.

Ting, Y., 1958. The Origin of Cultivated Rice Species and their Differentiation in China, in, Agrobiologiya, 1, pp. 27-43. (in Russ.), *cited in Nayar, N.M., 1973*, pp. 159, 290.

Tripathi, R.S. 1960. *History of Ancient India*. Delhi.

Turner, R.L. 1966. *A Comparative Dictionary of the Indo-Aryan Language*. London.

Vaidya, P.L. (Ed). 1960. *Aranya Kanda.* Baroda.

Vasu, S.C, 1962. *Astadhyayi of Paṇini.* Delhi.

Vavilov, N.I. 1951. *Origin, Variation, Immunity and Breeding of Cultivated Plants.* London.

Vijarnava, S.C.V. 1933. *Brihadaranyaka Upanishad.* Allahabad.

Vishvabandhu (Ed.), 1960-2, *Atharvaveda (Sannaka) with the Pada Path and Sayanacarya's Commentary.* (4 parts), Hoshiarpur.

Vishavabandhu (Ed). 1964-5, *Rig Veda with Commentaries of Skandasvamin, Udgitha, Venkara Madhava aud Mudgala* (8 Parts). Hoshiarpur.

Vishnu-Mittre, 1966. Kaundinyapur plant economy in Proto-historic and Historic times, *The Palaeobotanist*, Vol. XV, No. 1 & 2, pp. 152-156.

Vishnu-Mittre, 1969. Remains of rice and millet, in Sankalia, H.D., Deo, S.B., and Ansari, Z.D., *Excavations at Ahar, 1961-2*, Poona, pp. 229-235.

Vishnu-Mittre, 1971. Plant remains, in, Nagaraja Rao, M.S., *Proto-historic Cultures of the Tungabhadra Valley*, Dharwar, pp. 125-131.

Vishnu-Mittre, 1972. Neolithic plant remains at Chirand, Bihar, *The Palaeobotanist*, No. I, pp. 18-22.

Vishnu-Mittre, 1974. The beginnings of agriculture, palaeo-botanical evidence in India, in, Hutchinson, J. (Ed.), Evolutionary Studies in World Crops : Diversity and Change *in the Indian Subcontinent*, Cambridge, pp. 3-33.

Vishnu-Mittre, 1976. Comments on Sir J. Hutchinson's paper, India ; local and introduced crops, in, *Phil. Trans. R. Soc.*, London, B, p. 275.

Vishnu-Mittre and Gupta, H.P. 1968. Ancient Plant Economy at Paunar, Maharashtra, in, Deo, S. B., and Dhavalikar, M. K., *Paunar Excavation, 1967*, Nagpur, pp. 128-130.

Vishnu-Mittre, Prakash, U. and Awasthi, N., 1972. Ancient Plant Economy at Ter, Maharashtra, in, *Geophytology*, I (2), pp. 170-77.

Vishnu-Mittre and Savithri, R. 1974. Ancient Plant Economy at Noh, *Purattatva*, No. 7 pp. 77-80.

Vishnu-Mittre and Savithri, R. 1975. Supposed remains of rice (Oryza sp.) in the terracotta Cakes and Pai at Kalibangan, Rajasthan, the *Palaeobotanist.* Vol. XXII (I), pp. 124-126.

Waldschmidt, E. and Mehendale, M. A. (Rev.), 1963. *Corpus Inscriptionum Indicarum*, Vol. VI, Part I.

Watabe, T. 1972, 1974. *Preliminary Report, Tottori University's Scientific Survey, 1971. Origin and Alteration of Cultivated Rice in the Indian Sub Continent.* (2 Vols.). Tottori Univ. Japan.

Watt, G. 1908. *The Commercial Products of India,* Reprint Ed., 1966, Delhi.

Wealth of India, 1966. A Dictionary of Indian Raw Materials and Industrial Products, Vol. VII, CSIR, Delhi.

Whyte, R.H. 1972. The Graminae, wild and cultivated, of monsoonal and equatorial Asia in South Asia, *Asian Perspect,* 15, pp. 127, 157.

Whyte, R.H. 1974. The evolution and status of the Graminae in Asia, in, Pl. Genet. Res. Newslett. *cited in Oka, 1974.* p. 486.

Wilson, H.H., 1972. *The Vishnu Purana,* Calcutta.

Winternitz, M. 1972. *History of Indian Literature,* (2 Vols.). Delhi.

Yeh, B.P. and Henderson, M.T. 1961. Cytogenetic relationship between cultivated rice, Oryza sativa L. and five wild diploid forms of Oryza, *Crop. Sci.,* 1, pp. 445-50.

Zide, N.H. aud Zide, A.K. 1973. Semantic reconstructions in Proto Munda cultural vocabulary, *Indian Linguistics* No. 34 (1), pp. 1-24.

Zohary, D, 1970. Centres of diversity and centres of origin, in, Frankel, O.H., and Bennett, E. (Ed.), *Genetic Resources in Plants : Their Exploration and Conservation,* Oxford, pp. 33-43.

Zurovskij, P.M. 1950. *Cultivated Plants and their Wild Relatives.* London.

Index